Taxcafe.co.uk Tax Guides

Salary versus Dividends

& Other Tax Efficient Profit Extraction Strategies

Nick Braun PhD

Important Legal Notices:

Published by:
Taxcafe UK Limited
67 Milton Road
Kirkcaldy KY1 1TL

Email: team@taxcafe.co.uk

ISBN 978-1-911020-65-3

22nd edition, June 2021

Disclaimer
Before reading or relying on the content of this tax guide please read the disclaimer.

Disclaimer

1. This guide is intended as **general guidance** only and does NOT constitute accountancy, tax, investment or other professional advice.

2. The author and Taxcafe UK Limited make no representations or warranties with respect to the accuracy or completeness of this publication and cannot accept any responsibility or liability for any loss or risk, personal or otherwise, which may arise, directly or indirectly, from reliance on information contained in this publication.

3. Please note that tax legislation, the law and practices of Government and regulatory authorities (e.g. HM Revenue & Customs) are constantly changing. We therefore recommend that for accountancy, tax, investment or other professional advice, you consult a suitably qualified accountant, tax advisor, financial adviser, or other professional adviser.

4. Please also note that your personal circumstances may vary from the general examples provided in this guide and your professional adviser will be able to provide specific advice based on your personal circumstances.

5. This guide covers UK taxation only and any references to 'tax' or 'taxation', unless the contrary is expressly stated, refer to UK taxation only. Please note that references to the 'UK' do not include the Channel Islands or the Isle of Man. Foreign tax implications are beyond the scope of this guide.

6. All persons described in the examples in this guide are entirely fictional. Any similarities to actual persons, living or dead, or to fictional characters created by any other author, are entirely coincidental.

About the Author & Taxcafe

Dr Nick Braun founded Taxcafe in 1999, along with Aileen Smith. As the driving force behind the company, their aim is to provide affordable plain-English tax information for private individuals, business owners and professional advisors.

Over the past 21 years Taxcafe has become one of the best-known tax publishers in the UK and has won several prestigious business awards.

Nick has been a specialist tax writer since 1989, first in South Africa, where he edited the monthly *Tax Breaks* publication, and since 1999 in the UK, where he has authored several tax books including *Small Business Tax Saving Tactics* and *Pension Magic*.

Nick also has a PhD in economics from the University of Glasgow, where he was awarded the prestigious William Glen scholarship and later became a Research Fellow.

Contents

Introduction

This guide answers the most common question asked by company owners: "What's the best way to take money out of my company if I want to pay less tax?"

In Part 1 we kick off with a plain English guide to how *companies* are taxed.

In the March 2021 Budget the Government announced that corporation tax will increase from 1st April 2023. Calculating your company's tax bill will also become a bit more complicated and, as a result, new tax planning opportunities will arise.

The corporation tax changes are covered in detail in this part of the guide and, throughout the guide, we explain how the changes will affect your profit extraction decisions in the years ahead.

In Part 1 we also explain how *company owners* are taxed. As a director/shareholder you can choose the best <u>mix</u> of salary and dividends. We examine the pros and cons of each type of income.

Company owners can also choose the most tax efficient <u>level</u> of income.

We explain how, by smoothing your income, or varying it significantly from year to year, you may be able to cut your tax bill considerably.

Tax-Free Salaries & Dividends

In Part 2 we reveal how much tax-free salary and dividend income you can withdraw from your company this year.

You'll discover how to calculate the "optimal" tax–efficient salary and how couples in business together can receive £29,140 this year without paying any income tax.

In Part 3 we explain how much dividend income you can take taxed at just 7.5% and how to avoid paying tax at 32.5%.

This part of the guide also contains important tax saving strategies for parents who want to avoid the child benefit tax charge.

This kicks in when your income exceeds £50,000 but many company owners will be able to avoid it completely or in part.

There is also important tax planning information for high income earners (those with income over £100,000 or £150,000).

Income from Other Sources

In Part 4 we turn to company owners who have significant amounts of income from other sources (e.g. rental income, interest income, income from another business and stock market dividends).

We explain why you may need to adjust your company salary or dividends to avoid the higher tax rates that kick in when your income reaches certain key thresholds (£50,000, £50,270, £100,000 and £150,000).

We also examine some tax planning techniques that can be used to reduce or eliminate the tax payable on your income from other sources.

Company owners who are also landlords need to be aware of the new restriction to tax relief on mortgage interest. Fortunately, company owners have more flexibility than other landlords when it comes to avoiding some of the worst effects of this tax change.

Company owners can also enjoy much more tax-free interest than other taxpayers (up to £6,000 per year). Additional tax savings can be enjoyed by allocating some of your personal allowance from your interest income to your dividend income.

Splitting Income with Family Members

Part 5 explains how company owners can gift shares in the business to their spouses, partners or children and save over £10,000 in tax this year, with similar savings every year.

We also show how additional savings can be achieved by paying tax-free salaries to family members, including your minor children.

There are, however, many traps to avoid when it comes to splitting income with family members and these are fully covered in this part of the guide.

For example, we examine the danger of gifting shares that have fewer rights than ordinary shares and the danger of using dividend waivers to divert income to your spouse.

Alternative Profit Extraction Strategies

Part 6 looks at alternative profit extraction strategies:

- **Directors' loans** – How they can be used to reduce or postpone tax.

- **Rent** – Why getting your company to pay you rent is more tax efficient than a dividend in many circumstances.

- **Interest** – How to receive up to £6,000 of tax-free interest from your company.

- **Charity** – Who should donate: you or the company?

- **Pension contributions** – Why they're better than dividends, who should make them (you or the company), plus a chapter on putting property into a pension.

- **Company Cars, Vans & Motoring Costs** – a Plain English guide to the tax rules.

- **Mobile Phones** – Getting your company to pay the cost.

- **Capital gains** – How to pay 10% tax when you sell or wind up your company; How to pay 0% tax when you sell your company to an employee ownership trust.

In Part 7 we turn to some of the practical issues and dangers that may be experienced when extracting money from your company:

- How to avoid the minimum wage regulations

- How to make sure your salary is a tax deductible expense

- Making sure your company has sufficient distributable profits to declare dividends

- How to declare dividends properly and avoid an HMRC challenge

- The circumstances in which HMRC may try to tax your dividends as earnings

Other Tax Saving Strategies

In Part 8 we show how company owners, by altering the amount of income they withdraw from their companies, can reduce the amount of capital gains tax payable when assets like rental properties are sold.

In this part we also explain how you may be able to completely avoid tax by emigrating, including details of the statutory residence test. There is also a chapter explaining how you can reduce your income tax bill by investing in venture capital trusts.

Using This Guide & Limitations

This tax guide deals primarily with the 2021/22 tax year, starting on 6th April 2021 and finishing on 5th April 2022.

There are references to other tax years, for example when discussing the advantages and disadvantages of postponing income to a future tax year.

However, it is important to emphasise that the tax rates and tax laws that will apply in future tax years are not known with any degree of certainty.

Tax rates and tax laws (including HMRC's interpretation of those laws) are continually changing. The reader must bear this in mind when reading this guide.

Please note that, although owners of small trading companies are this book's main target audience, this is NOT supposed to be a do-it-yourself (DIY) tax planning guide.

My purpose in writing this guide is to explain in plain English how companies and company owners are taxed and provide some tax planning ideas that can be taken to an accountant or other professional advisor for further discussion.

I do not recommend 'going it alone' when it comes to this type tax planning and there are several reasons for my cautious approach.

Firstly, although the guide covers a fair amount of ground, it does not cover every possible scenario – that would be impossible without making the guide much longer and possibly much more difficult to digest.

In other words, in places I have had to sacrifice definitiveness in favour of making the guide a manageable and hopefully enjoyable read for the average small company owner.

Companies come in many different shapes and sizes, as do their owners, so it is possible that the information contained in this guide will not be relevant to your circumstances.

In particular, please note that this guide is aimed mainly at UK resident director/shareholders who own and work for UK resident companies.

Secondly, the main focus of this tax guide is *income tax* planning: helping company owners pay less tax on their salaries, dividends and other income. There are, however, other taxes that often have to be considered, including capital gains tax and inheritance tax.

Steps that you take to reduce one type of tax can have an adverse impact on your liability to pay other taxes. While some mention is made of other taxes in this guide, I cannot guarantee that all interactions are covered.

Thirdly, there are potential risks involved when it comes to structuring your affairs to reduce the tax payable on salaries, dividends and other payments made by your company.

While most of the tax planning ideas contained in this book are widely used by many accountants and other professional advisers, and have been for many years, this does not mean they have the blessing of HM Revenue & Customs!

There are some grey areas when it comes to this area of tax planning and there are no guaranteed tax savings.

In other words, we cannot be certain that some of the tax planning ideas contained in this book will not be subject to some sort of attack from HMRC, even if only at some point in the future.

For example, in the chapters that follow we will show that the most tax-efficient mix of income for most company owners is a small salary coupled with a larger dividend. While this may be the *mathematically* optimal income mix for many company owners, the tax savings are not guaranteed.

There is a danger that HMRC will seek to tax dividends as earnings in some circumstances and may frown on any reduction in an existing salary – see Chapters 35 and 36 for more information.

Fourthly, there are also *non-tax* factors that have to be considered when deciding how much money you withdraw from your company and in what form. In some instances other considerations will outweigh any potential tax savings.

For all of these reasons it is vital that you obtain professional advice before taking any action based on information contained in this guide. The author and Taxcafe UK Ltd cannot accept any responsibility for any loss which may arise as a consequence of any action taken, or any decision to refrain from taking action, as a result of reading this guide

The General Anti-Abuse Rule

Something called the general anti-abuse rule (GAAR) came into operation on 17 July 2013.

Tax arrangements are "abusive" if they cannot reasonably be regarded as a reasonable course of action – this is commonly referred to as the double reasonableness test.

Clearly it's very subjective and HMRC has sought to reassure taxpayers that there will be a "high threshold" for showing that tax arrangements are abusive:

"In respect of any particular arrangement there might be a range of views as to whether it was a reasonable course of action: it is possible that there could be a reasonably held view that the tax arrangements were a reasonable course of action, and also a reasonably held view that the arrangement is not a reasonable course of action. In such circumstances the tax arrangements will not be abusive for the purposes of the GAAR."

An indicator that tax arrangements may not be abusive is if they were "established practice" when entered into and HMRC indicated its acceptance of that practice at the time.

Tax arrangements may be abusive if, for example, the tax result is different to the real economic result, for example tax deductions or tax losses that are significantly greater than actual expenses or real economic losses.

If you think that all of the above is a bit vague and subjective, you are not alone. Even the best tax brains in the land don't know what this test means in practice. When legislation contains words like "reasonable" and "abusive" you know you have to be on your guard!

The question being asked by some tax advisers is this: will the anti-abuse rule be used to attack the sort of 'normal' or 'mainstream' tax planning carried out by thousands of small company owners, for example taking small salaries and dividends?

Many tax experts believe that well-established, conventional tax planning will not be attacked by HMRC using the GAAR. Instead the focus will be on the extreme end, for example 'aggressive' or 'artificial' tax avoidance schemes.

This view seems to be backed up by HMRC guidance published in January 2015 which says the following about small company dividends:

"Just as it is essential to understand what the GAAR is targeted at, so it is equally essential to understand what it is not targeted at. To take an obvious example, a taxpayer deciding to carry on a trade can do so either as a sole trader or through a limited company whose shares he or she owns and where he or she works as an employee. Such a choice is completely outside the target area of the GAAR, and once such a company starts to earn profits a decision to accumulate most of the profits to be paid out in the future by way of dividend, rather than immediately paying a larger salary, is again something that should in any normal trading circumstances be outside the target area of the GAAR."

Nevertheless, at present the simple truth is that no one knows how HMRC will apply the general anti-abuse rule to company owners in the years ahead and whether it will eventually affect certain tax planning practices that many regard as mainstream, including some of those contained in this guide.

Scottish Taxpayers

The Scottish Parliament now has the power to tax most types of income. The vast majority of the information contained in this guide is relevant to Scottish taxpayers and there is quite a lot of information specific to them. However, unless stated to the contrary, all examples, tables and calculations assume that the taxpayer concerned is not a Scottish taxpayer.

Part 1

How Companies & Company Owners Are Taxed

Chapter 1

How Companies Are Taxed

Companies pay corporation tax on both their income and capital gains.

For the current financial year, starting on 1st April 2021, all companies (except some in the oil and gas sector) will pay corporation tax at the same flat rate of 19%.

The corporation tax rate will also be 19% for the financial year which starts on 1st April 2022.

From 1st April 2023 the main rate of corporation tax will be increased to 25%. This was announced in the March 2021 Budget.

Calculating the Company's Effective Tax Rate

Not only will corporation tax be increased, it will also become more complicated, just like it was a few years ago. From 1st April 2023 there will be two official corporation tax rates:

- Small profits rate   19%
- Main rate   25%

The practical effect is that companies will pay tax as follows:

- **Profits £50,000 or less** – Company will continue to pay 19% tax on all of its profits

- **Profits between £50,000 and £250,000** – Company will pay 19% tax on the first £50,000 and 26.5% on the remainder

- **Profits greater than £250,000** – Company will pay 25% tax on all of its profits

Some sample corporation tax bills and overall corporation tax rates are shown in Table 1.

TABLE 1
Overall Corporation Tax Rates
After the Increase

Profits	Corporation Tax	Corporation Tax Rate
£50,000	£9,500	19.00%
£60,000	£12,150	20.25%
£70,000	£14,800	21.14%
£80,000	£17,450	21.81%
£90,000	£20,100	22.33%
£100,000	£22,750	22.75%
£110,000	£25,400	23.09%
£120,000	£28,050	23.38%
£130,000	£30,700	23.62%
£140,000	£33,350	23.82%
£150,000	£36,000	24.00%
£160,000	£38,650	24.16%
£170,000	£41,300	24.29%
£180,000	£43,950	24.42%
£190,000	£46,600	24.53%
£200,000	£49,250	24.63%
£210,000	£51,900	24.71%
£220,000	£54,550	24.80%
£230,000	£57,200	24.87%
£240,000	£59,850	24.94%
£250,000	£62,500	25.00%

A company with profits of £100,000 will pay 19% on the first £50,000 and 26.5% on the final £50,000. The total tax bill will be £22,750 which means the company will have an overall tax rate of 22.75% (£22,750/£100,000).

A company with profits of £150,000 will pay 19% on the first £50,000 and 26.5% on the remaining £100,000. The total tax bill will be £36,000 which means the company will have an overall tax rate of 24% (£36,000/£150,000).

A company with profits of £20,000 (i.e. less than £50,000) will simply pay £3,800 (19%). A company will profits of £300,000 (i.e. more than £250,000) will simply pay £75,000 (25%).

Non-Resident Companies

Only companies that are UK resident will be able to benefit from the 19% small profits rate. A non-resident company that earns rental income from UK properties, for example, will therefore have to pay 25% corporation tax on all of its UK rental profits.

Accounting Periods vs Financial Years

Because of the way corporation tax is calculated, the corporation tax increase will begin to affect some companies' profits as early as May 2022.

A company's own tax year (also known as its accounting period) can end on any date, for example 31st December, 31st March etc.

Corporation tax, on the other hand, is calculated according to financial years. Financial years run from 1st April to 31st March. The 2023 financial year is the year starting on 1st April 2023 and ending on 31st March 2024.

This matters when it comes to calculating how much tax your company will pay when the corporation tax rate changes.

For example, on 1st April 2023 the main rate of corporation tax will increase from 19% to 25%. A company with profits of more than £250,000 whose accounting period runs from 1 January 2023 to 31 December 2023 will therefore pay corporation tax as follows:

- 3 months to 31 March 2023   19%
- 9 months to 31 December 2023   25%

The company will therefore pay 19% corporation tax on roughly one quarter of its profits (3/12) and 25% tax on roughly three quarters of its profits (9/12). (It doesn't matter at what point during the financial year the profits are actually made.)

This means the company's overall corporation tax rate for this year will be 23.5%. (Note, in practice corporation tax is calculated using days not months and this will result in a tiny difference to the overall tax rate which largely disappears in the rounding. For example, the above rate correctly calculated using days not months would be 23.52%.)

Smaller Profits

If the company has profits of less than £250,000 the calculation will be a bit more complicated. For example, a company with profits of £150,000 whose accounting period runs from 1st January 2023 to 31st December 2023 will pay corporation tax as follows:

- 3 months to 31st March 2023   19%
- 9 months to 31st December 2023   24%

24% is taken from Table 1 and is simply the new overall tax rate payable by a company with profits of £150,000.

The practical effect is that the company will pay 19% corporation tax on approximately one quarter of its profits and 24% tax on approximately three quarters of its profits.

This means the company's overall corporation tax rate for this year will be 22.75%.

(As explained above, in practice, the actual calculation must be performed in days rather than months. Also, 2024 is a leap year, which has a further small effect on the calculation for companies with profits under £250,000, which I have ignored for simplicity.)

Another Example

Let's say the company has profits of £100,000 and an accounting period that runs from 1st May 2022 to 30th April 2023. It will pay corporation tax as follows:

- 11 months to 31st March 2023   19%
- 1 month to 30th April 2023   22.75%

22.75% is taken from Table 1 and is simply the new overall tax rate payable by a company with profits of £100,000.

The practical effect is the company will pay 19% corporation tax on approximately 11/12ths of its profits and 22.75% tax on the remaining 1/12th. This means the company's overall corporation tax rate for this year will be 19.31%.

This example shows how the corporation tax increase will begin to affect some companies' profits from as early as May 2022.

Marginal Tax Rate Planning

When the corporation tax rate increases many companies will pay more tax on their profits. The upside of this is companies will also enjoy more corporation tax relief on their spending.

At present companies enjoy 19% corporation tax relief no matter how much profit they make or when they spend their money. If a company incurs an additional £1,000 of tax deductible spending this will reduce its taxable profits by £1,000, saving it £190 in corporation tax.

When the corporation tax increase is in full force, the amount of tax relief a company enjoys will depend on its profits:

- A company with profits of £50,000 or less will have a marginal tax rate of 19% and will continue to enjoy 19% tax relief on its spending.

- A company with profits of between £50,000 and £250,000 will have a marginal tax rate of 26.5% and will enjoy 26.5% tax relief on its spending. (However, if the company's spending pushes its profits below £50,000 it will start to receive just 19% tax relief on any additional spending.)

- A company with profits of more than £250,000 will have a marginal tax rate of 25% and will enjoy 25% tax relief on its spending. (However, if the company's spending pushes its profits below £250,000 it will start to receive 26.5% tax relief on any additional spending.)

In Table 1 we listed the new overall tax rates companies will face. For example, a company which makes a profit of £100,000 will have an overall tax rate of 22.75%. Note, the overall rate is NOT used for most tax planning purposes, for example calculating the amount of tax a company will save if it spends some more money. Instead it is the company's marginal tax rate.

This makes sense when you consider a simple example. A company which anticipates making a profit of £100,000 and incurs an additional £10,000 of tax deductible expenditure will reduce its taxable profits by £10,000. This will reduce its tax bill by £2,650 (26.5%). The company's overall tax rate of 22.75% does not tell us how much tax the company will save.

Periods Straddling the Date of Change

A company will have a slightly lower marginal tax rate for the year that straddles 1st April 2023, the date corporation tax changes.

In other words, spending in that year will attract more tax relief than at present but not quite as much as when the corporation tax increase is in full force.

Take a company whose tax year runs from 1st January to 31st December 2023 and has profits of between £50,000 and £250,000. Its marginal tax rate for that year is calculated as follows:

1st January to 31st March	90/365 x 19%	4.685%
1st April to 31st December	275/365 x 26.5%	19.966%
Marginal rate		24.65%

Thus, if the company incurs an additional £10,000 of tax deductible spending between 1st January 2023 and 31st December 2023 its corporation tax bill will be reduced by £2,465.

Note, it doesn't matter when during the year the spending takes place (it doesn't matter whether it's between January and March or between April and December).

If the company has profits of more than £250,000 its marginal tax rate will be 19% for the first three months and 25% for the final nine months. Its overall marginal tax rate for the year will therefore be 23.52%.

Appendix A contains all the marginal tax rates that apply to companies with different accounting periods, all straddling April 2023, the date corporation tax increases.

Companies with profits of £50,000 or less will continue to have a marginal tax rate of 19% and will therefore receive 19% tax relief on their spending.

The fact that many companies will see their marginal rates of corporation tax increase from the current level of 19% raises a number of questions for their owners:

Should My Company Postpone Spending?

At present companies enjoy 19% tax relief on their spending. When the corporation tax increase is in full force some companies will enjoy 26.5% tax relief on their additional spending and some will enjoy 25% tax relief.

Thus a company that postpones some of its discretionary spending will enjoy up to an additional 7.5 percentage points of tax relief, saving it up to £750 for every £10,000 it postpones.

Unfortunately, however, the company may have to wait quite some time to enjoy the maximum tax relief.

Take a company whose accounting period runs from 1st January to 31st December and has taxable profits of between £50,000 and £250,000 per year. The company faces the following marginal rates of corporation tax:

- Year ended 31st December 2021   19%
- Year ended 31st December 2022   19%
- Year ended 31st December 2023   24.65%
- Year ended 31st December 2024   26.5%

Only spending from January 2024 onwards can enjoy 26.5% tax relief, although spending between January and December 2023 can enjoy up to 24.65% tax relief.

Some company owners may be willing to postpone certain types of spending for this amount of time, others will not.

Super Tax Deduction for Companies

The Government was concerned that companies would postpone some of their *investment* spending until after the increase in corporation tax. Thus in the March 2021 Budget the Government also introduced a 'super deduction' of 130% for investment spending that takes place before 1st April 2023, the date corporation tax changes.

Thanks to the super deduction companies can currently enjoy roughly 25% tax relief on their investment spending. For example, a company spending £1,000 on a qualifying asset will see its taxable profits reduced by £1,300, saving it £247 in corporation tax (at 19%).

The super deduction covers things like computer equipment, vans and office furniture. However, only spending on *new* assets qualifies; second-hand goods do not qualify. It also does not cover spending on cars.

For more information about the super deduction see the new Taxcafe guide *The Company Tax Changes*.

In summary, if you are thinking about postponing any investment spending until your company's corporation tax rate increases, remember that the spending may currently qualify for the temporary 130% super tax deduction.

Will the Tax Increase Affect Salaries, Dividends etc?

If your company pays you a salary, rental income, interest income or makes pension contributions on your behalf these are all tax deductible expenses for the company.

Thus the tax relief the company enjoys on all of these expenses will increase when corporation tax increases (assuming it has profits of more than £50,000).

By contrast dividends are paid out of a company's *after-tax profits*. Thus the total amount of tax paid on dividend income will increase.

We will take a look at how the corporation tax change will affect company owners' profit extraction decisions in the chapters that follow.

However, the main focus of this guide is the current 2021/22 tax year so in most of the corporation tax calculations in this guide we use the current 19% rate.

Multiple Companies

Company owners often think about setting up a second company, to keep a new venture separate from an existing business. Often there are sound commercial reasons for using more than one company, including to:

- Reduce risk (limit liability)
- Involve different shareholders
- Enable a stand-alone sale of each business
- Make it easier to borrow money

Using more than one company allows you to reduce your risk – if one business goes bankrupt, the other venture housed in a separate company should be protected because each company has limited liability status.

Using more than one company is also ideal when you want each business to have different shareholders. It's not uncommon for business owners to engage in different projects with different people.

Using separate companies may also make it easier to exit each business. For example, someone who owns an ecommerce business and a restaurant chain may wish to keep them in separate companies to make it easier to sell each business to a different buyer in the future.

When it comes to borrowing money, it's not uncommon for property investors to put their properties in a separate stand-alone company and lenders often insist on this. Mortgage lenders tend not to like companies that have 'trading' activities which are perceived as being more risky than property investment.

Saving Tax

Using separate companies may also be attractive when it comes to saving capital gains tax and inheritance tax – in particular when one business is a trading business and the other is not. Companies that own too many non-trading assets, like rental property, can lose important tax reliefs, including Business Asset Disposal Relief (previously known as Entrepreneurs Relief), Holdover Relief and Business Property Relief.

For example, someone who owns a software company and a property rental business may wish to keep them in separate companies so that the trading business (the software company) is not 'contaminated' by the non-trading business (the property rental business).

Using separate companies has drawbacks too. For example, if you initially expect losses from a new trading activity, those losses can usually be set off against the profits from an existing activity, if both businesses are in the same company. This is generally not possible if the businesses are in separate companies (unless you form a group).

Many taxpayers may also be asking whether, when corporation tax increases, they can benefit from more than one company each enjoying up to £50,000 of profit taxed at just 19%.

The answer is generally no if the companies are controlled by the same people.

Associated Company Rules

When the corporation tax increase comes into force, to prevent people artificially spreading their business activities across multiple companies, the £50,000 lower limit and £250,000 upper limit will be divided up if there are any 'associated companies'.

A company will be associated with another company if:

- One company controls the other company
- Both are under the control of the same person or persons

For example, if you own all of the shares in two companies these companies will be associated. Each company will start paying corporation tax at 26.5% when its profits exceed £25,000 (i.e. £50,000/2). Each company will pay 25% tax on all of its profits if its profits are greater than £125,000 (£250,000/2).

If there are three associated companies, each company will start paying corporation tax at 26.5% when its profits exceed £16,667 (£50,000/3)... and so on.

Example

Let's assume the new higher rates of corporation tax are in operation. Jamie owns Company 1 which has annual profits of £100,000. He then decides to start a second business and is trying to decide whether to house it in Company 1 or set up Company 2. Let's say the new business makes a profit of £30,000. If he keeps it in Company 1 the additional profit will be taxed at 26.5% producing a total tax bill of £30,700.

If Jamie decides to house the new business in Company 2, the two companies will be associated if we assume he controls them both. The companies will pay corporation tax as follows:

Company 1: £25,000 x 19% + £75,000 x 26.5% = £24,625
Company 2: £25,000 x 19% +   £5,000 x 26.5% = £6,075
Combined tax bill: £30,700

The total corporation tax bill will be the same whether Jamie uses one company or two. Jamie will still benefit from having £50,000 of profits taxed at 19% (£25,000 in each company).

If Company 2 has profits of less than £25,000, Jamie will effectively be penalised for running two companies. For example, if Company 2 breaks even (i.e. has a profit of exactly £0) he will pay £1,875 more tax with two companies. This is because Company 1 will have just £25,000 instead of £50,000 taxed at 19%.

What is an Associated Company?

Companies are associated if one company controls the other company or both companies are under the control of the same person or persons.

Example

If you own 51% or more of the shares of Company A, you control Company A.

If you own 51% or more of the shares of Company B, you control Company B.

The two companies are controlled by the same person and are therefore associated. Each company can only have £25,000 of profits taxed at 19%.

Example

Katie and her husband Jamie each own 50% of Company A.

They also each own 50% of Company B.

Thus Katie and Jamie together control Company A and together they control Company B.

The companies are associated because they are controlled by the same two persons. Each company can only have £25,000 of profits taxed at 19%.

Note, control isn't just about ownership of the company's share capital. If a person or persons together have either control of the affairs of the company, control through voting power, control over the company's income, control of the company's assets or the right to receive the greater part of the company's assets (for example when the company is wound up) that person or persons will have control of the company.

A loan creditor may have control of a company. For example, if one company lends money to another company, the company that makes the loan may have control of the other company and the two companies will then be associated.

When Companies Are Not Associated

An associated company is ignored if it has not carried on a trade or business at any time during the year.

This means dormant companies are disregarded, as are companies that only receive interest from a bank account and certain companies that are passive holding companies.

Similarly, a company that exists only to hold property (e.g. a second home) and does not rent out the property will not usually need to be counted as an associated company.

Subject to the above points, foreign companies are included, however.

Family Members and Business Partners

It's quite common for married couples to have an interest in more than one company. For example, there may be a trading company and a property company that holds rental properties. Or there may be two trading companies, for example a web design company and a garden landscaping company.

If the husband owns 51% or more of company 1 and his wife owns 51% or more of company 2 the two companies may not be associated. This means each company may be able to enjoy £50,000 of profit taxed at just 19%.

However, this will only be possible if there is not 'substantial commercial interdependence' between the companies.

This is because your 'associates' interests in a company are treated as your own if there is substantial commercial interdependence between the companies. Associates include:

- Your spouse or civil partner
- Close relatives (parents, grandparents, brothers and sisters, children, grandchildren etc.)
- Business partners

Substantial Commercial Interdependence

There are three types of links that determine if there is substantial commercial interdependence between two companies:

- **Financial interdependence** – Two companies are interdependent if one gives financial support to the other (for example a loan) or each has a financial interest in the same business.

- **Economic interdependence** – Two companies are economically interdependent if they have the same economic objective or the activities of one help the other or they have common customers.

- **Organisational interdependence** – Two companies are organisationally interdependent if they have common management, employees, premises or equipment.

It is not necessary for all three types of links to exist. For example, if there is a sufficient financial link, one company will be an associated company of another, even if no economic or organisational links exist.

HMRC guidance states that even if there is not substantial commercial interdependence, two companies may still be associated. Take the example of a husband and wife who separately own and run two completely different companies. Let's assume the husband has made a loan to his wife's company and as part of that loan is entitled to the company's assets if it is wound up. The two companies will be associated even though there is not substantial commercial interdependence. This is because the husband will control both companies through his shareholding and rights to assets on winding up.

Unmarried Couples

Lots of couples are not legally married but raise children, start businesses and buy property together. However, unmarried couples are not treated as associates by the tax legislation

An unmarried couple will therefore each be able to own their own company and benefit from a total of up to £100,000 of profits taxed at 19% between them, *even if there is substantial commercial interdependence between the two companies.*

Alternatively, one member of the couple may be able to own, say, 51% of company 1 and 49% of company 2 (and vice-versa for the other person) without the companies being treated as associated.

Corporation Tax Quarterly Instalments

The associated company rules will also be relevant in deciding whether a company has to pay corporation tax in quarterly instalments. Instalments are generally payable by companies whose profits exceed £1.5 million but this amount will be divided up if there are any associated companies. Whereas small companies currently only have to pay their corporation tax nine months after the financial year has ended, companies subject to instalments have to start paying tax half way through the year.

Trading Companies vs Investment Companies

In tax jargon a 'trading' company is one involved in, for want of a better word, 'regular' business activities, e.g. a company that sells goods online, a catering company or a firm of garden landscapers.

Common types of *non-trading* company include those that hold substantial investments in property or financial securities or earn substantial royalty income.

Corporation Tax

If your company is engaged mainly in non-trading activities it will currently pay corporation tax at the same rate as most other companies – 19%.

However, when the new corporation tax rates come into effect, some of these companies will have to pay corporation tax at the main rate of 25% on all of their profits.

This is because a company classed as a close investment holding company (CIC) will not able to benefit from the small profits rate. It will be forced to pay corporation tax at the main rate on all of its profits.

For example, a company that is set up to buy and sell stock market shares will currently pay 19% tax but when the new corporation tax rates come into effect it will pay 25%, even if it only makes a small amount of profit.

Companies that mainly derive their profits from renting property to unconnected third parties (i.e. not to family members, etc) are excluded from the CIC provisions. Hence, the vast majority of property investment companies will be allowed to enjoy the small profits rate.

Capital Gains Tax

If a company has too many non-trading activities (including most property investment and property letting) it may lose its trading status for capital gains tax purposes.

This will result in the loss of two important CGT reliefs:

- Business Asset Disposal Relief (Entrepreneurs Relief)
- Holdover Relief

Business Asset Disposal Relief allows you to pay CGT at just 10% (instead of 20%) when you sell your company or wind it up.

Holdover Relief allows you to give shares in the business to your children, common-law unmarried partner, or other individuals and postpone CGT. (You don't need Holdover Relief to transfer shares to your spouse because such transfers are always exempt.)

A company will only lose its trading status for CGT purposes if it has 'substantial' non-trading activities. Unfortunately to HMRC 'substantial' means as little as 20% of various measures such as:

- Assets
- Turnover
- Expenses
- Profits
- Directors' and employees' time

HMRC may attempt to apply the 20% rule to *any* of the above measures.

Inheritance Tax

Shares in trading companies generally qualify for business property relief which means they can be passed on free from inheritance tax. However, if the company holds investments (including rental property) this could result in the loss of business property relief.

The qualification criteria are, however, more generous than for CGT purposes and a company generally only loses its trading status for inheritance tax purposes if it is 'wholly or mainly' involved in investment related activities.

To be on the safe side you may want to ensure that the company's qualifying activities exceed 50% of each of the measures listed above (e.g. turnover, time, profits etc).

For more information see our guide *How to Save Inheritance Tax*.

Making Tax Digital (MTD)

The Government is making painful changes to the way businesses manage their taxes, including compulsory digital record-keeping and, worst of all, quarterly reporting of results to HMRC.

At the time of writing the Government was still consulting on MTD for corporation tax. It says it will not make it compulsory before 2026.

If and when MTD for corporation tax does come about, companies will have to use MTD compatible software to provide quarterly summary updates of their income and expenses to HMRC plus an annual corporation tax return plus four quarterly VAT returns.

After that we can expect the Government to ask companies to make more regular corporation tax payments too, instead of just one payment many months after the end of their tax year. HMRC launched a consultation on this very topic in March 2021.

MTD is absolutely bonkers and we at Taxcafe have said this from day one. There won't be a single business in the land that will benefit. All in all we welcome all delays and setbacks to this ridiculous project.

Chapter 2

How Directors Are Taxed: Employment Income

When HMRC and tax professionals talk about 'employment income', they are referring to salaries and bonuses.

Salaries and bonuses are subject to income tax and national insurance. They are also generally a tax deductible expense for the company.

Income Tax

For the 2021/22 tax year, starting on 6 April 2021, most individuals pay income tax as follows on their salaries:

- 0%   on the first   £12,570   Personal allowance
- 20%   on the next   £37,700   Basic-rate band
- 40%   above   £50,270   Higher-rate threshold

If you earn more than £50,270 you are a higher-rate taxpayer; if you earn less you are a basic-rate taxpayer.

The number £50,270 is important to remember because it will be mentioned repeatedly in the chapters that follow.

Transferable Personal Allowance

It is possible to transfer 10% of your personal allowance to your spouse or civil partner (£1,260 during the current 2021/22 tax year).

Only basic-rate taxpayers can benefit from this tax break, so the potential tax saving is £252 (£1,260 x 20%).

Unmarried couples are excluded – this was the rather feeble attempt by David Cameron (remember him?) to use the tax system to reward marriage.

Married couples can generally only benefit from this tax break if:

- One person earns less than £12,570 (not including savings interest under £5,000) and is therefore wasting some of their personal allowance

- The other person earns less than £50,270 (£43,662 in Scotland)

Both individuals must have been born on or after 6 April 1935.

You have to register to use it:

www.gov.uk/marriageallowance

Potential winners are married couples where one person does not work (e.g. full-time parents) or only has a part-time job.

Example
In 2021/22 Bill earns a salary of £30,000 and his wife Daphne earns £6,000 working part time. Daphne has £6,570 of unused personal allowance. She can transfer £1,260 of this to Bill which means Bill no longer has to pay tax on £1,260 of his income. This will save him £252 in tax (£1,260 x 20%).

Company owners have more scope than regular salaried employees to benefit from this tax giveaway, as we shall see in Chapter 21.

Income over £100,000

When your taxable income exceeds £100,000 your income tax personal allowance is gradually withdrawn. For every additional £1 you earn, 50p of your personal allowance is taken away.

What this means is that, when your income reaches £125,140 this year, your personal allowance will have completely disappeared.

It also means that those who earn salary income between £100,000 and £125,140 face a marginal income tax rate of 60%.

Example

Caroline, a company director, has received salary income of £100,000 so far during the current tax year. If she receives an extra £100 of salary she will pay an extra £40 of income tax. She will also lose £50 of her income tax personal allowance, so £50 of previously tax-free salary will now be taxed at 40%, adding £20 to her tax bill.

All in all, she pays £60 in tax on her extra £100 of salary, so her marginal income tax rate is 60%.

Income above £150,000

Once your taxable income exceeds £150,000, you will pay 45% income tax on any extra employment income. This is known as the additional rate of tax. It used to be 50%.

National Insurance

For the current 2021/22 tax year individuals pay national insurance as follows on their salary income:

- 0%   on the first   £9,568   Primary threshold
- 12%   on the next   £40,702
- 2%   above   £50,270   Upper earnings limit

The Government's stated ambition is to align the primary threshold with the personal allowance.

Combined Tax Rates

The combined marginal rates of income tax and national insurance applying to salaries in 2021/22 are as follows:

Income up to £9,568	0%
Income from £9,568 to £12,570	12%
Income from £12,570 to £50,270	32%
Income from £50,270 to £100,000	42%
Income from £100,000 to £125,140	62%
Income from £125,140 to £150,000	42%
Income over £150,000	47%

Employer's National Insurance

Most employees don't lose sleep over their employer's national insurance bill. However, as a company director/shareholder, the company's money is effectively your money so this extra tax is an important consideration.

Companies pay 13.8% national insurance on every single pound of salary the director/shareholder earns over the 'secondary threshold'. The secondary threshold is £8,840 for 2021/22.

Employer's national insurance is a tax deductible expense. So if a company pays £100 of national insurance, this will reduce its taxable profits by £100, currently saving the company £19 in corporation tax. Thus the net overall cost is actually £81.

There is no employer's national insurance on salaries paid to under 21s and apprentices under 25 provided they are not higher-rate taxpayers (i.e. they must earn less than £50,270). Note, the exemption is not lost if the employee earns more than £50,270. Employer's national insurance is only payable on the excess salary.

The Government has introduced a national insurance holiday for employers taking on military veterans from April 2021. The holiday will be for the employee's first year of civilian employment. The exemption applies to salary up to the higher-rate threshold. For further details go to:

https://tinyurl.com/veteransNI

£4,000 Employment Allowance

Most businesses qualify for the employment allowance which was increased from £3,000 to £4,000 in April 2020.

From April 2020 the allowance is only given to employers whose national insurance bill was less than £100,000 in the previous tax year. Fortunately, therefore, most small businesses will be unaffected and will continue to enjoy this tax break.

The reason for covering the employment allowance in this guide is because it may affect some company owners' own salary choice. For example, two company owners who have no other employees can pay themselves a salary of £23,332 each this year without having to pay any employer's national insurance.

But is it a good idea to take this much salary to avoid wasting the £4,000 employment allowance? We'll answer this question in Chapter 8. In this section we'll take a brief look at some of the employment allowance rules.

One Man Band Companies

Unfortunately the employment allowance is not available to "one man band" companies where there is just one director who is the only employee.

According to HMRC guidance, the employment allowance also cannot be claimed if there are other employees BUT the director's salary is the only one on which employer's national insurance is payable.

This is to prevent directors of one-man band companies employing friends or family and paying them a token amount in order to claim the employment allowance for their own salaries.

At least one of the additional employees must be paid more than the secondary threshold. For example, a company that employs a seasonal worker who earns above the secondary threshold in a week (£170 for 2021/22) will be eligible for the employment allowance for the whole tax year.

The second employee can be another director (e.g. your spouse) provided both directors' salaries exceed the *annual* secondary threshold (£8,840 for 2021/22 or pro rata if the directorship begins after the tax year has started).

If circumstances change during the tax year and the director becomes the only employee paid above the secondary threshold, the employment allowance can still be claimed for that tax year.

If a company with just one director who earns less than the national insurance threshold employs just one other person (not a director), the company can claim the employment allowance if the employee earns more than the national insurance threshold.

It should be pointed out that several expert commentators, including the Institute of Chartered Accountants, believe HMRC has not interpreted the law correctly and that it should be possible to claim the employment allowance even if the second employee receives a small salary on which no employer's national insurance is payable.

However, to play it safe it would be advisable to pay any second employee a salary slightly higher than the secondary threshold.

Other Employment Allowance Rules

The employment allowance can only be used against class 1 national insurance and not against class 1A national insurance. Class 1A is due on most taxable benefits in kind provided to employees, e.g. company cars.

If your company belongs to a group of companies, only one can claim the allowance. If your business runs multiple PAYE schemes, the allowance can only be claimed against one scheme.

The allowance is claimed as part of the payroll process. The full £4,000 can be claimed in month one of the tax year if your employer's class 1 national insurance exceeds £4,000 per month.

You can start claiming the allowance after the tax year has started and make a catch-up claim which can also be offset against your other PAYE costs.

If you claim the allowance at the end of the tax year and your remaining PAYE costs are not sufficient to use the entire allowance, the unclaimed balance can be carried forward to the next tax year.

Connected Companies

A company cannot claim the employment allowance if a 'connected company' already claims it.

Companies are connected if one company has control of the other company or both companies are controlled by the same person.

A person is generally considered to have control of a company if they hold more than 50% of the company's share capital or voting power or if they are entitled to more than 50% of the company's distributable income or assets if the company is wound up.

For example, if you own all the shares in two companies you will only be entitled to one employment allowance, even if the two companies are completely separate businesses with, for example, separate premises and staff.

If the company that claims the employment allowance has employer's class 1 national insurance of less than £4,000, the balance cannot be claimed by the other company.

Where there is 'substantial commercial interdependence' between two or more companies (see Chapter 1) the holdings of close relatives and other 'associates' are added together to determine whether the companies are controlled by the same person or group of persons.

For example, if you own all the shares in company X and your spouse owns all the shares in company Y, your spouse's holding in company Y is attributed to you and you are treated as controlling company X and Y, as is your spouse.

However, the two companies will only be treated as connected companies if there is substantial commercial interdependence between them.

If the two companies are completely unrelated then two employment allowances can be claimed. If there is substantial commercial interdependence between the companies then only one allowance can be claimed.

Case Study – Total Tax Payable on Salary

Jane earns a salary of £60,000. Her income tax for 2021/22 can be calculated as follows:

- 0%   on the first   £12,570   =   £0
- 20% on the next   £37,700   =   £7,540
- 40% on the final   £9,730   =   £3,892

Total income tax bill: £11,432

Her national insurance for 2021/22 can be calculated as follows:

- 0%   on the first   £9,568   =   £0
- 12% on the next   £40,702   =   £4,884
- 2%   on the final   £9,730   =   £195

Jane's national insurance bill: £5,079.

Her company claims the £4,000 employment allowance but this is used up paying salaries to other employees. Her company's national insurance bill on her salary is therefore:

- 0%   on the first £8,840   =   £0
- 13.8% on the next £51,160   =   £7,060

The company's national insurance bill is £7,060. Because the company pays corporation tax at 19%, its national insurance bill, net of corporation tax relief, is £5,719.

The total tax paid by Jane and her company is as follows:

	£
Income tax	£11,432
Employee's national insurance	£5,079
Employer's national insurance	£5,719
Total taxes	£22,230

When you include employer's national insurance, it's startling how much tax is paid on Jane's income. Her £60,000 salary is not low by any standards but you wouldn't describe her as a high income earner either. Nevertheless an amount equivalent to 37% of her salary is paid in direct taxes on her *whole* income.

TABLE 2
Total Tax Payable on Salary 2021/22

Salary	Income Tax	Employee NI	Employer NI	Total	%
10,000	0	52	130	182	2
20,000	1,486	1,252	1,247	3,985	20
30,000	3,486	2,452	2,365	8,303	28
40,000	5,486	3,652	3,483	12,621	32
50,000	7,486	4,852	4,601	16,939	34
60,000	11,432	5,079	5,719	22,230	37
70,000	15,432	5,279	6,836	27,547	39
80,000	19,432	5,479	7,954	32,865	41
90,000	23,432	5,679	9,072	38,183	42
100,000	27,432	5,879	10,190	43,501	44
110,000	33,432	6,079	11,308	50,819	46
120,000	39,432	6,279	12,425	58,136	48
130,000	44,460	6,479	13,543	64,482	50
140,000	48,460	6,679	14,661	69,800	50
150,000	52,460	6,879	15,779	75,118	50
160,000	56,960	7,079	16,897	80,936	51
170,000	61,460	7,279	18,014	86,753	51
180,000	65,960	7,479	19,132	92,571	51
190,000	70,460	7,679	20,250	98,389	52
200,000	74,960	7,879	21,368	104,207	52
225,000	86,210	8,379	24,162	118,751	53
250,000	97,460	8,879	26,957	133,296	53
275,000	108,710	9,379	29,751	147,840	54
300,000	119,960	9,879	32,546	162,385	54
350,000	142,460	10,879	38,135	191,474	55
400,000	164,960	11,879	43,724	220,563	55
450,000	187,460	12,879	49,313	249,652	55
500,000	209,960	13,879	54,902	278,741	56
600,000	254,960	15,879	66,080	336,919	56
700,000	299,960	17,879	77,258	395,097	56
800,000	344,960	19,879	88,436	453,275	57
900,000	389,960	21,879	99,614	511,453	57
1,000,000	434,960	23,879	110,792	569,631	57

Table 2 shows the total tax payable on a whole range of salaries. In each case we assume the director's salary is subject to employer's national insurance which is not reduced by the £4,000 employment allowance. The employer's national insurance cost has been reduced by deducting 19% corporation tax relief.

Once again, it's startling how much tax is paid on salaries, especially when you look at the overall tax rate (the last column).

Future Income Tax Changes

In his March 2021 Budget speech Chancellor Rishi Sunak promised that "this government is not going to raise the rates of income tax, national insurance, or VAT."

We were then told that pretty much every important tax threshold and allowance will be frozen until April 2026 – giving the Government five years to let inflation slowly erode their value. Saying you're not going to raise tax rates and then freezing tax thresholds is a bit like a mugger telling you he's not going to shoot you just before he sticks a knife in your belly.

Example
*Chavez earns a salary of £60,000 in 2021/22 and pays income tax of £11,432. This means his overall tax rate is **19%**.*

*His salary simply increases with inflation and by 2025/26 is £67,500. His pay does not increase in real terms, so he is no better off than before. Because the Government has decided to freeze income tax thresholds, Chavez's income tax bill will be £14,432 in 2025/26 and his overall tax rate will be **21%**.*

Thus by 2025/26 his overall tax rate has increased by 2 percentage points.

The Government is taking a bigger share of his income, even though his income is exactly the same as before in real inflation-adjusted terms. (Remember the tax system is supposed to tax you more heavily as your income goes up… but only if your income goes up in *real terms*.)

The two percentage point tax increase Chavez suffers will probably be permanent. If the Government adjusts income tax bands for inflation in 2026/27 this will simply stop his overall tax rate from increasing further. To reduce it back to 19% they would have to adjust tax bands by much more than inflation.

In other words, it is possible Chavez's overall tax rate will be 2% higher for the rest of his working life.

Note in this example I have assumed that inflation will be 3% per year over the next five years. Personally I don't think this is an outlandish assumption. With total Government debt hovering around £2 trillion, allowing higher than normal inflation may be the only way to erode the burden.

Fiscal austerity (cutting spending or a broad-based tax increase) is politically unpalatable and can only go so far.

Scottish Income Tax

The Scottish Parliament has complete power to set income tax rates and thresholds for most types of income including salaries, self-employment income, rental income and pensions.

It does NOT have the power to tax interest and dividend income (including small company dividends). These types of income continue to be taxed using UK rates and thresholds.

The Scottish Parliament also does not have the power to set the personal allowance. National insurance and most other taxes, including corporation tax, capital gains tax and inheritance tax, remain the preserve of the UK Government.

Scottish Income Tax 2021/22

The following income tax rates apply for 2021/22:

£0 - £12,570	0%	Personal allowance (PA)
£12,570 - £14,667	19%	Starter rate
£14,667 - £25,296	20%	Basic rate
£25,296 - £43,662	21%	Intermediate rate
£43,662 - £100,000	41%	Higher rate
£100,000 - £125,140	61.5%	PA withdrawal
£125,140 - £150,000	41%	Higher rate
£150,000 +	46%	Top rate

Coupled with national insurance (set by the UK Government), the combined tax rates on salary income are as follows:

£0 to £9,568	0%
£9,568 to £12,570	12%
£12,570 to £14,667	31%
£14,667 to £25,296	32%
£25,296 to £43,662	33%
£43,662 to £50,270	53%
£50,270 to £100,000	43%
£100,000 to £125,140	63.5%
£125,140to £150,000	43%
Over £150,000	48%

Table 3 compares Scottish income tax with the rest of the UK. "Income" does not include dividends or interest.

Many Scottish taxpayers will pay more tax than those in the rest of the UK thanks to the extra 1% tax paid at many income levels and the lower higher-rate threshold (£43,662 compared with £50,270 in the rest of the UK).

For example, someone earning £50,000 in Scotland will pay £1,494 more tax than someone living elsewhere in the UK; someone earning £100,000 will pay £2,048 more tax.

Note, however, that Scottish taxpayers who earn less than £27,393 will pay less tax than those living elsewhere in the UK.

To date income tax increases in Scotland have been relatively timid because the Scottish Government has been worried about chasing away high earners. However, I strongly suspect that the 46% top rate will be increased again at some point in the future.

Table 3
Income Tax: Scotland vs Rest of UK
2021/22

Income	Scotland	Rest of UK	Difference
£20,000	£1,465	£1,486	-£21
£30,000	£3,512	£3,486	£26
£40,000	£5,612	£5,486	£126
£50,000	£8,980	£7,486	£1,494
£60,000	£13,080	£11,432	£1,648
£70,000	£17,180	£15,432	£1,748
£80,000	£21,280	£19,432	£1,848
£100,000	£29,480	£27,432	£2,048
£125,000	£44,855	£42,432	£2,423
£150,000	£55,133	£52,460	£2,673
£175,000	£66,633	£63,710	£2,923
£200,000	£78,133	£74,960	£3,173

Who is a Scottish Taxpayer?

Someone is a Scottish taxpayer if their sole or main place of residence is in Scotland. For example, someone who rents a flat in London where they work during the week will probably be treated as a Scottish taxpayer if their spouse and children live in the family home in Edinburgh and most of their friends and other social links are also in Edinburgh.

In some cases it may be difficult to establish where the main residence is located.

Where no close connection to Scotland can be identified (for example, because it is not possible to establish the person's main place of residence), Scottish taxpayer status will be determined through day counting.

You will be a Scottish taxpayer if you spend more days during the tax year in Scotland than you spend in Wales, Northern Ireland or England (taking each country separately).

Scottish Company Owners

Scottish company owners who pay themselves a small tax-efficient salary (see Chapter 8) and take the rest of their income as dividends are completely immune from Scottish income tax. They pay exactly the same amount of tax as company owners living in the rest of the UK.

This is because the Scottish Parliament cannot change the income tax personal allowance or national insurance threshold and cannot tax dividend income.

This assumes that the company owner does not have any other income subject to Scottish income tax, for example rental income.

Being subject to Scottish income tax is not necessarily a bad thing. It's only when Scottish company owners have salary income and other income subject to Scottish tax of more than £27,393 that they will pay more tax than those living elsewhere in the UK.

Welsh Income Tax

Since April 2019 the National Assembly for Wales has been able to vary the income tax rates payable by Welsh taxpayers.

However, for the current 2021/22 tax year, taxpayers in Wales will pay exactly the same income tax as taxpayers in England and Northern Ireland.

As in Scotland, the powers are limited with the UK Government retaining responsibility for the income tax personal allowance and the taxation of savings and dividend income. The UK Government also retains control of most other taxes such as national insurance, VAT, corporation tax, capital gains tax and inheritance tax.

Chapter 3

How Directors Are Taxed: Dividend Income

Dividends are subject to income tax but not national insurance. Also, the income tax rates on dividends are lower than the income tax rates on salaries because dividends are paid out of a company's *after-tax* profits: the money has already been taxed in the company's hands, whereas salaries are a tax deductible expense.

The tax treatment of dividends was completely changed on 6th April 2016.

Dividend tax credits have been abolished, so it's no longer necessary to gross up your cash dividends to calculate your tax. All tax calculations now work with cash dividends only and are therefore a lot simpler.

(I generally refer to the amount of dividend actually paid, or deemed to be paid, as the "cash" dividend. This does not necessarily mean that it is literally paid in cash, as dividends are sometimes paid by way of accounting entries.)

While simpler tax calculations are the good news, the bad news is that the current tax rates for cash dividends are 7.5% higher than the previous ones.

The first £2,000 of dividend income you receive is, however, tax free thanks to the "dividend nil rate band", also known as the "dividend allowance". The dividend allowance was cut from £5,000 to £2,000 in 2018/19.

For those receiving dividends in excess of the £2,000 dividend allowance, the following income tax rates apply (the old effective rates are included for comparison):

	Old	**Current**
Basic-rate taxpayers	0%	7.5%
Higher-rate taxpayers	25%	32.5%
Additional-rate taxpayers	30.6%	38.1%

Overall Tax Rates on Dividend Income

Because income paid out as dividends is taxed twice (first in the hands of the company and second in the hands of the shareholder) it's easy to lose sight of how much tax is being paid overall.

As a company owner you are likely to be equally concerned about your company's tax bill as your own, so it's worth showing the overall combined tax rates on dividend income.

With companies currently paying 19% corporation tax, the total tax rates on dividend income are as follows:

	Total Tax Rate (rounded)
Basic-rate taxpayers	25%
Higher-rate taxpayers	45%
Additional-rate taxpayers	50%

For example, a company with £100 of profit will pay £19 corporation tax, leaving £81 to pay out as dividends. Ignoring the £2,000 dividend allowance, a higher-rate taxpayer will pay £26 tax on this income (£81 x 32.5%), so the total tax bill on the £100 profit is £45, which is 45%.

The above tax rates are higher than the regular income tax rates that apply to most types of income (20% for basic-rate taxpayers, 40% for higher-rate taxpayers and 45% for additional-rate taxpayers).

This is because the Government wanted to level the playing field between company owners (who often don't pay any national insurance) and self-employed business owners and regular employees, who pay national insurance on most of their earnings.

From a tax planning perspective, once a company owner has used up the £2,000 dividend allowance they are usually better off paying themselves income that is taxed at the "regular" income tax rates in preference to dividends, wherever possible.

Examples include rental income and interest income. A small salary also fits the bill, as long as the additional national insurance cost is mitigated.

After the Corporation Tax Increase

When corporation tax increases (see Chapter 1) the combined tax rates on dividend income will also naturally increase for many company owners. For example, where a company has profits greater than £250,000 and pays 25% tax on all of its profits, the total tax rates on dividend income will be:

	Total Tax Rate
Basic-rate taxpayers	30.63%
Higher-rate taxpayers	49.38%
Additional-rate taxpayers	53.58%

The corporation tax increase will thus make it even more attractive for company owners to pay themselves other types of income that are taxed at the "regular" 20%, 40% and 45% income tax rates in preference to dividends.

Company owners whose companies have profits of £50,000 or less will continue to face the total tax rates listed on the previous page.

For companies with profits of between £50,000 and £250,000, the combined tax rates on dividend income will vary according to the amount of profit the company makes. For example, a company with profits of £100,000 will face a total corporation tax bill of £22,750 (see Table 1), leaving £77,250 to pay out as dividends. If higher-rate tax at 32.5% is payable on all of this income the total tax bill on the £100,000 profit will be £47,856, which is 47.86%.

Table 4 contains the total tax rates that will apply at different profit levels and different income tax rates. (Note in all of these calculations we ignore the £2,000 dividend allowance.)

Some of these tax rates are unrealistically low if we assume that all of the company's profits are paid out in a single year to a single director.

For example, if a company has pre-tax profits £200,000 it would be impossible for its after-tax profits of £150,750 to be paid out to just one director in one tax year with just 7.5% basic-rate income tax payable (resulting in a total tax rate of just 30.28%).

TABLE 4
Total Tax Rates on Dividend Income
after the Corporation Tax Increase

Profits	Tax Rate @ 7.5%	Tax Rate @ 32.5%	Tax Rate @ 38.1%
£50,000	25.08	45.33	49.86
£60,000	26.23	46.17	50.63
£70,000	27.06	46.77	51.19
£80,000	27.68	47.22	51.60
£90,000	28.16	47.58	51.92
£100,000	28.54	47.86	52.18
£110,000	28.86	48.09	52.39
£120,000	29.12	48.28	52.57
£130,000	29.34	48.44	52.72
£140,000	29.53	48.58	52.85
£150,000	29.70	48.70	52.96
£160,000	29.84	48.81	53.05
£170,000	29.97	48.90	53.14
£180,000	30.09	48.98	53.21
£190,000	30.19	49.06	53.28
£200,000	30.28	49.12	53.34
£210,000	30.36	49.18	53.40
£220,000	30.44	49.24	53.45
£230,000	30.50	49.29	53.49
£240,000	30.57	49.33	53.54
£250,000	30.63	49.38	53.58

However, this tax rate could be payable if dividends are paid to several directors who are all basic-rate taxpayers, or if the profits are paid out over a number of years.

Similarly, some of the total tax rates are unrealistically high if the director does not have income from other sources. For example, if a company has pre-tax profits of just £50,000 this would never result in additional rate tax at 38.1% being payable if the director has no other source of income. If, however, the director does have a significant amount of income from other sources, it is possible the total tax rate on some or all of their dividend income will be 49.86%.

Marginal Tax Rates

The total tax rates listed in Table 4 are calculated using the total corporation tax and income tax payable if all of the company's after-tax profits are paid out as dividends.

However, for companies with profits between £50,000 and £250,000 these are not the ones we would typically use to make tax planning decisions. For these purposes we would use the company's *marginal tax rate*.

Remember companies with profits between £50,000 and £250,000 will pay 19% on the first £50,000 and 26.5% on the rest. 26.5% is the company's marginal tax rate. Its total (average) tax rate will be lower because some of its profits will be taxed at 19%.

For companies with profits of £50,000 or less the total tax rate and the marginal tax rate will be the same: 19%. Similarly, for companies with profits of more than £250,000 the total tax rate and the marginal tax rate will also be the same: 25%. (However, if the company spends enough money to take its profits below £250,000, it will start to have a marginal tax rate of 26.5%.)

Marginal Tax Rate Planning and Dividends

Take a company owner who is a higher-rate taxpayer and anticipates that, as things stand, his company will make a profit of £60,000. Let's say the company already pays him rent to use an office property that he owns personally and he wants to know whether he'll be better off paying himself an additional £1,000 of rent, or taking the money as a dividend instead.

If he pays himself rent this will be a tax deductible expense for the company, so the whole £1,000 will be paid out and after paying 40% income tax he will be left with £600.

Alternatively the company will pay 26.5% corporation tax on this final £1,000 of profit, leaving £735 to pay out as dividend income. After paying income tax at 32.5% he will be left with £496.

The total tax payable on the additional dividend income is £504 which is 50.4%. Clearly in this case additional rental income is more attractive.

Note, 50.4% is higher than the 46.17% rate in Table 4 for a company with profits of £60,000. That total tax rate is calculated using the company's total corporation tax rate. Most of its profits are taxed at just 19%, so the total tax rate in the table is lower.

The rate we've used in this example, however, is the company's 26.5% marginal tax rate, the rate which applies to the final £1,000 of profit we are looking at.

In summary, the total tax rates listed in Table 4 give you some idea of the total amount of corporation tax and income tax that will be payable if all of a company's after-tax profits are paid out as dividends. But when it comes to choosing between a dividend and some other type of income, the marginal tax rate is more relevant.

For company owners whose companies have profits of between £50,000 and £250,000 the combined marginal tax rate (corporation tax and income tax) on dividend income will be as follows after the corporation tax increase:

	Combined Marginal Tax Rate
Basic-rate taxpayers	32%
Higher-rate taxpayers	50.4%
Additional-rate taxpayers	54.5%

The £2,000 Dividend Nil Rate Band

Company owners do not enjoy an additional standalone amount of £2,000 tax free. Instead, the dividend nil rate band typically uses up some of your basic-rate band.

If you have a £55,000 dividend and no other income, the first £12,570 will be tax free thanks to your personal allowance and the next £2,000 will be tax free thanks to the dividend nil rate band. Only £35,700 of your remaining income will be taxed at 7.5% because the £2,000 dividend nil rate band uses up part of your £37,700 basic-rate band. The final £4,730 will be taxed at 32.5%.

The dividend nil rate band only uses up your basic-rate band if, like many company owners, you have dividend income subject to basic-rate tax. As we shall see later, it works differently if you have a lot of other income and all your dividends are subject to higher-rate tax.

Dividend Taxation – Examples

Let's take a look at some sample dividend tax calculations for the current 2021/22 tax year. To keep things simple we'll assume that the company owners take a small salary of £9,568 and the rest of their income as dividends. There may be £100 of employer's national insurance payable by the company on this salary. See Chapter 8 for a discussion as to why this amount of salary may nevertheless be the most tax efficient.

We'll also assume that the company owners have no other taxable income. The examples apply equally to Scottish company owners.

Example – Basic-Rate Taxpayer

Stuart is a company owner with a salary of £9,568 and cash dividend of £20,000. His total income is thus £29,568.

His salary is tax-free because it is covered by his personal allowance. The first £3,002 of his dividend income is tax free, being covered by the remainder of his personal allowance (£12,570 - £9,568).

The next £2,000 of his dividend income is also tax-free thanks to the dividend allowance. The final £14,998 of his dividend income is taxed at 7.5%, producing a total tax bill of £1,125.

Example – Higher-Rate Taxpayer

Robert is a company owner with a salary of £9,568 and dividend of £50,000. His total income is thus £59,568.

His salary is tax-free as it is covered by his personal allowance, as is the first £3,002 of his dividend (£12,570 - £9,568).

The next £2,000 of his dividend is also tax-free thanks to the dividend allowance. The dividend allowance uses up £2,000 of his £37,700 basic-rate band so just £35,700 of his dividend income is taxed at 7.5%, producing a tax bill of £2,678. The final £9,298 of his dividend income takes him over the higher-rate threshold and is taxed at 32.5%, producing a tax bill of £3,022.

Robert's total tax bill is £5,700.

Example – Personal Allowance Withdrawal

Alpesh is a company owner with a salary of £9,568 and dividend of £100,000. His total taxable income is thus £109,568. His personal allowance is reduced from £12,570 to £7,786. Thus £1,782 of his salary is taxed at 20% (£9,568 - £7,786), producing a tax bill of £356.

The first £2,000 of his dividend income is tax free, being covered by the dividend allowance. The next £33,918 of his dividend income is covered by his remaining basic-rate band (£37,700 - £1,782 - £2,000) and taxed at 7.5%, producing a tax bill of £2,544.

The remaining £64,082 of his dividend income is taxed at 32.5%, producing a tax bill of £20,827.

His total tax bill is therefore £23,727.

Example – Additional-Rate Taxpayer

Maeve is a company owner with a salary of £9,568 and dividend of £200,000. Her total income is thus £209,568. Because her income exceeds £150,000 she is an additional-rate taxpayer.

The first £2,000 of her dividend income is tax free but her income tax personal allowance is completely withdrawn. This means she will pay 20% income tax on her salary – £1,914 – and her remaining basic-rate band will be reduced to just £26,132 (£37,700 - £9,568 salary - £2,000 dividend allowance). She will thus pay 7.5% tax on £26,132 of her dividend income (£1,960).

The next £112,300 of her dividend (£150,000 less £37,700) is subject to higher-rate tax at 32.5%, resulting in additional tax of £36,498. The remaining £59,568 of dividend income takes her over the £150,000 threshold and is taxed at 38.1%, resulting in additional tax of £22,695.

Maeve's total tax bill is £63,067.

Taxpayers with Lots of Non-Dividend Income

It's important to explain how the dividend nil rate band operates when you have lots of non-dividend income, for example a big salary or a significant amount of rental income.

The dividend nil rate band only forms part of your basic-rate band if you have dividend income that falls into the basic-rate band. It works differently if your basic-rate band is completely used up by other income, e.g. salary or rental income.

The way to think about it is like this: dividends are always treated as the top slice of your income and taxed at your highest marginal rate. The dividend nil rate band exempts the bottom £2,000 of that income from tax. So if you have dividend income taxed at both 7.5% and 32.5%, the dividend allowance will exempt some of the income taxed at 7.5%.

But if ALL of your dividend income is taxed at 32.5% (because you have lots of other income, e.g. rental income) the dividend nil rate band will be part of your higher-rate band and you'll pay 0% tax instead of 32.5% tax on £2,000 of your dividend income.

Example
In 2021/22 Julia has a £60,000 salary and £30,000 dividend. Her salary uses up her personal allowance and basic-rate band, taking her over the higher-rate threshold. The first £2,000 of her dividend is tax free; £28,000 is taxed at the 32.5% higher rate.

The dividend allowance does not form part of her basic-rate band as none of her dividend income falls into the basic-rate band.

Example
In 2021/22 Leon has a £130,000 salary and £50,000 dividend. With this much income his personal allowance is completely withdrawn.

The first £2,000 of his dividend income is covered by the dividend allowance, leaving £18,000 taxed at the 32.5% higher rate. Along with his salary this takes Leon up to the £150,000 additional-rate threshold. The final £30,000 of his dividend income is taxed at 38.1%.

Leon has dividend income taxed at both the higher rate and additional rate. The dividend allowance reduces the amount of his dividend income taxed at the 32.5% higher rate.

Example

In 2020/21 Martin has a £100,000 salary, £50,000 of rental income and £50,000 dividend. With this much income his personal allowance is completely withdrawn.

His salary and rental income take him up to the £150,000 additional-rate threshold. The first £2,000 of dividend income is covered by the dividend allowance leaving £48,000 taxed at the 38.1% additional rate.

All of Martin's dividend income is taxable at the additional rate. The dividend allowance therefore reduces the amount of his dividend income taxed at the additional rate.

Scottish Taxpayers

The Scottish Government can tax most types of income but not dividends or interest. It also cannot change the personal allowance or national insurance.

This means:

- Scottish company owners pay exactly the same amount of tax on their dividend income as company owners living in the rest of the UK.

- Scottish company owners who also pay themselves a small tax-efficient salary (no higher than the £12,570 personal allowance) are completely immune from Scottish income tax, assuming they do not have any other income subject to Scottish tax.

- Scottish company owners whose salary income, rental income and other income (except interest and dividends) exceeds £12,570 will pay Scottish income tax.

  However, if this income is less than £27,393 they will pay less tax on this income than people living elsewhere in the UK. If this income exceeds £27,393 they will pay more tax.

  They will pay the same amount of tax on their dividend income as company owners living in the rest of the UK.

(See Chapter 16 for more information for high income earners.)

Example

Alan is a company owner living in Scotland. He has salary and rental income of £30,000 and dividend income of £25,000.

He is subject to Scottish income tax on his salary and rental income. As we saw in Table 3 in Chapter 2, this means he will pay £26 more tax on this income than someone living elsewhere in the UK.

And what about his dividend income?

Although the higher-rate threshold is £43,662 in Scotland, it is the UK higher-rate threshold (£50,270) that applies to his dividend income.

The first £2,000 is tax free thanks to the dividend allowance. This leaves him with £18,270 of basic-rate band (£50,270 - £30,000 - £2,000). This income will be taxed at 7.5%.

The remaining £4,730 of his dividend income takes him over the £50,270 higher-rate threshold and will be taxed at 32.5%.

Will Dividend Tax Rates be Increased Again?

When the dividend tax increase was announced in the July 2015 Budget the documentation stated that:

"These changes will also start to reduce the incentive to incorporate and remunerate through dividends rather than through wages to reduce tax liabilities."

Use of the word "start" hinted that further dividend tax increases were on the horizon. In the March 2017 Budget the threat became reality when it was announced that the dividend allowance would be reduced from £5,000 to £2,000 in April 2018.

Policymakers have a bee in their bonnets about the different amounts of tax paid by salaried employees, the self-employed (sole traders and partnerships) and company owners.

It's quite clear that those in charge of tax policy do not believe that entrepreneurs should be given special tax treatment to foster economic growth. We at Taxcafe think they should!

This is also why the rate of class 4 national insurance paid by the self-employed was increased in the March 2017 Budget. This tax increase was later cancelled when the media pointed out that it broke the 2015 election pledge to not increase tax rates. None of the dividend tax increases were reversed, however.

In the March 2021 Budget Chancellor Rishi Sunak promised that "this government is not going to raise the rates of income tax, national insurance, or VAT."

Instead the Government decided to freeze the personal allowance and higher-rate threshold for five years which is much the same as a permanent income tax increase (see the example with Chavez in Chapter 2).

Furthermore, the increase in corporation tax from April 2023 will result in an increase in the total combined tax rates on dividend income.

Following the huge surge in Government spending to support the economy during the coronavirus pandemic, we would definitely not rule out an increase in income tax rates (including dividend tax rates) at some point in the future.

However, given Rishi Sunak's promise, this is highly unlikely until after the next General Election (expected in May 2024) and no earlier than the 2025/26 tax year which starts on 6th April 2025.

Dividend Tax Terminology

Note that the 0% tax rate applying to the £2,000 dividend nil rate band is known officially as the "dividend nil rate". The 7.5% rate is known as the "ordinary rate", the 32.5% rate is known as the "upper rate" and the 38.1% rate as the "additional rate".

I do not use these terms much in this guide, preferring the terms basic rate, higher rate and additional rate.

Chapter 4

Making the Most of Your Personal Allowance

In all of the examples so far the taxpayer's personal allowance has been deducted from his salary rather than his dividends. This isn't mandatory – tax legislation states that your personal allowance can be used in the way that reduces your tax bill most.

Allocating some of your personal allowance from your salary to your dividend income is usually not worth doing but in a limited number of cases will produce further tax savings:

Example

In 2021/22 Antonia has salary income of £48,270 and dividend income of £50,000. If all of her personal allowance is allocated to her salary, her income tax will be calculated as follows:

Salary		**Tax**
Personal allowance	£12,570	£0
Taxed at 20%	£35,700	£7,140

Dividend		
Dividend allowance	£2,000	£0
Taxed at 32.5%	£48,000	£15,600
Total tax		£22,740

If instead Antonia allocates £2,000 of her personal allowance to her dividend income, her tax bill will be calculated as follows:

Salary		**Tax**
Personal allowance	£10,570	£0
Taxed at 20%	£37,700	£7,540

Dividend		
Personal allowance	£2,000	£0
Dividend allowance	£2,000	£0
Taxed at 32.5%	£46,000	£14,950
Total tax		£22,490

By reallocating her personal allowance, Antonia's tax bill falls by £250.

Why? Because she now pays 20% tax on £2,000 more salary BUT pays 32.5% tax on £2,000 less dividend income.

Does this means everyone should allocate some of their personal allowance to their dividend income? No because there is something else that usually increases your tax bill, although not in Antonia's case.

If you have £2,000 more salary taxed at 20% this means £2,000 of your basic-rate band will be used up by your salary. This means £2,000 more of your dividend income will be pushed over the higher-rate threshold and taxed at 32.5% instead of 7.5%, adding a further £500 to your tax bill.

The reason Antonia's tax bill does not increase is thanks to the precise salary we gave her, close to the higher-rate threshold. In her case it doesn't matter if £2,000 of her dividend income is pushed over the higher-rate threshold because this is the dividend income that is always tax free thanks to her dividend allowance.

In Chapter 20 we will examine how a far greater number of taxpayers with <u>interest income</u> could benefit from having their personal allowance reallocated.

Chapter 5

Don't Forget about Payments on Account

Many company owners having to make payments on account.

Payments on account are made twice a year and allow HMRC to collect some of the tax you owe early. Common victims include sole traders and landlords, i.e. those whose income tax is not collected at source.

Most salary earners do not have to make payments on account because their tax is collected almost immediately through PAYE.

Before the increase in dividend tax rates, the only small company owners who had to make payments on account were higher-rate taxpayers and additional-rate taxpayers. Basic-rate taxpayers didn't pay any tax on their dividends and therefore didn't have to make any payments on account.

This has all changed. Basic-rate taxpayers now pay 7.5% tax on their dividends and so many now have to make twice yearly payments on account.

Note, payments on account are not extra tax but they do affect your cashflow.

How Payments on Account Are Calculated

If you paid yourself a dividend during the previous tax year, which started on 6th April 2020 and ended on 5th April 2021, the income tax is normally payable by 31st January 2022 – almost 10 months after the tax year has ended.

For example, let's say a company owner paid himself a salary of £12,500 and dividend of £22,000 and had no other taxable income.

To keep the example simple let's also assume that he has never had to make any payments on account in the past.

No income tax was payable on his salary because it was fully covered by his personal allowance and the first £2,000 of his dividend income is tax free thanks to the dividend allowance.

The remaining £20,000 of his dividend income is taxed at 7.5%, producing a total income tax bill of £1,500 which has to be paid by 31st January 2022.

2021/22 Tax Year

Now let's move forward to the 2021/22 tax year which started on 6th April 2021 and ends on 5th April 2022.

We will assume our company owner pays himself a tax-free salary of £12,570 and a dividend of £25,000. His income tax bill will be £1,725 but this time he cannot wait until 31st January 2023 to pay his tax.

On 31st January 2022, when he pays his 2020/21 tax bill, he will also have to make a £750 payment on account for 2021/22 and another one on 31st July 2022. Thus his total tax payments will be as follows:

- 31st January 2022   £1,500 + £750 = £2,250
- 31st July 2022   £750

Each payment on account is half the previous year's (2020/21) self assessment tax.

In January 2023 he will have to make a final tax payment for 2021/22 but will be able to deduct the two payments on account.

In this example he will have an additional £225 to pay (£1,725 - £1,500 payments on account) because his payments on account will not fully cover his tax bill.

If he takes a much smaller dividend in 2021/22 he may be entitled to a tax refund (if his payments on account end up being too big).

Postponing Tax

Making payments on account is still much better than paying tax through the PAYE system.

Take a look at our company owner's tax payments for 2021/22.

The first payment is due around *10 months* after the start of the tax year (January 2022), the second payment is due around *16 months* after the start of the tax year (July 2022) and the third payment is due around *22 months* after the tax year has started (January 2023).

This means that if you pay yourself a dividend at the start of the tax year, you will have free use of the taxman's money for well over a year.

That money could be invested in a cash ISA or an offset mortgage or some other low-risk investment. The returns are likely to be better than those available from your company's bank account.

Who Has to Make Payments on Account?

Payments on account are all about the tax you paid in the *previous tax year*.

You only have to make payments on account if your self-assessment tax (i.e. ignoring tax deducted at source) for the previous tax year was more than £1,000.

For example, if during the current 2021/22 tax year you pay yourself a salary of £12,570 and a dividend of £15,000 your total income tax bill will be £975 and you will not have to make any payments on account in January and July 2023.

Of course, if you have income from other sources (e.g. rental income from property) this will have to be factored into the equation too.

You do not have to make payments on account, however, if more than 80% of your total tax from the previous year was covered by tax deducted at source.

How to Reduce Payments on Account

Where your self-assessment liability for the current year can reasonably be expected to be less than that for the previous year, you can apply to reduce your payments on account to the appropriate level (i.e. half of the anticipated liability for the current year).

For example, if you take a much smaller dividend in 2021/22 than you took in 2020/21, you can apply to reduce your payments on account due on 31 January and 31 July 2022.

You can do this when you submit your 2020/21 tax return.

You have to be careful when doing this, however. If you claim a reduction in your payments on account and then find that you have more tax to pay than you expected, you will have to pay interest on the underpayment and potentially a penalty.

Chapter 6

Salary versus Dividends: The Basics

Unlike self-employed business owners (sole traders and partnerships), company owners are in the fortunate position of wearing two caps.

On the one hand, you can reward your work as a director; on the other hand, you can reward your entrepreneurship as a shareholder.

As a company director and shareholder you can split your income into salary and dividends and this can generate income tax and national insurance savings.

For example, while national insurance is payable on salaries, it is not payable on shareholder dividends.

By structuring distributions from your company carefully and taking the 'optimum' amount of salary and dividends, you could end up with a significantly higher after-tax income than a regular salaried employee who earns a higher income before tax.

However, while saving income tax will be an important consideration, other factors are important too.

Salaries & Dividends: What's the Difference?

The major differences between a salary and dividend are the following:

Salaries Are Tax Deductible

Salaries usually qualify for corporation tax relief, dividends do not.

If the company pays you a salary, its taxable profits will be reduced and it will pay less corporation tax.

Dividends are paid out of a company's after-tax profits, so paying a dividend does not reduce the *company's* tax bill.

This is an important point to remember because most company owners are concerned about both their own and their company's tax bill.

For example, if a company has a taxable profit of £10,000 it will currently pay £1,900 corporation tax (19%), leaving £8,100 to distribute as dividends.

This corporation tax must be added to any income tax paid by the shareholder on his dividend income when calculating the total tax suffered.

Dividends Require Profits

Only companies that have made profits can pay dividends. Profits are usually calculated when the company's annual accounts are drawn up (often many months after the end of the company's financial year).

So dividends will usually be paid out of profits made in a previous accounting period. It is, however, possible to pay dividends out of profits made during the current year, for example if accurate management accounts are drawn up to determine the level of the company's distributable profits (see Chapter 37).

Salaries can be paid even if the company is making tax losses.

National Insurance

Salaries are generally subject to national insurance, dividends are not. Both the director and the company may be subject to national insurance.

Income Tax

Salaries and dividends are subject to different rates of income tax.

Tax Payment Dates

The income tax and national insurance payable on salaries is collected almost immediately via PAYE. The income tax on dividends is collected via self assessment – generally at a later date.

Earnings

Salaries are classed as 'earnings' which is important if you want to make significant pension contributions personally. Dividends are not classed as earnings.

Chapter 7

Company Owners Can Control
Their Income Tax Bills

In Chapter 6 we mentioned that a company owner can often decide whether any distribution of the company's money is classified as salary or dividend.

Another advantage of being a company owner is that you have complete control over *how much* income you withdraw in total. This gives you significant control over your income tax bill.

Unlike sole traders, who pay tax each year on ALL the profits of the business, company owners only pay income tax on the money they actually withdraw from the company.

This allows company owners to reduce their income tax bills by adopting the following strategies:

- 'Smooth income'
- 'Roller-coaster income'

Smooth Income

With smooth income, the company owner withdraws roughly the same amount of money each year, even though the company's profits may fluctuate considerably.

'Smooth income' allows the director/shareholder to stay below any of the following key income tax thresholds that could result in a higher income tax bill:

- £50,000/£50,270   Child benefit tax charge + Higher-rate tax
- £100,000   Personal allowance withdrawal
- £150,000   Additional rate tax

We will return to how you can plan your salary and dividend withdrawals around these key income tax thresholds in the chapters that follow.

The higher-rate threshold generally increases each year with inflation but has now been frozen until 5th April 2026. The other thresholds have *never* been increased. This means more taxpayers have been dragged into a higher tax bracket, even though their income has not increased in real terms.

The £100,000 and £150,000 thresholds were introduced in April 2010. If they had gone up with inflation you would only start losing your personal allowance with an income of around £135,000 today and you would only start paying 45% tax with an income of £200,000 today.

The child benefit tax charge was introduced in 2013. If the £50,000 threshold where it kicks in had gone up with inflation, you would only start paying the extra tax with an income of around £60,000 today.

By freezing these thresholds the Government has decided to deploy "fiscal drag" to raise taxes. Fiscal drag occurs when an increase in your income, which is purely down to inflation, pushes up your tax rate. At Taxcafe we call fiscal drag the Silent Killer.

Roller-coaster Income

With 'roller-coaster income', the company owners take a bigger or smaller salary or dividend than would normally be required to fund their lifestyles. Roller-coaster income could save you tax in the following circumstances:

Income Tax Rates Are Going Up Or Down

If the Government announces that income tax rates will *rise* during a future tax year, you may wish to pay yourself more income now and less income later on. And if your tax rate will *fall* during a future tax year, you may wish to pay yourself less income now and more income later on.

Note, the fact that corporation tax is increasing from April 2023 is NOT a reason to take bigger dividends now and smaller dividends after the increase. Dividends do not alter a company's corporation tax bill because they are paid out of profits that have already been taxed.

You Want to Save Capital Gains Tax

It may also make sense for company owners to pay themselves less income during tax years in which they sell assets subject to capital gains tax such as rental properties.

Why? This may allow some of your basic-rate band (£37,700 this year) to be freed up, which means some of your capital gains will be taxed at 10% or 18% instead of 20% or 28% (see Chapter 41).

Living Abroad

If you intend to move abroad and become non-resident in the future, you could consider withdrawing less income from your company while you are UK resident and more income after you become non-resident.

Providing you move to a country with favourable income tax rates, this strategy could potentially save you significant amounts of UK income tax (but see Chapter 42 for potential dangers).

Pension Income

When you reach age 55 you may decide to start withdrawing money from any private pension scheme you belong to, for example a self-invested personal pension (SIPP). Any amount you withdraw over and above your 25% tax-free lump sum will be subject to income tax.

Fortunately, with a drawdown arrangement you can vary the amount of income you withdraw from your pension scheme every year and there are no limits placed on the amount of income you can withdraw.

Coupled with the fact that you can vary the amount of income you withdraw from your company, this could allow you to minimise your income tax bill by staying below any of the income tax thresholds listed earlier.

Part 2

Tax-free Salaries
& Dividends

Chapter 8

Tax-free Salaries

After reading the preceding chapters you should have a good understanding of how salaries and dividends are taxed.

The next question is: What is the most tax-efficient mix of salary and dividends for directors who want to extract money from their companies?

In this chapter we will attempt to calculate the "optimal" amount of salary you should withdraw from your company.

The answer depends on various factors including whether your company's £4,000 national insurance employment allowance is used up paying salaries to other employees.

All amounts are for the current 2021/22 tax year which ends on 5th April 2022. However, at the end of the chapter we also take a look at how the corporation tax increase will affect the decision. The answer changes every year, so it's important to stay up to date.

Assumption: No Other Taxable Income

We will assume for now that the company owner has no other taxable income. This keeps the number crunching as simple as possible.

It's not a totally unrealistic assumption either. Although most company owners will have at least some other taxable income, for example bank account interest or stock market dividends, many will have no more than a few hundred pounds.

For those company owners who do have significant amounts of other taxable income, for example rental profits from a portfolio of properties, more information is provided in Part 4.

Why a Small Salary Is Tax Efficient

The first point to make is that most company owners should pay themselves a small salary. They should not take all of their income as dividends.

The first few thousand pounds of either salary or dividend income you receive are tax free. However, a dividend is not as tax efficient for the *company*. This is because dividends are paid out of the company's *after-tax* profits, once corporation tax has been paid. So every dividend has a corporation tax bill attached to it.

(As a company owner you should be equally concerned about your company's tax position as your own personal tax position.)

A salary, on the other hand, is a tax deductible expense for the company.

In summary, a small salary is more tax efficient than a dividend. Not only is it potentially tax free in the hands of the company owner, it provides a corporation tax saving for the company as well.

What if You Don't Need the Money?

Because a small salary is so tax efficient most company owners should take one, even if they don't need the income. The money can always be left inside the company until a decision is made to withdraw it.

The general rule is that remuneration can only be deducted from a company's current taxable profits if it is 'paid' within nine months of the company's year end. However, HMRC will accept that remuneration is paid when it is credited to the director's loan account. So if you don't need the cash, there's nothing to stop you running your salary through the monthly payroll as normal and crediting the amounts to your director's loan account.

The fact that small salaries are so tax efficient is also why company owners should consider paying salaries to their spouses or partners and children, including their minor children wherever possible (see Part 5).

How Much Salary?
Companies with Employees
(i.e. with no spare employment allowance)

We'll start off with owners of companies whose £4,000 employment allowance (see Chapter 2) is used up paying salaries to other employees, i.e. there is no spare employment allowance for the directors' own salaries.

This section also applies to "one man band" companies with just one director who is the only employee and other companies that are not entitled to the employment allowance (see Chapter 2).

So how much salary should a company owner in this position take? There are three relevant thresholds for the 2021/22 tax year:

- Employer's national insurance   £8,840
- Employee's national insurance   £9,568
- Income tax   £12,570

For 2021/22 the "optimal" salary for many directors of companies with no spare employment allowance is £9,568.

I placed the word "optimal" in inverted commas because every company and company owner is different. Clearly, a salary of £9,568 will not be optimal for every single company owner in the land. There are many factors that may influence a salary decision.

At first glance a salary of £8,840 looks better because there isn't any national insurance payable. By contrast, a salary of £9,568 will result in a small amount of employer's national insurance:

$$£9,568 - £8,840 = £728 \times 13.8\% = £100$$

However, the extra salary and employer's national insurance will attract corporation tax relief, currently at 19%:

Corporation tax relief on extra salary: £728   x 19% = £138
Corporation tax relief on employer's NI: £100   x 19% = £19

The extra corporation tax relief (£157) outweighs the national insurance cost (£100) by £57.

Extra tax on dividends

That's not the end of the story. To get his hands on this additional £57 sitting in the company's bank account the director will have to pay additional income tax. If the director is a basic-rate taxpayer additional income tax of roughly £4 will be payable, assuming the money is taken as a dividend taxed at 7.5%. If the director is a higher-rate taxpayer additional income tax of roughly £19 will be payable (£57 x 32.5%).

The net effect is that basic-rate taxpayers will typically be £53 better off by taking a salary of £9,568 instead of £8,840 and higher-rate taxpayers will typically be £38 better off.

Summary

The additional saving is not significant and some company owners may prefer to take a salary of £8,840 to avoid the hassle or having to make any national insurance payments. This would include owners of one-man band companies that don't have any employees but don't enjoy the benefit of the £4,000 employment allowance for the director's own salary.

Most other company owners have nothing to lose by paying themselves a salary of £9,568. If the company has other employees and is making monthly national insurance payments anyway, there is no extra effort involved adding a national insurance payment on behalf of the directors.

Salary of £12,570?

Why not take a salary of £12,570 instead of £9,568 to use up your personal allowance (i.e. an additional £3,002)? To answer this we have to examine the tax position of the company and the director:

The Company

Employer's national insurance (£3,002 x 13.8%)	£414
Corporation tax relief on extra salary (£3,002 x 19%)	£570
Corporation tax relief on employer's NI (£414 x 19%)	£79

The corporation tax relief outweighs the national insurance cost by £235.

The Director

That's not the end of the story. To get his hands on this additional £235 sitting in the company's bank account the director will have to pay additional income tax (£18 as a basic-rate taxpayer and £76 as a higher-rate taxpayer).

The director will also have to pay employee's national insurance of £360 on the additional salary (£3,002 x 12%).

Thus basic-rate taxpayers will typically be £143 worse off taking a salary of £12,570 instead of £9,568 (£235 - £18 - £360 = -£143). Higher-rate taxpayers will typically be £201 worse off.

Having to pay *both* employee's and employer's national insurance on any salary payment will usually make it unattractive.

Summary

Clearly the extra tax cost is not significant, so whether you take a salary of £9,568 or £12,570 (or £8,840 for that matter) won't make a huge amount of difference.

Some company owners may wish to pay themselves a salary of £12,570 because, although strictly speaking not "optimal", this lets them take a bigger chunk of income out of the company on a regular basis, without some of the hassle that comes with paying dividends (for example, making sure the company has sufficient distributable profits and that dividends are properly declared).

Some owners of one-man band companies may prefer to take a salary of £8,840 to avoid having to make any national insurance payments at all.

Although the tax savings are fairly trivial, this juggling act gets to the heart of the salary/dividend question: as a company owner you have to compare the tax cost to you *personally* with the tax cost and tax relief enjoyed by your *company*.

For the remainder of this guide we will assume that directors whose companies have no spare employment allowance (for example, where it is used up paying salaries to other employees) take a salary of £9,568 during the 2021/22 tax year.

How Much Salary?
Companies with No Employees
(i.e. with spare employment allowance)

In this section we'll take a look at companies that do NOT use up their £4,000 employment allowance paying salaries to other employees, i.e. there is spare employment allowance for the directors' own salaries.

This group includes companies with no employees other than the directors and companies with just a couple of low-paid employees (please see Chapter 2 for more information about which companies qualify for the employment allowance).

Directors of these companies may be able to pay themselves higher salaries without having to worry about *employer's* national insurance. The question is, should they?

Salary of £9,568?

A salary of £8,840 will not attract any employer's or employee's national insurance and will also be free from income tax, providing the director has no other income.

But a salary of £9,568 will not attract any national insurance or income tax either, so in most cases it makes sense to pay yourself a salary of £9,568 instead of £8,840 this year.

Salary of £12,570?

If the company owner takes a salary of £12,570 instead of £9,568 no national insurance will be paid by the company itself but the extra salary will result in a national insurance bill of £360 for the director personally (£3,002 x 12%). That's the bad news.

The good news is that, by increasing the director's salary from £9,568 to £12,570, £570 of additional corporation tax relief is obtained for the company (£3,002 x 19%).

However, to get his hands on the additional £570 sitting in the company's bank account the director will have to pay additional income tax (£43 as a basic-rate taxpayer and £185 as a higher-rate taxpayer).

The net effect of all this is that basic-rate taxpayers will typically save £167 by taking a salary of £12,570 instead of £9,568 and higher-rate taxpayers will typically save £25.

In summary, for company owners with spare employment allowance, a salary of up to £12,570 will generally be more tax efficient than a salary of £9,568.

Salary over £12,570?

A company with no employees and two directors (e.g. a husband and wife) can pay the directors a salary of £23,332 each with no employer's national insurance liability.

But is it worth paying salaries of more than £12,570 to avoid wasting the £4,000 employment allowance? From a strict comparison of tax bills the answer is typically no.

For example, if a salary of £23,332 is taken instead of £12,570 the additional income tax (at 20%) and employee's national insurance (at 12%) will outweigh the additional corporation tax relief (currently at 19%) by £1,399.

However, the £10,762 of additional salary will reduce the amount of after-tax profit available to distribute as dividends by £8,717 (£10,762 less 19% corporation tax). This will reduce the amount of dividend income on which the directors have to pay income tax.

If the directors are basic-rate taxpayers, the income tax payable on their dividend income will fall by £654 (£8,717 x 7.5%). So overall they will be worse off by £745 (£1,399 - £654) by taking a salary of £23,332 instead of £12,570.

Many may consider this a tax cost worth paying for the convenience of taking a larger salary without some of the restrictions and hassle that comes with paying dividends.

If the directors are higher-rate taxpayers, on the plus side they'll have £8,717 less dividend income taxed at 32.5%, saving them £2,833. Against this, the additional salary will use up £10,762 of their basic-rate bands which means they'll have £10,762 more dividend income taxed at 32.5% instead of 7.5%, costing them £2,691.

Overall, many directors who are higher-rate taxpayers will be worse off by £1,257 (£2,833 - £2,691 - £1,399) by taking a salary of £23,332 instead of £12,570. Again, some may consider this a tax cost worth paying for the convenience of taking a larger sum of money out of their companies on a more regular basis.

In summary, for the 2021/22 tax year the most tax efficient salary for directors of companies with spare employment allowance is £12,570.

A director who takes a £12,570 salary will receive £12,210 after tax (£12,570 less £360 employee's national insurance).

Some directors may find it more convenient to take a somewhat larger salary (e.g. £23,332) even if the tax cost is higher.

Is a Lower Salary Preferable?

Although a salary of £12,570 may be "optimal" for company owners with spare employment allowance, a lower salary may be preferable in some cases.

For example, if the company doesn't have any other employees, the directors may decide to pay themselves a salary of £9,568 each to avoid the hassle of having to make any national insurance payments (for example, to avoid late payment penalties).

Although a salary of £9,568 is completely tax free, it still has to be reported to HMRC as part of the normal payroll process (although it may be possible to make a single annual payroll submission in some circumstances – see Chapter 37).

It's also important to remember that there's a limit to the number of directors' salaries of £12,570 that can be paid before the £4,000 national insurance employment allowance is used up (almost 8).

Higher Salaries

Although the salaries discussed in this chapter are "optimal" from a strict comparison of tax rates and thresholds, there may be other tax and non-tax reasons why you may wish to pay yourself a higher salary (see Part 7).

After the Corporation Tax Increase

From 1st April 2023 the corporation tax rate for many companies will increase (see Chapter 1). The upside of this is that many companies will enjoy more tax relief on directors' salaries and the employer's national insurance payable on those salaries.

Does this mean that the directors of these companies should pay themselves higher salaries after the corporation tax increase?

In some cases the answer is yes but in many cases the answer is no. In many cases the additional corporation tax relief will not outweigh the additional national insurance cost.

Employer's National Insurance Payable

Let's take the example of a director who pays himself a salary of £9,568 this year and whose company usually has profits of between £50,000 and £250,000 and will therefore have a marginal corporation tax rate of 26.5% after the increase.

We'll also assume that employer's national insurance would be payable on any additional salary the director receives.

Increasing his salary by £3,002 from £9,568 to £12,570 will have the following tax consequences:

The Company

Employer's national insurance (£3,002 x 13.8%)	£414
Corporation tax relief on extra salary (£3,002 x 26.5%)	£796
Corporation tax relief on employer's NI (£414 x 26.5%)	£110

The corporation tax relief outweighs the national insurance cost by £492.

Higher-Rate Taxpayers

That's not the end of the story. To get his hands on this additional £492 sitting in the company's bank account the director will have to pay additional income tax. If we assume that he is a higher-rate taxpayer, additional income tax of £160 will be payable (£492 x 32.5%).

The director will also have to pay employee's national insurance of £360 on the additional salary (£3,002 x 12%).

Thus a higher-rate taxpayer will typically be £28 worse off taking a salary of £12,570 instead of £9,568 (£492 - £160 - £360 = -£28).

Having to pay *both* employee's and employer's national insurance outweighs the additional corporation tax relief at 26.5%.

However, the additional tax cost is not significant so many directors may decide to pay themselves a salary of £12,570 and perhaps a bit higher than £12,570.

(Note, at present we don't know what the national insurance thresholds will look like when the corporation tax increase starts to take effect. There's a good chance the primary threshold will be higher than £9,568 because it increases each year with inflation.)

Note 26.5% is the maximum amount of tax relief any company will receive after the corporation tax increase. Companies with profits of more than £250,000 will receive 25% tax relief; companies with profits of £50,000 or less will continue to receive 19% tax relief.

Furthermore, for accounting periods that straddle 1st April 2023, companies will receive tax relief at rates ranging from between 19.49% and 25.87% (see Chapter 1 and Appendix A).

What all this seems to imply is that it will not be strictly speaking "optimal" for any company owner who is a higher-rate taxpayer to pay himself a salary greater than the national insurance primary threshold after the corporation tax increase.

Basic-Rate Taxpayers

By contrast, a basic-rate taxpayer director whose company has a marginal tax rate of 26.5% after the corporation tax increase will be £94 better off overall taking a salary of £12,570 instead of £9,568 (£47 better off if the company has a marginal tax rate of 25%).

Some directors may decide to pay themselves a salary higher than £12,570. For example, where the company has a marginal tax rate of 26.5%, paying a salary of £13,570 will have almost exactly the same tax cost as a salary of £9,568.

Employer's National Insurance NOT Payable

As we saw earlier in this chapter, where the company has spare employment allowance (i.e. employer's national insurance is not payable on the directors' own salaries), a salary of £12,570 is more tax efficient this year than a salary of £9,568.

After the corporation tax increase these higher salaries will be even more attractive because they will enjoy more corporation tax relief than they do at present.

The question is: should directors pay themselves salaries even higher than £12,570 after the corporation tax increase?

Higher-Rate Taxpayers

A higher-rate taxpayer director whose company has a marginal tax rate of 26.5% after the corporation tax increase will be £177 better off overall taking a salary of £12,570 instead of £9,568.

Paying an even higher salary will not be strictly speaking 'optimal' but the additional tax cost may be something the director is happy to pay if he prefers a higher salary.

For example, taking a salary of £15,000 will have an overall tax cost that is only £160 higher than a salary of £12,570 (£185 if the company has a marginal tax rate of 25%).

Basic-Rate Taxpayers

A basic-rate taxpayer director whose company has a marginal tax rate of 26.5% after the corporation tax increase will be £376 better off overall taking a salary of £12,570 instead of £9,568.

Paying an even higher salary will not produce any additional tax savings but will also not be any more expensive than taking additional income as dividends. This is because the combined marginal corporation tax and income tax rate on dividend income will be 32% (see Chapter 3). This is identical to the combined income tax and employee's national insurance payable on salary income (20% + 12% = 32%).

Thus basic-rate taxpayers will be able to pay themselves as much salary income as they wish without any adverse tax consequences – as long as the salary is fully covered by the company's employment allowance (i.e. there is no employer's national insurance payable).

In Chapter 2 we saw that two company owners who have no other employees can pay themselves a salary of £23,332 each this year without having to pay any employer's national insurance.

After the corporation tax increase it will be possible to do this without paying any more tax than someone who takes a salary of £12,570.

Where the company has a marginal corporation tax rate that is lower than 26.5% a salary higher than £12,570 will come with an additional tax cost but in many cases this may be worth paying. For example, where the company has a marginal tax rate of 25% (profits over £250,000) a salary of £23,332 will be just £148 more expensive than a salary of £12,570.

Summary

Once the corporation tax increase takes effect, salaries will attract more tax relief than they do at present. However, in many cases company owners will not save any more tax by paying themselves a salary that is higher than what is currently "optimal". Taking a salary higher than what is currently optimal will often not result in a significant additional tax cost.

Chapter 9

Older & Younger Directors

Younger Directors

You can be a company director as long as you are 16 or older. When you turn 16 you also become subject to *employee's* national insurance.

However, if you are under 21 there is no *employer's* national insurance payable on your salary, as long as it does not exceed the higher-rate threshold (currently £50,270). Employer's national insurance is only payable on the portion that exceeds £50,270.

For young directors, a salary of £12,570 is generally more tax efficient than a salary of £9,568 (for the same reason that it is more tax efficient when the company has spare employment allowance – see previous chapter).

Older Directors

If a company director is over state pension age there is no *employee's* national insurance payable on their salary.

Employer's national insurance is still payable, however.

For these older directors a salary of £12,570 is, at first glance, more tax efficient than a salary of £9,568.

However, as we shall see in Part 4, if you have income from other sources (including a state pension), you should take this other income into account when deciding how much salary to pay yourself.

In many cases, if employer's national insurance is payable, a salary of £9,568 will still be more tax efficient than a salary of £12,570.

National Insurance Free Salaries

A company director can receive a salary of more than £9,568 with no national insurance payable at all if:

- The director is over state pension age

- The company has spare employment allowance

It may be possible for a director in these circumstances to receive a salary of up to £37,825 with no national insurance liability at all (for example, when there is just one other low-paid, part-time employee who earns £1 more than the secondary national insurance threshold).

Where there are two directors over state pension age, and no other employees, it will be possible for the directors to receive salaries of £23,332 each with no national insurance liability at all.

The only tax payable will be income tax at 20% once the director's personal allowance has been exhausted.

In some cases an overall saving of over £1,000 can be achieved by taking a larger national insurance free salary in preference to a smaller salary and dividends.

The only tax payable on the salary will be 20% income tax, compared with the combined 25% tax rate on dividend income once the dividend allowance has been exhausted – see Chapter 3).

Chapter 10

Salaries: Pension Benefits

Apart from being tax efficient a salary confers two extra benefits on the director/shareholder:

- State pension entitlement
- Ability to make private pension contributions

State Pension Entitlement

To protect your state pension entitlement you should pay yourself a salary that is greater than the national insurance 'lower earnings limit'.

For 2021/22, the lower earnings limit is £120 per week which requires a total annual salary of at least £6,240.

If you want to protect your state pension entitlement, a salary of at least £6,240 should be paid in 2021/22 in preference to taking dividends or any other types of income.

Private Pension Contributions

Everyone under the age of 75 can make a pension contribution of £3,600 per year. The actual cash contribution would be £2,880, with the taxman adding £720 to bring the total gross contribution to £3,600.

If you want to make bigger pension contributions the contributions you make *personally* (as opposed to contributions made by your company) must not exceed your 'relevant UK earnings'. Salaries count as earnings but dividends, rental income and interest income do not.

For a company director taking the "optimal" tax-free salary of £9,568, the maximum pension contribution he or she can make is £9,568.

This is the maximum *gross* contribution. The director would personally invest £7,654 (£9,568 x 0.8) and the taxman will top this up with £1,914 of basic-rate tax relief for a gross contribution of £9,568.

Similarly, a director taking a salary of £12,570 can make a maximum pension contribution of £12,570. The director would personally invest £10,056 (£12,570 x 0.8) and the taxman will top this up with £2,514 of basic-rate tax relief for a gross contribution of £12,570.

Company owners can also get their companies to make pension contributions, instead of making them personally. And as we shall see in Chapter 28, company pension contributions are more tax efficient than contributions made personally in many circumstances.

Chapter 11

Tax-free Dividends

If a company owner needs more income this year than the small "optimal" salary, as most probably do, the most tax-efficient solution is generally to take a dividend rather than a bigger salary.

In this chapter we'll take a look at how much tax-free dividend income you can take and then in the next chapter we'll look at how much dividend income you can take taxed at just 7.5%.

We know from Chapter 3 that dividends attract no national insurance and are free from income tax to the extent they're covered by the director's personal allowance and £2,000 dividend nil rate band.

Companies with Employees
(i.e. with no spare employment allowance)

A director/shareholder who takes a tax-free* salary of £9,568 and has no other income can take a tax-free dividend of £5,002.

The first £3,002 will be covered by their remaining personal allowance and the final £2,000 will be tax free thanks to the dividend nil rate band.

Combined with the tax-free salary, this gives the director/shareholder the maximum total tax-free income for 2021/22 – £14,570:

- £9,568   Tax-free salary
- £5,002   Tax-free dividend

* By "tax free" I mean in the hands of the director. As we saw in Chapter 8, there is £100 of employer's national insurance payable by the company on this level of salary.

The Corporation Tax Bill

Although a dividend of £5,002 can be paid with no tax consequences for the director/shareholder, the payment is not completely tax free.

Dividends are paid out of a company's after-tax profits. So for a company that currently pays 19% corporation tax, a dividend of £5,002 will have a corporation tax bill of £1,173:

Pre-tax profits	£6,175
Less: corporation tax @ 19%	£1,173
After-tax profits/dividend	£5,002

So while dividends are tax efficient they are NOT tax free. This is an important point to remember, especially if you want to grow your business rather than extract income from it.

If, for example, a company incurs £6,175 of tax deductible expenditure before the end of its accounting period, its corporation tax bill will be reduced by £1,173. This will leave less after-tax profit to distribute as dividends but such a strategy may appeal to some business owners who would prefer to re-invest profits and minimise all taxes, including corporation tax.

The fact that dividends come with a corporation tax bill is why company owners should consider other profit extraction strategies, for example paying interest or making company pension contributions (Chapters 25 and 27). Some payments like these can be both tax free in the hands of the director and provide corporation tax relief. This is the best case scenario when it comes to extracting money from your company.

Having said this, most company owners need to extract additional cash from their companies every year to cover their living costs. This means some tax will usually always be payable, either by the company or the director personally. The key is to minimise it.

Finally, please note the corporation tax rate was reduced from 20% to 19% on 1 April 2017. Thus it's possible any dividend you receive this year will be paid partly out of profits that have been taxed at 20% or an effective rate of between 19% and 20% – see Chapter 1. We use the current 19% rate in most of the examples in this guide to keep things simple.

Companies with No Employees
(i.e. with spare employment allowance)

Company owners with no other income who decide to take a salary of £12,570 (because the company has spare employment allowance or because the director simply wants a larger salary) can take a tax-free dividend of £2,000.

Combined with an after-tax salary of £12,210 (£12,570 less £360 employee's national insurance), this gives the director/shareholder a total income of £14,210 in 2021/22:

- £12,210   After-tax salary
- £2,000   Tax-free dividend

Doubling the Tax-Free Income
(Companies owned by couples)

Many companies are started and run by married or unmarried couples.

For couples in business together, the salaries and tax-free dividends outlined above can be doubled up.

In other words, where salaries of £9,568 are taken:

Tax-free salaries	£19,136
Tax-free dividends	£10,000
Total tax-free income	£29,136

Where salaries of £12,570 are taken (£12,210 after employee NI):

Salaries	£24,420
Tax-free dividends	£4,000
Total income	£28,420

Spouses/Partners Brought into the Business

Of course, not all companies are started or managed by couples. In some cases the business may have been started before the couple met. In other cases, one member of the couple may not want to become actively involved in the business, for example if they have their own career or do not work at all.

In these cases the questions from a tax planning perspective are:

- Can a spouse/partner be employed in the business?

- Can shares in the company be transferred to a spouse/partner?

- How much tax will the above two strategies save?

We'll return to these important tax planning issues in Chapter 21.

Use it or Lose It!

A company owner may decide to not withdraw the maximum tax-free dividend for several reasons. However, it really is a case of use it or lose it: if you don't take the maximum tax-free dividend this year, you cannot take a bigger tax-free amount next year.

Company Directors Tax Returns

Note that, even if you don't have any income tax to pay on your salary and dividends, you will still have to complete a tax return.

All company directors have this duty.

The Next Step: Taxable Dividends

The tax-free salaries and dividends listed above will not provide enough income for the vast majority of company owners, even if the amounts are doubled up where the company is owned by a couple. Those that require more income will have to pay income tax on any additional dividends withdrawn, as we shall now see.

Part 3

How to Extract More Income Tax Efficiently

Chapter 12

The Next Step: Dividends Taxed at Just 7.5%

So far we've shown that a company owner who has no other income and takes a tax-free salary of £9,568 can also take a tax-free dividend of £5,002 for a total tax-free income of £14,570.

A company owner who takes a salary of £12,570 can take a tax-free dividend of £2,000 for a total income of £14,210 (net of employee's national insurance).

These amounts can be doubled up where the company is owned by a couple.

Of course, most company owners will require more income and the most tax-efficient route is normally to take a bigger dividend.

Any additional dividend income you take will be taxed, however as long as you keep your total income below the £50,270 higher-rate threshold you will pay just 7.5% income tax. If you take any more dividend income the tax rate jumps to 32.5%!

Salary of £9,568

If you've taken a salary of £9,568 and tax-free dividend of £5,002 the maximum amount of additional dividend income you can take taxed at just 7.5% is £35,700. The income tax payable on this additional dividend income will be £2,678.

In summary, you can take a salary of £9,568 and a total dividend of £40,702 for a total pre-tax income of £50,270. After paying £2,678 tax you'll be left with an after-tax income of £47,592.

These amounts can be doubled up if the company is owned by a couple, leaving them with a total after-tax income of £95,184 and a total tax bill of £5,356.

Salary vs Dividends

Even though the additional dividend income is taxed, it is still much more tax efficient than taking a bigger salary.

To end up with the same after-tax income of £47,592, a director/shareholder would require an additional salary payment of £54,057, on top of the £9,568 already paid and the maximum tax-free dividend of £2,000.

Overall, the director would end up with the same amount of after-tax income but the company would end up with £11,127 less cash (because it has to make such a large salary payment to cover all the extra tax, especially national insurance).

The table below illustrates this effect in two companies: one paying a small salary and dividends, the other paying a big salary plus a £2,000 tax-free dividend.

In each case the director ends up with £47,592. The company paying the big salary ends up with £11,127 less cash.

	Small Salary £	Big Salary £
Company's tax		
Company profit	100,000	100,000
Less: Salary	9,568	63,625
Less: Employer's NI	100	7,560
Net Profit	90,332	28,815
Less: Corporation tax @ 19%	17,163	5,475
After-tax profit	73,169	23,340
Less: Dividend	40,702	2,000
Company cash	32,467	21,340
Director's tax		
Total income	50,270	65,625
Income tax	2,678	12,882*
National insurance	0	5,151
After-tax income	47,592	47,592

* £1,684 higher for Scottish taxpayers

Salary of £12,570

If you've taken a salary of £12,570 and tax-free dividend of £2,000 the maximum amount of additional dividend income you can take taxed at just 7.5% is £35,700. The income tax payable on this additional dividend income will be £2,678.

In summary, you can take a salary of £12,570 and a dividend of £37,700 for a total pre-tax income of £50,270. After paying £360 national insurance on your salary and £2,678 income tax on your dividend income you'll be left with an after-tax income of £47,232.

These amounts can be doubled up if the company is owned by a couple, leaving them with a total after-tax income of £94,464 and a total tax and national insurance bill of £6,076.

Company Owners with Bigger Salaries

Of course not all company owners take a salary of £9,568 or £12,570. Some take a bigger salary because it suits them to do so, even if this is not the most tax efficient or "optimal" thing to do.

For example, a company owner who takes a salary of £30,000 can still take a tax-free dividend of £2,000 plus additional dividend income of up to £18,270 taxed at 7.5% (£50,270 - £30,000 - £2,000).

A company owner who takes a salary of £50,000 can still take a tax-free dividend of £2,000. However, because their total taxable income exceeds the higher-rate threshold any additional dividend income will be subject to tax at the higher rate of 32.5%.

Chapter 13

Making the Most of the 7.5% Tax Rate

So far we have shown that a company owner who takes a salary of £9,568 can receive dividend income of £5,002 tax free and a further £35,700 taxed at 7.5%.

A company owner who takes a salary of £12,570 can receive dividend income of £2,000 tax free and a further £35,700 taxed at 7.5%.

Company owners who extract more money from their companies will go over the £50,270 higher-rate threshold and start paying income tax at 32.5% on their dividends, which is a big leap!

(Remember, at this point, to keep things simple, we are assuming the company owner does not have any income from other sources.)

An important tax planning question is whether you should pay yourself as much dividend income as you can taxed at 7.5%, even if you don't need the money immediately?

It's impossible to provide a definitive answer to this question because every company owner is different. However, I will attempt to outline the main benefits and drawbacks in this chapter.

One of the main reasons why you may NOT want to pay yourself the maximum amount taxed at 7.5% this year is if you expect to be able to withdraw the same money tax free next year or in another tax year.

We've shown that a couple who take salaries of £9,568 each can also pay themselves tax-free dividends of £5,002 each – a total tax-free income of £29,140 in 2021/22.

Although some company owners may be able to survive on the tax-free amounts, most will not and will have to withdraw at least some dividend income each year taxed at 7.5%.

Arguably you then have fairly little to lose by withdrawing the maximum amount you can have taxed at 7.5% this year (£35,700).

The main drawback is you will end up paying income tax earlier than may be necessary.

In other words, the extra money you pay in income tax will earn interest in the taxman's bank account instead of your company's bank account!

Most company bank accounts pay paltry amounts of interest at present so the potential loss is very small. Anything you lose can probably be more than made up by investing the extra dividend income in a cash ISA (the rates are typically far higher than for company bank accounts).

So what are the benefits of paying tax early? By paying yourself the maximum dividend taxed at 7.5% you stand to protect against:

- Further dividend tax increases
- Business risk
- Becoming a higher-rate taxpayer

It is possible, although by no means certain, that dividend tax rates will be increased again at some point in the future. This is because the Government's covid spending splurge has left the public finances in a mess.

Thus it may be better to withdraw as much income as you can taxed at 7.5% in case the rate is increased to, say, 10%.

Some company owners may also wish to remove surplus cash from their companies to protect against business risk (arguably your money is at greater risk in the company's bank account than your own).

It may also be worth paying yourself the maximum dividend taxed at 7.5% if you think you may become a higher-rate taxpayer in the future.

In other words, it may be better to *definitely* pay 7.5% tax this year rather than *possibly* 32.5% in a future tax year.

Avoiding 32.5% Tax

Why would you expect to become a higher-rate taxpayer in the future? Perhaps you expect the profits of your business to grow significantly or you expect to receive more income from other sources, e.g. an inheritance.

In fact, thanks to a cunning Government tax proclamation, it is possible that many basic-rate taxpayers will become higher-rate taxpayers, even if their real income does not increase at all.

In the March 2021 Budget the Government announced that the higher-rate threshold will remain fixed at £50,270 for the five year period ending on 5th April 2026. Thus it is possible that many basic-rate taxpayers will become higher-rate taxpayers even if their income simply increases because of inflation.

Although you may never become a higher-rate taxpayer, you arguably have very little to lose by paying yourself the maximum dividend taxed at 7.5%. If you do become a higher-rate taxpayer you'll save 25% (by paying 7.5% tax this year rather than 32.5% in the future). If you're wrong, you will lose nothing (because you will pay 7.5% tax this year rather than 7.5% in the future).

Reasons to Pay Smaller Dividends

A company owner may decide to not withdraw the maximum dividend taxed at 7.5% for several reasons:

- The company hasn't made enough profit
- The company needs the cash to grow
- The company owner doesn't need the money
- The company is forced to restrict its dividends
- The company owner has taxable capital gains

The Company Hasn't Made Enough Profit

The company doesn't need to have made any profit to pay *salaries* and tax-efficient salaries should be paid wherever possible because they are also a tax deductible expense and reduce the company's corporation tax bill (even if this is only at a later date if the company is currently not making profits). For example, a salary of £9,568 will currently reduce a company's tax bill by £1,818.

Dividends, on the other hand, can only be declared if the company has sufficient distributable profits.

It is not necessary for the company to actually make a profit in the year the dividend is paid, as long as there are sufficient accumulated profits (after tax) from previous years.

(See Chapter 37 for more information.)

The Company Needs the Cash to Grow

Even if the company has made sufficient profits, the directors may wish to hold onto the company's cash to grow the business.

If you prefer to retain the cash in your company, it may be possible for a dividend to be declared but not paid out. The dividend can simply be credited to the director's loan account and withdrawn at a later date when it is more convenient.

This may be more tax efficient than reducing dividends during one year and then declaring bigger dividends taxed at 32.5% in another year.

Note that the director will generally be subject to income tax on any dividend that has been declared but not paid out. In practice, this means that it may be necessary to pay out a portion of the dividend to help the director pay his tax bill.

The Company Owner Doesn't Need the Money

A company owner may decide to take a smaller dividend if he has other resources, such as inherited money or proceeds from selling another business or from selling other assets like property and shares. The company owner may also have a spouse/partner who earns enough income to support the family.

In these circumstances the company owner may believe it is sensible to limit the amount taken as dividends to avoid paying tax at 7.5%. In reality, the company owner may simply be storing up an income tax problem for the future. If accumulated profits are eventually paid out as a large dividend, an income tax charge of 32.5% or 38.1% could be payable on a significant portion of any dividend declared.

If income is withdrawn on a more regular annual basis, even if not required immediately, income tax can be restricted to 7.5%.

There is one important exception. If the company owner has taxable income from other sources, it may be prudent to take a smaller dividend. So far we have been assuming that the company owner has no other taxable income. If there is other taxable income that uses up some or all of the director's basic-rate band, it may be necessary to restrict dividends to avoid paying income tax at 32.5%. (More about directors with other income in Part 4.)

The Company is Forced to Restrict its Dividends

Lenders may place restrictions on dividend payments to protect their interests (i.e. to stop cash leaking out of the company that should be going to them). In these circumstances it may be difficult for the company owners to structure their dividend payments to mitigate tax.

The Company Owner Has Taxable Capital Gains

If you have taxable capital gains you may want to reduce the amount of income you withdraw from your company to free up some of your basic-rate band. This may allow you to pay less capital gains tax – see Chapter 41.

Alternatives to Dividends

Although paying tax at 7.5% is a lot better than paying tax at 32.5%, it's important to remember that dividends are paid out of income that has already been subjected to corporation tax.

Thus, if you are a basic-rate taxpayer, the true effective tax rate on your dividend income is currently 25%, not 7.5% (see Chapter 3).

This means dividends are less tax efficient than certain other types of income that you may be able to extract from your company. And they will become even less attractive after the increase in corporation tax (see Chapter 1).

Take rental income for example. If your company pays you rent of £10,000 the amount will be a fully deductible expense, providing the rent is reasonable. If you're a basic-rate taxpayer you will pay 20% tax on the amount, leaving you with £8,000.

If, on the other hand, your company does not pay you rent it will have additional profits of £10,000 on which it will currently pay 19% corporation tax, leaving £8,100 to distribute as dividends. After paying 7.5% tax you will be left with £7,493.

Clearly, rental income is a fair bit more tax efficient than dividend income in this situation (see Chapter 24 for more information).

I also suspect some directors have been getting their companies to make bigger pension contributions since dividend tax rates were increased in 2016. If your company contributes £10,000 to your pension it can claim corporation tax relief, again providing the amount is reasonable. Ignoring investment growth, when you retire you will be able to withdraw 25% tax free and the rest will be taxed at 20% if you are basic-rate taxpayer (as most retirees are).

After tax you'll be left with £8,500, compared with £7,493 from a dividend (see Chapter 27 for more on pension contributions).

Clearly, there's a tension between paying dividends and other types of income. These other amounts will often be a tax deductible expense for the company which means they will reduce the company's profits and therefore the amount that can be paid out as dividend income in the future.

If a company has already realised profits and incurred corporation tax, arguably the most tax efficient thing to do is distribute the after-tax profits as a dividend, especially if it will be either tax free or taxed at just 7.5%.

However, paying dividends may also limit the financial resources available to the company to make other tax efficient payments during the current year, e.g. rental income and pension contributions.

Chapter 14

Making the Most of the 32.5% Tax Rate

Summary So Far

So far we have shown that a company owner who takes a tax-free salary of £9,568 can extract a tax-free dividend of £5,002 and a dividend of £35,700 taxed at 7.5%, leaving him with an after-tax income of £47,592.

A company owner who takes a salary of £12,570 (£12,210 after national insurance) can extract a tax-free dividend of £2,000 and a dividend of £35,700 taxed at 7.5%, leaving him with an after-tax income of £47,232.

In both scenarios the company owner ends up with a taxable income of £50,270 and is on the cusp of being a higher-rate taxpayer.

These amounts can be doubled in the case of companies owned and run by couples.

If you generally do not require more income, you may be able to adopt an 'income smoothing' strategy – taking the maximum tax-free salary and dividend plus the maximum dividend taxed at 7.5% every year where possible, regardless of whether the company has made bigger than normal profits or lower than normal profits.

Taking Bigger Dividends

If you want more income the optimal strategy is to take additional dividends rather than salary, in order to avoid the national insurance payable on employment income. However, now that you have reached the £50,270 higher-rate threshold you will pay a whopping 32.5% income tax on any additional dividend income you take.

You also have to watch out for two further tax stings:

- Child benefit tax charge – Income over £50,000
- Personal allowance withdrawal – Income over £100,000

In this chapter we will assume that the company owner (or their spouse/partner) is not claiming any child benefit. We will return to child benefit in the next chapter.

If no child benefit is being claimed, the next threshold to watch out for is £100,000, where your personal allowance starts to be withdrawn. The personal allowance currently saves higher-rate taxpayers up to £5,028 in tax, so many company owners will want to keep their income below £100,000 to avoid losing it.

Maximum Income

With total income of £50,270 the director can take additional dividend income of up to £49,730 taxed at 32.5% before the £100,000 threshold is reached.

A director who takes a salary of £9,568 and the rest of his income as dividends will be left with total after-tax income of £81,160:

£9,568 salary + £90,432 dividend - £18,840 tax = £81,160

A director who takes a salary of £12,570 (£12,210 after national insurance) will be left with a total after-tax income of £80,800:

£12,210 salary + £87,430 dividend - £18,840 tax = £80,800

If the company is owned and managed by a couple, the above amounts can potentially be doubled up.

Don't Forget the Corporation Tax Bill!

It's tempting to think that company owners who pay themselves any of the above amounts are paying relatively little tax. After all, a total of £100,000 is being extracted from the company with a total income tax bill of just £18,840. The effective income tax rate is less than 19%!

However, it's important to remember that dividends are always paid out of a company's *after-tax* profits.

To pay a dividend of £90,432 the company will have had to make taxable profits of £111,644, resulting in a corporation tax bill of £21,212. Coupled with an income tax bill of £18,840, the total tax bill attached to the dividend is £40,052.

Alternatives to Dividends

In Chapter 3 I pointed out that, if you are a higher-rate taxpayer, the total tax rate on your dividend income is currently 45%. With the tax rate at this level, some small company owners may have decided to not pay themselves any dividend income which takes them over the higher-rate threshold. Instead they may simply roll up cash inside their companies, possibly until the business is sold or wound up.

At this point it may be possible to pay just 10% capital gains tax on the funds extracted if the company owner qualifies for Business Asset Disposal Relief. We'll explore this issue more in Chapter 32.

Other company owners may have decided to pay themselves less dividend income and focus on other techniques to extract money from their companies, e.g. pension contributions.

For example, if your company contributes £10,000 to your pension the payment will be a tax deductible expense for the company. Ignoring investment growth, when you retire you will be able to withdraw 25% tax free and the rest will be taxed at 20% if you are basic-rate taxpayer (as most retirees are).

After tax you'll be left with £8,500, compared with £5,468 if instead a dividend is taken now and taxed at 32.5% (see Chapter 27 for more on pension contributions).

When the corporation tax rate goes up, the total tax rate on dividend income will rise even further. For many company owners who are higher-rate taxpayers the combined marginal tax rate on dividend income will rise to roughly 50% (see Chapter 3).

This will make it even more attractive than it is at present to extract other types of income from your company (for example rental income and interest income) or focus on other profit extraction techniques such as pension contributions.

If your total tax rate will rise from 45% to around 50%, does this mean you should pay yourself bigger dividends now, before the increase? No because dividends do not affect the amount of corporation tax your company pays – dividends are paid out of the company's *after-tax* profits.

The amount of dividend income you take is mostly an *income tax* planning decision, based on your personal tax position.

What the corporation tax increase does mean for tax planning is that company owners should consider postponing certain types of discretionary spending, wherever possible, in order to enjoy corporation tax relief at 25% or 26.5% in the future, instead of 19% at present.

In most cases it is not possible to postpone paying yourself things like rent (if your company uses a property you own) or interest (if your company owes you money). For tax purposes these types of expense are generally allocated to the period they relate to.

It may, however, be possible to postpone making pension contributions and various other expenses.

Postponing and Bringing Forward Dividends

Back in 2016/17 the higher-rate threshold was just £43,000 but the Government announced that it would be increased to £50,000 over the next few years.

We therefore advised readers to postpone taking more than £43,000 out of their companies, where possible, until the higher-rate threshold was increased. This way it would be possible to avoid paying 32.5% tax on some of their dividend income.

The higher-rate threshold has now been increased to £50,270 which means couples can now withdraw £14,540 more dividend income taxed at 7.5% instead of 32.5%, saving them £3,635 in tax.

Now we have the opposite situation – the Government has announced that the higher-rate threshold will remain frozen at £50,270 until 5th April 2026.

Company owners who regularly extract dividends taxed at 32.5% have very little incentive to hold back paying themselves even more dividend income taxed at 32.5% (unless they can extract money from their companies in a more tax efficient manner).

With the public finances in such a perilous state it seems very unlikely that the higher-rate threshold will be increased significantly in the future or that the 32.5% tax rate will be cut.

In fact, company owners whose taxable income is anywhere close to £100,000 should consider paying themselves as much dividend income as they can taxed at 32.5%. This is because, once your income rises above £100,000, your marginal income tax rate will rise from 32.5% to 53.5% (see Chapter 16).

For example, if you expect your taxable income to be, say, £85,000 this year it may be better to pay yourself an additional £15,000 this year instead of in a future tax year when your income has risen to £100,000.

The £100,000 threshold has not been increased since it was introduced in April 2010 and we don't expect it to be increased any time soon. As a result more and more taxpayers will probably have their personal allowances withdrawn in the years ahead.

Sample Tax Bills

For company owners who want to withdraw more than £50,270 *this year*, Table 5 contains some sample income tax bills.

It's assumed that a tax-free salary of £9,568 or £12,570 is taken, with the remaining income taken as dividends. The table goes up to £100,000 – beyond that your personal allowance is withdrawn.

The numbers are fairly easy to calculate. The first £12,570 is tax free thanks to the personal allowance and the next £2,000 of dividend income is also tax free thanks to the dividend allowance. The next £35,700 of dividend income is taxed at 7.5%, resulting in

TABLE 5
Income between £50,270 and £100,000

Income £	Income Tax £	After-tax Income £
50,270	2,678	47,592
55,000	4,215	50,785
60,000	5,840	54,160
65,000	7,465	57,535
70,000	9,090	60,910
75,000	10,715	64,285
80,000	12,340	67,660
85,000	13,965	71,035
90,000	15,590	74,410
95,000	17,215	77,785
100,000	18,840	81,160

Notes:
1. Salary of £9,568 or £12,570 taken with rest of income as dividends
2. Where salary is £12,570 national insurance of £360 must also be included
3. For income over £50,270 the extra tax is simply 32.5% of the excess
4. Table may contain small rounding errors

tax of £2,678. At this point the company owner has income of £50,270 and is on the higher-rate threshold. Any additional dividends will be taxed at 32.5%. Someone who extracts £75,000 will pay £2,678 on the first £50,270 and £8,037 on the final £24,730 (£24,730 x 32.5%), resulting in a total tax bill of £10,715.

In all cases the amounts listed in Table 5 can be doubled for companies owned and run by couples. For example, a couple can withdraw £150,000 (£75,000 each) with a total income tax bill of £21,430 (£10,715 each).

Income Smoothing

If your company makes bigger than normal profits during one accounting period you may be tempted to pay yourself a bigger dividend, even if this results in income tax being payable at a higher rate on some of the dividend income.

Paying a bigger than normal dividend is perfectly acceptable from a tax planning perspective IF you expect the company's profits to remain at a higher level or continue to grow.

If, however, you expect the company's profits to fall back, it may be wiser to 'smooth' your income and withdraw any bumper profits gradually, paying tax at no more than 7.5%.

Chapter 15

How to Protect Your Child Benefit

If you wish to withdraw more than £50,270 income from your company *and* you are the highest earner in a household that receives child benefit, you will be subject to two tax stings:

- 32.5% tax on your dividend income, and
- The High Income Child Benefit Charge

To avoid *both* you have to keep your salary and dividends below £50,000.

Child benefit is gradually withdrawn when any member of your household has over £50,000 income. This is done by imposing a child benefit charge on the highest earner in the household. Once the highest earner's income reaches £60,000, all of the child benefit is effectively taken away in higher tax charges.

The £50,000 threshold does not increase with inflation and, in fact, has never been increased since the child benefit charge was introduced back in 2013. This means that more and more households have been drawn into its net.

Why the £50,000 threshold was not increased this year to align it with the £50,270 higher-rate threshold is anyone's guess.

The child benefit charge has important implications for company owners who want to determine how much income to withdraw from their companies during the current and future tax years.

Child Benefit: How Much is it Worth?

Child benefit is a valuable *tax-free* handout from the Government. Those who qualify will receive the following payment in 2021/22:

- £1,099.80 for the first child
- £728 for each subsequent child

Depending on the number of children, a family can expect to receive the following total child benefit payment:

Children	Total Child Benefit
1	£1,100
2	£1,828
3	£2,556
4	£3,284

plus £728 for each additional child

How Long Do Child Benefit Payments Continue?

Child benefit generally continues to be paid until your children are 16 years old.

The payments will continue until age 20 if the child is enrolled in full-time 'non-advanced' education, including:

- GCSEs
- A levels
- Scottish highers
- NVQ/SVQ level 1, 2 or 3
- BTEC National Diploma, National Certificate, 1st Diploma

So if your child is 16, 17, 18 or 19 and enrolled in one of the above courses, child benefit will continue to be paid.

Once the child is 20 years old all child benefit payments will cease.

The following courses do NOT qualify:

- Degrees
- Diploma of Higher Education
- NVQ level 4 or above
- HNCs or HNDs
- Teacher training

In other words, if your children are 16, 17, 18 or 19 and enrolled in any these courses, you will not receive any child benefit.

Total Value of Child Benefit

Child benefit payments continue for between 16 and 20 years. Based on current child benefit rates, the total amount you can expect to receive over the total period your child qualifies is:

- £17,600 to £22,000 tax free for the first child
- At least £11,648 tax free for each additional child

These are very much 'back of the envelope' figures because they ignore the potential danger that child benefit may not hold its real value if it doesn't increase with inflation (as has happened in recent years).

Furthermore, the amount received for second and subsequent children will vary from family to family. When your first child ceases to qualify your second child will step into their shoes and receive the higher payment. In other words, when you stop receiving £1,100 for your first child, the payment for your second child will increase from £728 to £1,100.

Thus families will receive different overall amounts depending on the age difference between their children and where they study.

The above overall figures nevertheless illustrate how valuable child benefit is over many years and why it is worth protecting.

How the Child Benefit Charge is Calculated

For every £100 of income over £50,000 an income tax charge equivalent to 1% of the child benefit is levied on the highest earner in the household.

For example, if the highest earner in the household has income of £52,500, the tax charge will be equivalent to 25% of the child benefit claimed.

If the highest earner in the household has income of £55,000, the tax charge will be equivalent to 50% of the child benefit.

And if the highest earner has income of £60,000 or more the tax charge will be equivalent to 100% of the child benefit.

Income between £50,270 & £60,000: 1970s Style Tax Rates

Once your income goes above £50,270 you will have to pay the child benefit charge _and_ 32.5% tax on your dividend income.

For the highest earner in the household the child benefit charge creates the following marginal tax rates on dividend income in the £50,270-£60,000 tax bracket:

Children	Marginal Tax Rate on Dividends
1	43%
2	51%
3	58%
4	65%

Plus 7% for each additional child.

Example

David, a company owner, has taken a salary and dividends totalling £50,000 so far in 2021/22. He is the highest earner in a household claiming child benefit for two children.

David decides to withdraw additional dividend income of £10,000. His total income will be £60,000 so he will face the maximum child benefit charge. The tax payable on the additional dividend is £5,010, calculated as follows:

£270 dividend x 7.5%	_£20_
£9,730 dividend x 32.5%	_£3,162_
£1,828 child benefit x 100%	_£1,828_
Total additional tax	_£5,010_

Before he decided to take the additional £10,000 dividend he was paying just 7.5% income tax on his dividend income. The overall tax rate on the additional £10,000 dividend is 50%.

Clearly David should think twice about withdrawing the additional income, especially if he does not need the money urgently.

Income between £60,000 and £100,000

If you have more than £60,000 of income you will already be paying the maximum child benefit charge. Income between £60,000 and £100,000 does not incur any further charge.

Dividends between £60,000 and £100,000 are simply taxed at 32.5%.

Once your income rises above £100,000 you face a fresh tax sting: withdrawal of the income tax personal allowance.

How to Avoid the Child Benefit Charge

Clearly taxpayers have an incentive to escape the much higher tax rates that apply to dividends when the child benefit charge is payable.

Company owners may find it easier than other taxpayers to escape the child benefit charge because they can alter the amount of dividend income they pay themselves each year.

Some company owners will be able to *mostly* avoid the charge and the 32.5% tax rate applying to dividend income by paying themselves no more than £50,270 this year. But it's probably worth paying yourself no more than £50,000 because that final £270 will be taxed at 26% if you have two children, compared with the 7.5% rate that generally applies to basic-rate taxpayers.

Other company owners, including those who usually withdraw more than £60,000 each year, may be able to avoid the charge in some tax years but not others, or partly reduce the charge.

Company owners can also spread their income among family members, for example, by gifting shares in the business to their spouses (see Chapter 21).

For the current and future tax years, the following dividend strategies could be considered:

Smooth Income

If the income you withdraw is currently somewhere *below* £50,000 and you expect your income to continue growing above £50,000, you should consider extracting approximately £50,000 for several tax years, where possible.

This may mean that you pay yourself more income than you need to begin with and less income than you need later on, but by doing so you may be able to avoid the child benefit charge (and the 32.5% tax rate that kicks in after £50,270) for several years.

In other words, it's better to pay 7.5% tax now rather than, say, 51% in the future.

For example, if you withdrew £40,000 from your company last year you should consider withdrawing £50,000 this year even if this is more money than you need. The extra income will be taxed at just 7.5%.

Roller-Coaster Income

If you plan to withdraw *more than* £60,000 from 2021/22 onwards, you could consider taking big dividends during some tax years and smaller ones in other tax years.

For example, instead of withdrawing a total income of £75,000 every year, consider taking £100,000 every second year, if possible, and £50,000 in the intervening years. This will allow you to avoid the child benefit charge every second year.

Similarly, a company owner who normally takes around £60,000 every year could consider taking £70,000 in year 1 and £50,000 in year 2, where possible.

Austerity

If your taxable income is normally over £50,000, you could consider keeping your income below £50,000 for several years to avoid the child benefit charge.

For example, let's say you have three children and your taxable income is normally around £60,000. If for the next three years you can afford to withdraw just £50,000, you may be able to protect over £7,668 of child benefit.

Other Issues

When paying yourself dividends that are smaller than normal or bigger than normal there may be lots of other issues to consider.

For example, you can only declare bigger dividends if the company has sufficient distributable profits.

If you postpone taking some of your dividends until a future tax year, you may leave yourself exposed to any future increase in tax on company owners. Remember tax rules are constantly changing.

If you take a smaller than normal dividend this may have other financial repercussions, for example it may affect the size of mortgage you are able to get.

Chapter 16

Income over £100,000

Summary So Far

So far we have shown that a director/shareholder of a company that has no spare employment allowance can extract a tax-free salary of £9,568 and a dividend of £90,432 (with £5,002 tax free, £35,700 taxed at 7.5% and £49,730 taxed at 32.5%). Total pre-tax income: £100,000. Total after-tax income: £81,160.

If the company has spare employment allowance, a salary of £12,570 can be taken with a total national insurance cost of £360. On top of this, a dividend of £87,430 can be taken (with £2,000 tax free, £35,700 taxed at 7.5% and £49,730 taxed at 32.5%). Total pre-tax income: £100,000. Total after-tax income: £80,800.

The above amounts can be doubled up if the company is also owned and run by your spouse/partner.

The child benefit charge is payable if the highest earner in the household has income of more than £50,000 (see Chapter 15).

Income between £100,000 and £125,140

Many company owners will be satisfied with a net after tax income of around £80,000.

For those who wish to extract more cash, a dividend is often the best option. However, now you face an additional tax sting: withdrawal of your £12,570 income tax personal allowance.

Once your taxable income rises above £100,000, your personal allowance is gradually withdrawn. It is withdrawn at the rate of £1 for every £2 of additional income.

In other words, if you have income of £101,000 your personal allowance will be reduced by £500. Once your gross income reaches £125,140 you will have no personal allowance left at all.

Company owners with income in the £100,000-£125,140 bracket could end up paying income tax at an effective rate of over 50% on any additional dividends they withdraw.

Example

Annabel, a company owner, has already taken a salary of £9,568 and dividend of £90,432. Total income: £100,000. She decides to pays herself additional dividend income of £25,140. On the additional dividend she will pay 32.5% income tax: £8,171. She will also lose all of her personal allowance which means her salary of £9,568 will now be taxed at 20%. Additional tax: £1,914.

In addition, £3,002 of dividend income, previously covered by her personal allowance, will be taxed at 32.5%. Additional tax: £976. Finally, her salary uses up £9,568 of her basic-rate band which means £9,568 of dividends will be taxed at 32.5% instead of 7.5%. Additional tax: £2,392.

The total additional income tax is £13,453 which is equivalent to 53.5% of the £25,140 dividend.

Don't Forget the Corporation Tax Bill!

As always, it's important to remember that dividends are always paid out of a company's *after-tax* profits.

To pay an additional dividend of £25,140 the company will have had to make profits of £31,037, resulting in a corporation tax bill of £5,897. Coupled with an income tax bill of £13,453, the total tax bill on the £31,037 of profit is £19,350, i.e. 62%!

Income between £125,140 and £150,000

These extortionate tax rates do not apply to all dividend income over £100,000 – only income between £100,000 and £125,140.

Once your income exceeds £125,140 your personal allowance will have disappeared altogether and any additional dividends will be taxed at the regular rate applying to higher-rate taxpayers: 32.5%.

After that, the next threshold you have to watch out for is £150,000 where the additional rate of tax kicks in (see Chapter 17).

How to Avoid 53.5% Tax

Unlike regular salaried employees or owners of unincorporated businesses (sole traders and partnerships), company owners can avoid this extortionate tax rate by simply not paying themselves salary and dividends in excess of £100,000 per year.

Thus a company owner taking a salary of £9,568 should extract dividends not exceeding £90,432; a company owner taking a salary of £12,570 should extract dividends not exceeding £87,430.

A company owner whose income may fluctuate from year to year, in line with the company's profits, may want to consider smoothing income to avoid the £100,000 threshold. In other words, if possible try not to pay yourself a salary and dividend of £80,000 in year 1 and £120,000 in year 2. It may be better to pay yourself £100,000 during both tax years, to preserve all of your income tax personal allowance in year 2.

Bigger Companies

Owners of companies earning substantial profits face a dilemma. While they may choose to extract no more than £100,000 per year, ultimately they may end up with a lot of surplus cash inside their companies.

For example, if you are the only shareholder in a company that is making an after-tax profit of £200,000 per year, you may not wish to extract just £100,000 per year indefinitely, especially if the surplus cash is not needed to help grow the business.

Company owners who wish to pay themselves more than £100,000 per year may be able to occasionally keep their personal allowances by using the 'roller-coaster' strategy: paying bigger dividends in some tax years and smaller dividends in other years.

Remember, once your income exceeds £125,140 your personal allowance will have disappeared altogether and there is no additional penalty for taking additional dividend income, providing you keep your income below £150,000.

For example, let's say you withdraw a salary of £9,568 and dividend of £115,432 (total income £125,000). With this level of income almost all of your personal allowance will be withdrawn. If instead you pay yourself £100,000 in year 1 and £150,000 in year 2, this will allow you to keep all of your personal allowance in year 1. Potential tax saving: £5,219 (2021/22 tax rates).

Salary vs Dividends

If you intend to pay yourself one of the small salaries discussed in Chapter 8 (£9,568 or £12,570) and extract the rest of the company's profits as dividends, it *may* be possible to achieve a small additional saving by paying yourself an even smaller salary, if you expect to have taxable income of more than £100,000.

The potential tax savings depend on a number of factors, including how much profit the company makes and whether the company has spare national insurance employment allowance.

For example, we have seen that where a company does have spare employment allowance, the "optimal" salary for most company owners is typically £12,570. However, where a company owner's taxable income exceeds £100,000, it may be possible to achieve a tax saving of several hundred pounds by taking a salary equal to the £9,568 national insurance primary threshold instead. It may be tax efficient to take an even lower salary in some cases.

Where a company does not have any employment allowance available, the optimal salary for most company owners is typically £9,568. Where the company owner's taxable income exceeds £100,000, a small tax saving can sometimes be achieved by taking a smaller salary, such as £8,840 which is the employer's national insurance threshold, or an even lower salary in some cases.

The potential tax saving is often not very impressive – less than £100, which is a very small saving for someone with so much income. Nevertheless this may suit some company owners, for example owners of one man band companies that aren't entitled to the employment allowance and don't want the hassle of making any national insurance payments.

In some cases taking a smaller salary will result in a higher tax bill – the interactions are complex!

When You Should Not Reduce Your Salary

There are also various tax and non-tax reasons why you may not want to reduce your salary. In other words, what may be 'mathematically optimal' does not always make for sound tax planning.

Pensions are a case in point. Anyone who personally wants to make a pension contribution higher than £3,600 (the minimum contribution that can be made by anyone under age 75) requires earnings. Salaries count as earnings, dividends do not.

Furthermore, in order to protect your state pension entitlement, you should always make sure you receive a salary that exceeds the national insurance 'lower earnings limit'. For 2021/22, the lower earnings limit is £120 per week which requires a total annual salary of at least £6,240.

When it comes to reducing your salary to achieve additional tax savings the permutations are too many to provide any simple guidelines here. Any analysis would have to be performed on a case by case basis.

After the Corporation Tax Increase

When corporation tax increases (see Chapter 1) many companies will eventually enjoy 26.5% or 25% tax relief on salaries paid to directors.

Will this make a larger salary attractive if the director is earning over £100,000? Probably not.

Where the company has spare employment allowance, a salary of £9,568 will still be more tax efficient than a salary of £12,570 for most company owners whose taxable income exceeds £100,000.

Where a company does not have any employment allowance, a salary of £8,840 will still be a little bit more tax efficient than a salary of £9,568 for most company owners whose taxable income exceeds £100,000.

(Of course the national insurance thresholds may be slightly higher by the time corporation tax increases.)

Scottish Company Owners

In previous chapters I have stated that company owners in Scotland who take a small salary and the rest of their income as dividends are completely immune from Scottish income tax.

However, those with income over £100,000 will have their personal allowances gradually taken away, which means their salaries will become subject to Scottish income tax. Their dividends will continue to be taxed using UK rates and thresholds.

As it happens this is not necessarily a bad thing. As long as your salary and other income subject to Scottish tax (e.g. rental income) do not exceed £27,393 this year, you will pay a tiny bit less tax than company owners living elsewhere in the UK.

In this way the SNP Government has unwittingly handed a tax cut to company owners who have big dividends but only small salaries!

Chapter 17

Income over £150,000

Once your income rises above £150,000 you become an 'additional rate' taxpayer. Most people are familiar with the 45% tax rate (previously 50%) that applies to most types of income above this threshold.

However, if you are a company owner it's likely it will be your dividends that take you over the £150,000 threshold (dividends are always treated as the top slice of income – see Chapter 18).

Once your dividend income rises above £150,000, the income tax rate rises from 32.5% to 38.1%.

Don't Forget the Corporation Tax Bill

Although 38.1% is lower than the 45% rate most people associate with income over £150,000, we must not forget that dividends are paid out of profits that have already been subject to corporation tax.

For example, if a company currently pays £190 corporation tax on £1,000 of profit, that leaves £810 to distribute as dividends. If the director/shareholder then pays 38.1% income tax on the £810 distribution, the additional tax comes to £309. The total tax paid by the director and the company is £499 which is 49.9%!

Will the Additional Rate Be Abolished?

David Cameron's Government once stated that the additional rate of tax was "temporary" (it came into effect just weeks before Gordon Brown was booted out of office).

However, when the rate was reduced from 50% to 45% in 2012 (36.1% to 30.6% for dividends), no date was given for a further reduction. Instead the Government backtracked and increased the additional rate for dividends to 38.1% in April 2016.

Although Conservative governments used to be ideologically committed to lower taxes, that all ended with the pandemic. The increase in corporation has put any doubts to rest. Of all the taxes that can be increased, no government in favour of lower taxes would ever increase corporation tax. Plenty of research has shown that increasing this type of tax will raise revenues in the short term but harm economic growth in the long run.

If there are any tax cuts in the near future they certainly won't be ones that only benefit the "rich", such as cutting the additional rate of income tax.

In summary, I doubt any Government will ever reduce or abolish the additional rate. If anything it's far more likely that the rate will be increased at some point in the future.

In Scotland the top rate is 46% and we think it will be increased further in the future. However, the key thing to remember is that the Scottish Parliament can NOT tax dividend income, so many Scottish company owners will not be affected by the increase in the Scottish rate.

Avoiding the 38.1% Tax Rate

The simplest way to avoid paying 38.1% tax on your dividends is to keep your taxable income below £150,000 (e.g. by extracting higher than normal profits over more than one tax year). Fortunately, this is fairly simple for company owners to do because, unlike most other taxpayers, they can control their personal incomes to a large extent.

But owners of very profitable companies (who don't want to roll up profits inside the company indefinitely) should also remember that going over the additional-rate threshold is not as painful as going over the higher-rate threshold.

When your income rises above £50,270 the dividend tax rate goes from 7.5% to 32.5% and you start paying an extra £250 tax on every additional £1,000 of dividend income you receive. But when your income rises above £150,000 the dividend tax rate goes from 32.5% to 38.1% and you will pay just £56 more tax on every additional £1,000 of dividend income you receive.

When Paying the 38.1% Rate is a Good Idea

In some cases it is better to pay the 38.1% tax rate during one tax year in order to protect your income tax personal allowance during another tax year.

This is because losing your income tax personal allowance can be more costly than paying the additional rate.

Example
Sam owns a successful chain of gyms. He decides to take a salary of £9,568 and a dividend of £140,500. His total taxable income is £150,000, so he avoids paying the 38.1% additional rate of tax. He has been withdrawing exactly £150,000 for several years now.

With this much income he does, however, lose all of his income tax personal allowance every year. His total income tax bill will be £40,371. Over two tax years his total tax bill will be £80,742 (income tax rates and thresholds will be the same next year as this year).

Sam could instead consider withdrawing £200,000 during tax year 1 and £100,000 during tax year 2 – the same total income but split differently. If he does this his total tax bills will be £59,422 and £18,840 respectively: a total tax bill of £78,262.

Sam saves £2,480 by following this strategy. In tax year 1 he has to pay income tax of 38.1% on an extra £50,000 of dividend income: £19,050. However, in tax year 2 his taxable income falls by £50,000 to £100,000 so his income tax personal allowance is fully retained. He would have paid 53.5% tax on the first £25,140 of that income (see Chapter 16) and 32.5% on the final £24,860 – a total of £21,530. The difference is £2,480 (£21,530 - £19,050).

Sam could repeat this strategy, withdrawing income of £100,000 every second year in order to protect his personal allowance. The tax saving is not hugely impressive for someone with this amount of income but the example does show how company owners can use 'roller-coaster income' (see Chapter 7) to lower their tax bills.

Salary versus Dividends

From a strict comparison of tax rates, company owners who are additional-rate taxpayers may be able to save themselves some money at present by not paying themselves any salary at all and taking all of the company's profits as dividends.

Take a company that has profits of £250,000 and just one director/shareholder. If the owner takes a small salary of £9,568 the company will be left with profits of £194,669 to distribute as dividends (after paying 19% corporation tax). The company owner will then be left with £143,201 after paying income tax on the salary and dividends.

If no salary is taken and all of the company's profits are extracted as dividends the company owner will be left with £143,323, a total saving of £122.

Clearly the tax saving is tiny for someone with this much income and, as has been pointed out before, there are other reasons why taking a salary is desirable. For example, a salary of at least £6,240 this year is necessary to preserve your state pension entitlement.

Larger Salaries

In fact, some company owners may desire the convenience of a much larger salary, even if this is not strictly speaking "optimal". For example, if the company owner in the above example takes a salary of £30,000 instead of £9,568, and extracts the remaining profits as dividends, he or she will be £4,016 worse off overall.

Although this extra tax is not insignificant, for someone with taxable income of more than £200,000 a loss of £4,016 is relatively small in *percentage* terms.

Similarly, if the owner of a company with profits of £500,000 takes a salary of £50,000 instead of £9,568 he or she will be £6,833 worse off overall. After-tax income will fall by a relatively modest 2.5% from £268,549 to £261,716.

The extra tax cost will, of course, be smaller if the company has spare employment allowance which reduces the employer's national insurance payable on the company owner's own salary.

After the Corporation Tax Increase

When corporation tax increases (see Chapter 1) many companies will eventually enjoy 26.5% or 25% tax relief on salaries paid to directors.

This will probably mean that the "optimal" salary for most directors with income over £150,000 will be larger than at present.

For example, based on current national insurance thresholds, the optimal salary for most would be £8,840.

Using a Company versus Self-Employment

Most company owners probably realize that if they take all of their income as salary they could end up paying significantly more tax than a self-employed person (sole trader or partner) with the same income. This is because of the additional 13.8% employer's national insurance payable on most salary income.

It's interesting to note that, even if a company owner structures his pay in the most tax efficient manner, taking most or all of his income as dividends, he could still end up paying significantly more tax than a self-employed person. This situation will typically arise when the company owner withdraws most or all of the company's profits and is a high income earner.

Table 6 compares the total after-tax income of a company owner with the total after-tax income of a self-employed business owner at different profit levels. In each case the business owners have over £150,000 of income and are additional-rate taxpayers.

For the company owner, it is assumed that a salary of £6,240 is taken to protect state pension entitlement and all of the remaining after-tax profits are extracted as dividends.

The "Extra Income" column is the additional income enjoyed by the *self-employed* person. For example, when profits are £500,000 a self-employed person will enjoy £8,600 more income than a company owner.

TABLE 6
After-tax Income Compared
Company Owner vs Self Employed

Profits	Company Owner	Self-Employed	Extra Income
£200,000	£118,207	£118,224	£17
£250,000	£143,276	£144,724	£1,447
£300,000	£168,346	£171,224	£2,878
£400,000	£218,485	£224,224	£5,739
£500,000	£268,624	£277,224	£8,600
£600,000	£318,763	£330,224	£11,461
£700,000	£368,902	£383,224	£14,322
£800,000	£419,041	£436,224	£17,183
£900,000	£469,180	£489,224	£20,044
£1,000,000	£519,319	£542,224	£22,905

Notes:
1. Company owner withdraws all the profits of the business
2. Company owner takes £6,240 salary and remaining income as dividends
3. Company owner tax includes corporation tax and income tax
4. Self-employed tax includes income tax and national insurance
5. Self-employed tax bills are higher in Scotland

This doesn't necessarily mean that owners of companies with significant profits would be better off self-employed. If profits are kept inside the company to help it grow, the only tax payable will be corporation tax. Clearly paying just corporation tax (currently at 19% but up to 25% in future) is a lot better than the 47% tax paid by self-employed people who are additional-rate taxpayers (48% in Scotland).

It is in these circumstances – when profits are reinvested – that companies are most powerful as tax shelters. For example, where a company has profits of £500,000 and only half the after-tax profits are paid out as dividends, the total tax bill will be around £67,000 less than the tax paid by a self-employed person.

Alternative Profit Extraction Strategies

Company owners may wish to keep their income below £150,000 by using alternative profit extraction strategies, including:

- Gifting shares in the business to family members, including family members who are higher-rate taxpayers (see Part 5)

- Making personal or company pension contributions (see Chapters 27 and 28)

- Keeping cash inside the company until the business is sold or wound up (see Chapter 32). At this point it may be possible to pay just 10% capital gains tax on the extracted funds

Pension Contributions

Company owners who pay themselves small salaries can only make small pension contributions *personally* – your pension contributions cannot exceed your earnings (dividends don't count as earnings).

For example, if you pay yourself a salary of £9,568 in 2021/22 you can only make a pension contribution of £9,568 personally (£7,654 contributed by you, with a further £1,914 added to your pension by the taxman).

Company owners who wish to enjoy bigger pension contributions can either pay themselves higher salaries or get their companies to make the contributions on their behalf.

A higher salary usually comes with a punitive national insurance bill, so company pension contributions are often the preferred route.

Company pension contributions enjoy corporation tax relief, providing they are not excessive (see Chapter 28).

The Pension Taper

High income earners face another restriction. The annual allowance – the maximum amount that can be invested in a pension each year – can be reduced from £40,000 to just £4,000.

Fortunately, following an announcement in the March 2020 Budget, this pension taper now only kicks in at much higher income levels than previously.

As a result, many high earning company owners can benefit from much higher pension contributions than before.

The first thing you have to calculate is your "threshold income". If your threshold income is £200,000 or less you are completely exempt from tapering and can make pension contributions just like anyone else.

Your threshold income is, broadly speaking, your total taxable income. This includes your salary, dividends, rental profits, interest income and any other taxable income you receive.

From this you deduct any pension contributions you have made *personally* (you deduct the gross contributions).

You can also deduct other reliefs listed in Section 24 of the Income Tax Act 2007. These include things like trade loss relief.

Employer pension contributions are ignored when calculating threshold income. But you must add back any salary sacrificed in exchange for employer pension contributions after 8th July 2015.

The threshold used to be £110,000 but was increased to £200,000 with effect from 6th April 2020.

Example 1
Dirk takes a salary of £9,568 and a dividend of £190,432 out of his company. He has no other income so his total taxable income is £200,000. His company makes a pension contribution on his behalf but we ignore that when calculating his threshold income. He doesn't make any pension contributions personally so his threshold income is exactly £200,000. Dirk is unaffected by the tapered annual allowance. This means his annual allowance for the current tax year is £40,000.

Example 2

Beric is a company owner who pays himself salary and dividend income totalling £200,000. He also has taxable rental profits of £40,000, so his total taxable income is £240,000.

His company makes a pension contribution of £35,000 on his behalf but we ignore this when calculating his threshold income. He doesn't make any pension contributions personally.

Beric's threshold income is therefore £240,000. Because this exceeds £200,000, he is potentially affected by the tapered annual allowance.

If your threshold income exceeds £200,000 the next thing you have to calculate is your "adjusted income".

Broadly speaking, your adjusted income is your total taxable income *plus* any pension contributions made by your company.

You also add back any contributions to an occupational pension scheme under a net pay arrangement (where your contributions are deducted from your salary before calculating PAYE).

You can also deduct the reliefs listed in Section 24 of the Income Tax Act 2007.

Your annual allowance will only be reduced if your adjusted income exceeds £240,000 (previously £150,000).

Your annual allowance is reduced by £1 for every £2 your adjusted income exceeds £240,000. For example, an individual with adjusted income of £270,000 will have their annual allowance reduced by £15,000 (£30,000/2), giving them an annual allowance of £25,000.

The annual allowance cannot fall below £4,000 – this is the new minimum contribution that those affected by the taper can make.

Pension contributions that exceed the tapered annual allowance face the annual allowance charge. The excess contributions will be added to your income and taxed. If the charge exceeds £2,000 it may be possible to have it paid out of your pension savings. This may only be possible if total contributions to the scheme in question exceed the £40,000 annual allowance.

Example 2 continued

As we saw earlier, Beric has total taxable income of £240,000 and his company makes a contribution of £35,000 on his behalf.

Beric's adjusted income is £275,000 (£240,000 + £35,000)

His annual allowance is cut by (£275,000 - £240,000)/2 = £17,500

His annual allowance is therefore £40,000 - £17,500 = £22,500

Beric faces an annual allowance charge on £12,500:

£35,000 - £22,500 = £12,500

Calculating the Tapered Annual Allowance in Practice

Beric can avoid the charge by getting his company to make a smaller pension contribution (no more than £26,667).

Alternatively, he may be able to extract less income from his company (no more than £215,000) to benefit from a tapered annual allowance of £35,000. Company owners will find it easier than others to control their taxable income to reduce their threshold income and adjusted income. However, if they do this they may have to be wary of triggering a special tax anti-avoidance rule (see below).

Company owners will find it fairly easy to calculate their adjusted and threshold income when it comes to salaries and dividends. Problems may arise when the company owner has other income that is less predictable, for example rental income from properties. Company owners who are also landlords may not know precisely how much taxable income they have earned (and thus their tapered annual allowance) until *after* the tax year has ended. By then it will be too late to make pension contributions.

Those who wish to benefit from pension contributions and think they may be affected by the tapered annual allowance may therefore need to estimate their total taxable income just *before* the end of the tax year.

The Tapered Annual Allowance and Carry Forward

All is not lost if your pension contributions exceed your tapered annual allowance for the year. Those affected by the tapered annual allowance can still carry forward any unused annual allowance from the three previous tax years. For example, if your annual allowance this year is reduced from £40,000 to £30,000 and you make a £20,000 pension contribution, you will have £10,000 left to carry forward to next year (£30,000 - £20,000).

Carry forward could act as a lifeline for those whose pension contributions accidentally exceed the tapered annual allowance in any given year. Beric in the above example will avoid the annual allowance charge if he has at least £12,500 of unused annual allowance from the three previous tax years.

Example
Mario is a company owner with taxable income of £200,000. He gets his company to make a £60,000 pension contribution (carrying forward unused annual allowance).

His adjusted income is £260,000 but his threshold income is £200,000, so his annual allowance is not reduced.

If your threshold income does not exceed £200,000 you cannot be subject to the tapered annual allowance, even if your adjusted income is greater than £240,000.

Anti-Avoidance Rule

There is an anti-avoidance rule to prevent anyone entering into an arrangement which involves reducing their adjusted or threshold income and increasing their income in a different tax year.

The anti-avoidance provisions apply when it is reasonable to assume that the main purpose, or one of the main purposes of the arrangement, is to reduce the impact of the tapered annual allowance. If the anti-avoidance provisions apply, then the relevant arrangement will be ignored for the purposes of calculating the tapered annual allowance.

It is unclear how this anti-avoidance rule could be applied to company owners who vary their income from year to year.

Enjoying 49.9% Tax Relief

Thanks to the change announced in the March 2020 Budget many additional rate taxpayers are unaffected by the tapered annual allowance and can once again make fairly big pension contributions with full tax relief.

Any company owner with taxable income of between £150,000 and £200,000 can get their company to make a pension contribution of up to £40,000 every year with full tax relief.

Other high earning company owners can make the following maximum pension contribution:

Taxable Income	Maximum Pension Contribution*
£215,000	£35,000
£230,000	£30,000
£245,000	£25,000
£260,000	£20,000
£275,000	£15,000
£290,000	£10,000
£305,000	£5,000
£308,000+	£4,000

* Ignores potential carry forward from previous tax years

Additional-rate taxpayers currently face a combined marginal tax rate of 49.9% on their dividend income (corporation tax and income tax). So a company owner with £1,000 of pre-tax profit will be left with £501 after tax.

By contrast, with a pension contribution the whole £1,000 can be paid into the director's pension fund. Income tax will be payable when he eventually takes the money out but the effective tax rate could be no more than 15%, leaving him with £850 after tax.

Thus the director can choose between £501 today or £850 in the future. It is easy to see why pensions are such powerful tax shelters!

Part 4

Company Owners with Income from Other Sources

Chapter 18

Keeping Income Below the Key Thresholds

Introduction

In Chapter 7 we explained why company owners, when deciding how much income to withdraw from their companies, need to be aware of the following income tax thresholds and brackets:

- Over £50,270   Higher rate tax
- £50,000-£60,000   Child benefit tax charge
- £100,000-£125,140   Personal allowance withdrawal
- Over £150,000   Additional rate of tax

Basic-rate taxpayers generally pay no more than 7.5% income tax on their dividends. Once your income exceeds £50,270 you become a higher-rate taxpayer and start paying 32.5% tax.

However, dividend income that falls into the final three tax brackets is taxed at much higher rates:

- £50,270-£60,000   43% to 65% or more
- £100,000-£125,000   53.5% in some cases
- Over £150,000   38.1%

(Note: the £50,270-£60,000 bracket only applies to households in receipt of child benefit. The child benefit charge actually kicks in at £50,000, where basic-rate tax is still payable. For example, dividend income in the tiny £50,000-£50,270 bracket is taxed at 26% if you have two children. What unnecessary complication!)

When trying to avoid these extortionate tax rates, you must remember to include any other taxable income you receive. If you have taxable income from other sources it may force your company income, in particular your dividend income, into a higher tax bracket. To avoid a potential tax sting you may wish to reduce the amount of income you withdraw from your company or take other steps to reduce your tax bill.

The Order in which Income is Taxed

Income is taxed in the following order:

- Non-savings income:
  - ➢ Employment income
  - ➢ Self-employment income
  - ➢ Rental income
- Savings income
- Dividend income

Dividends are always treated as the top slice of income.

Let's say you expect to earn £10,000 of rental income during the current tax year but, so far, have not withdrawn any income from your company. As things stand, all of your rental income will be tax free, being covered by your income tax personal allowance.

Let's say you now decide to withdraw a salary of £12,570 and a dividend of £37,700 from your company (the maximum amount you can withdraw tax free or taxed at just 7.5%, in the absence of any other income).

The decision to take a salary means you now have £22,570 of non-savings income and your income tax bill will increase by £2,000:

£22,570 - £12,570 personal allowance = £10,000 x 20% = £2,000

And what about your dividends which are supposedly taxed at no more than 7.5%?

Thanks to your rental income, £10,000 of your dividend income will now be pushed into the higher-rate tax bracket and taxed at 32.5% instead of 7.5%, resulting in additional tax of £2,500.

In summary, having £10,000 of rental income increases the company owner's tax bill by £4,500!

Income from Other Sources

With the exception of self-employment income, it may be possible to extract all of the various types of income listed above from *your own company*: employment income, rental income, interest income, and dividend income.

We've already talked extensively about salaries (employment income) and dividends. If your company uses a property that you own personally (for example, an office or shop) it can also pay you rent; and if your company borrows money from you it can pay you interest.

In Chapters 24 and 25 we take a look at whether it is tax efficient to get your company to pay you rent or interest and how much.

In this part of the guide the focus is on company owners who have income from *other sources* – i.e. income that does not come out of their own company.

More specifically, the focus is on company owners who have income from other sources that is subject to *income tax*.

Some income (e.g. most interest income and stock market dividends) can be sheltered from income tax inside an ISA or pension scheme.

It is also possible to shelter assets from income tax inside another company. Many property investors do this. Corporation tax is still payable on any rental profits produced by the properties but the income tax position of the director/shareholder will be unaffected, unless those profits are extracted.

Those company owners who do have a significant amount of taxable income from other sources, and cannot shelter it from income tax, may wish to reduce the amount of income they withdraw from their own companies, so as to avoid paying income tax at some of the extortionate rates listed at the beginning of this chapter.

Other Income – Control

One of the benefits of being a company owner is you can control how much income you withdraw from your business. This allows you to control your income tax bill from year to year.

Income from other sources is often less easy to control. For example, it may not be possible to shift it from one tax year into another tax year. You may be able to control the dividends declared by your own company but you cannot force the board of Vodafone to increase or lower its dividend!

Company owners who want to keep their taxable income just below any of the key income tax thresholds may therefore have to increase or decrease their *company income* – it may not always be possible to alter the amount of income you receive from other sources.

Table 7 shows the maximum dividend you can withdraw during 2021/22 if you have other taxable income (including salary income) and want to avoid some of the key income tax thresholds.

For example, if you have other taxable income of £20,000 a dividend of no more than £30,270 will prevent your income going over £50,270 which means you will avoid paying 32.5% tax.

A dividend no higher than £30,000 will ensure that you avoid the child benefit tax charge, where relevant.

A dividend of up to £80,000 will ensure that your income does not exceed £100,000. A significant amount of your dividend income will be taxed at 32.5% and you may end up paying the maximum child benefit tax charge but you will not lose any of your personal allowance.

Note, Table 7 is equally relevant to Scottish taxpayers because it is the *UK* thresholds that apply to your dividend income.

For example, a Scottish taxpayer with £40,000 of salary and rental income can still receive a dividend of £10,270 without paying 32.5% tax because it is the UK higher-rate threshold that applies to dividend income.

TABLE 7
Avoiding the Tax Thresholds
Maximum Dividend 2021/22

Other Income	Threshold			
	£50,000	**£50,270**	**£100,000**	**£150,000**
£9,568	£40,432	£40,702	£90,432	£140,432
£12,570	£37,430	£37,700	£87,430	£137,430
£15,000	£35,000	£35,270	£85,000	£135,000
£20,000	£30,000	£30,270	£80,000	£130,000
£25,000	£25,000	£25,270	£75,000	£125,000
£30,000	£20,000	£20,270	£70,000	£120,000
£35,000	£15,000	£15,270	£65,000	£115,000
£40,000	£10,000	£10,270	£60,000	£110,000

Note: First £2,000 of dividend income tax free

Remember, no matter how much other income you have, you can always receive at least £2,000 of tax-free dividend income thanks to the dividend allowance.

For example, someone with other income of £50,000 can still receive a tax-free dividend of £2,000 without having to worry about paying 32.5% tax.

In some cases taking tax-free dividend income will have other negative tax consequences.

For example, someone with other income of £50,000 who receives a £2,000 tax-free dividend will end up with total income of £52,000 which means they could end up losing some of their child benefit.

Someone with other income of £100,000 can also receive £2,000 of tax-free dividend income. However, this will bring their total income to £102,000 which means they will lose some of their personal allowance.

Other Income – Predictability

At the start of a new tax year you may not know with complete certainty how much taxable income you will receive from other sources during the year. This could be problematic if you wish to withdraw dividends from your company *at the beginning of the tax year*.

If you withdraw dividends from your company and your other income then turns out to be higher than expected, you may end up paying more income tax than you expected on your company dividends.

Some types of income are, however, more predictable than others. For example, interest income, stock market dividends and rental income are arguably more predictable than, say, the profits of a sole trader business (self-employment income).

Some types of income, if not completely predictable, are more likely to end up being *less than expected*, rather than higher than expected. For example, a rental property that normally generates rental income of £1,000 per month may lie empty for three months, thereby producing an annual income of £9,000 rather than £12,000.

If your income from other sources turns out to be less than expected, you may be able to get your company to pay you additional dividend income before the end of the tax year.

If your income from other sources turns out to be *higher than expected* you generally cannot reverse any dividends you have already taken out of your company, although it may be possible to do some emergency year-end tax planning (see Chapters 20 and 43).

Company owners who have unpredictable income from other sources may therefore wish to postpone paying dividends until closer to the end of the tax year, if they are concerned that their dividend income may fall into a heavily taxed bracket.

Chapter 19

Should I Pay Myself a Smaller Salary?

So far we have shown that if you have income from other sources (e.g. rental income) you may wish to reduce your company *dividends* to avoid various tax thresholds.

Another important question is: "Should I pay myself a smaller salary?"

If you intend to pay yourself one of the small salaries discussed in Chapter 8 (typically £9,568 or £12,570) and extract the rest of the company's profits as dividends, it may be possible to increase your after-tax disposable income by reducing your company salary in some circumstances.

For example, in Chapter 8 it was shown that, where a company has spare national insurance employment allowance, the optimal salary for most company owners is £12,570.

However, where the company owner has taxable income from other sources that uses up his personal allowance, it may be possible to achieve a tax saving of a few hundred pounds by taking a salary equal to the £9,568 national insurance primary threshold instead.

In Chapter 8 it was also shown that, where a company has employees and does not have any spare employment allowance, the optimal salary for most company owners is £9,568.

Where the company owner has taxable income from other sources a small tax saving of around £50 can be achieved by taking a salary of £8,840 (the employer's national insurance threshold) instead of £9,568. It generally doesn't pay to reduce your salary any further.

A smaller salary may, however, be preferable when the company owner wishes to extract just a small amount of income in total from the company. This is because, if you have other income that uses up your personal allowance, the "optimal" salary/dividend profit extraction strategy is typically as follows:

- First, pay yourself a tax-free dividend of £2,000

- Second, pay yourself a salary up to the £8,840 employer's national insurance threshold (if there is no employment allowance available) or £9,568 (if there is spare employment allowance for the directors' salaries)

- Pay any further amounts as dividends

The reason a tax-free dividend is the first port of call is because the only tax payable is corporation tax, currently at 19%.

By contrast, if you have other income that uses up your personal allowance, any salary you pay yourself will effectively be taxed at a rate of 20%. And if your other income also uses up your basic-rate band, any salary you pay yourself will effectively be taxed at 40%.

So a tax-free dividend is better than salary in these circumstances.

If you want to extract more than your £2,000 tax-free dividend a salary is the best bet as long as there is no national insurance payable. Income tax will typically be payable at 20% or 40%, compared with the combined tax rates on additional dividend income of 25% or 45% – see Chapter 3.

Once you've exhausted your national insurance free salary dividends are generally better.

Having said all this, there are lots of reasons why you may not wish to reduce your salary or why it may not be practical to reduce your salary:

- To keep your earnings above the lower earnings limit (£6,240 in 2021/22) to protect your state pension entitlement (See Chapter 10).

- To make bigger pension contributions personally (see Chapter 28).

- Because your income from other sources may not be known at the beginning of the year, when you may wish to start making monthly salary payments.

- Because the taxman may question any reduction in your salary (see Chapter 39).

After the Corporation Tax Increase

When corporation tax increases (see Chapter 1) many companies will eventually enjoy 26.5% or 25% tax relief on salaries paid to directors.

However, this will probably not make taking a larger salary more tax efficient than it is at present, if the company owner has income from other sources.

Based on current national insurance thresholds, a salary of £9,568 will still, in most cases, be more tax efficient than a salary of £12,570 where the company has spare national insurance employment allowance.

Where the company does not have spare employment allowance, a salary of £8,840 will still be slightly more tax efficient than a salary of £9,568 in most cases.

Chapter 20

The Different Types of Income

Let's take a closer look at the different types of income you may earn from sources outside your company and how they may affect the income you decide to withdraw from your own company:

Employment Income

It is possible to have more than one source of employment income, for example:

- Salary from a second job with a separate employer, or
- Salary from a second company you own

If you have recently started out in business, it's possible you will have a second job (possibly a part-time job) to help pay the bills.

If you start a second company for a separate business venture there is, of course, nothing to stop you paying yourself a second salary.

For income tax purposes you are only entitled to one personal allowance (£12,570 at present). This generally means that you can only have one tax-free salary (unless, of course, the two salaries, when added together, total less than £12,570). Some or all of the second salary may be taxed at 20%.

National insurance is calculated differently. Employees who have more than one salary of £9,568 this year may not have to pay national insurance contributions at all. This is because the earnings from each job may be treated separately.

If the two businesses are "in association", however, the salaries will be added together and national insurance may be payable. Employers are considered to be in association if:

- The businesses serve a common purpose, and

- There is significant sharing of things like premises, personnel, equipment or customers

Following the increase in dividend tax rates, a second salary may be more tax efficient than a dividend, providing there is no national insurance payable.

If you wish to pay yourself two salaries it may be necessary to obtain professional advice to satisfy yourself that the companies will not be treated by HMRC as being in association, with resulting national insurance liabilities.

Finally, there may be other tax and non-tax reasons why you wish to pay yourself a second salary or a bigger second salary.

Salary from Other Job Exceeds £50,270

Where a company owner earns a salary of more than £50,270 (the upper earnings limit) from a different employment, it may be possible to reduce the employee's national insurance rate on the salary they receive from their own company.

In other words, instead of paying 12% national insurance it may be possible to pay just 2% on all of the second salary the director receives from his own company.

This is because there is a maximum amount of salary income on which you have to pay 12% national insurance each year (see Chapter 2). This year the maximum is £40,702 (£50,270 upper earnings limit minus £9,568 primary threshold).

Applications can be made using form CA72A, available from HMRC's website.

In Chapter 8 we saw that, where there is no *employer's* national insurance payable (because the company has spare employment allowance) a salary of £12,570 is generally optimal. Where, in addition, *employee's* national insurance is payable at just 2%, it is generally tax efficient at present to pay yourself as much salary as possible to exhaust the company's employment allowance. For example, two company owners who have no other employees can pay themselves a salary of £23,332 each this year without having to pay any employer's national insurance.

Even higher salaries will become tax efficient after the corporation tax increase (see Chapter 1).

Self-Employment Income

You may have self-employment income if you have another business that is not a company (i.e. you're a sole trader or belong to a partnership). Many entrepreneurs have multiple businesses and it's possible a second or third business will not be a company.

Companies can be wonderful tax shelters but unincorporated businesses have advantages of their own, including lower accountancy fees, more generous treatment of certain expenses and more generous capital allowances for cars used in the business.

Self-employment income may be difficult to predict – especially close to the beginning of a new tax year – making it difficult to decide how much income to withdraw from the other company business.

Fortunately, as far as your self-employment business is concerned, it may be possible to do some emergency year-end tax planning to reduce your tax bill (e.g. by making pension contributions or incurring other tax deductible expenditure).

Rental Income

When we use the term 'rental income' what we mean is rental *profit*. You may receive rents of £10,000 per year but your rental profit may only be £5,000, after deducting all the expenses property investors can claim.

Unlike interest income and stock market dividends, most rental income cannot be sheltered from income tax in an ISA, pension scheme or other tax shelter.

There are, however a couple of exceptions:

- Commercial property held in a pension scheme

- Residential or commercial property held in a company

Some business owners place their business premises inside a self-invested personal pension (SIPP) to avoid income tax and capital gains tax (see Chapter 29).

Others put their properties in a separate company. Corporation tax is payable on the company's income and capital gains but your own income tax bill will be unaffected, unless the property company's profits are extracted.

Apart from these two exceptions, most landlords own their properties *personally*, which means they are fully exposed to income tax on their rental profits. These rental profits may then need to be factored into the mix when deciding how much income you withdraw from your company.

For example, in 2021/21 if you take a salary of £9,568 and expect to have taxable rental profits of £20,000 you can take tax-free dividend income of £2,000 plus additional dividend income of £18,702 taxed at 7.5%. This takes you up to the £50,270 higher-rate threshold. Any additional dividend income you receive will be taxed at a rate of at least 32.5%.

If you take a salary of £9,568 and expect to have taxable rental profits of £50,000 you can still take tax-free dividend income of £2,000 (because everyone can benefit from the dividend nil rate band). However, on any additional dividend income you will pay at least 32.5% tax.

Rental losses

If you have rental losses brought forward from previous years you will not have to pay any income tax on the rental profit you make during the current tax year (providing, the loss brought forward is big enough to completely offset the current year's profit).

If the rental profit you make during the current tax year is not taxable it does not need to be factored into the mix when deciding how much income you withdraw from your company.

Changes to Mortgage Tax Relief

Tax relief for interest and finance costs paid by individual landlords who own residential properties is now restricted.

The new rules do not apply to commercial properties or furnished holiday lettings or to properties held inside companies.

Tax relief has been phased out over a period of four years and replaced with a 20% basic-rate "tax reduction" as follows:

- 2017/18   75% deducted as normal, 25% at basic rate only
- 2018/19   50% deducted as normal, 50% at basic rate only
- 2019/20   25% deducted as normal, 75% at basic rate only
- Later years   All relieved at basic rate only

Company owners who have a separate rental property business have had to contend with two major tax changes in recent times:

- Higher tax rates for dividends (2016/17 onwards)
- Reduced tax relief on mortgage interest (2017/18 onwards)

The reduced tax relief on mortgage interest means many landlords now have bigger taxable rental profits.

This in turn has pushed more of the dividend income they receive from their companies over the higher-rate threshold where it is subject to the 32.5% tax rate.

Example

Sinead owns a graphic design company and pays herself a salary of £12,570 and dividends of £40,000.

She's also a landlord and earns a rental profit of £35,700 before deducting her interest costs. She pays £12,000 interest on her buy-to-let mortgages, so her true rental profit is £23,700. However, with none of her mortgage interest tax deductible any more, her taxable rental profit will be £35,700. Along with her salary of £12,570 this will take her income up to £48,270.

Because this is still below the £50,270 higher-rate threshold all of her taxable rental profit will be taxed at 20%, with an offsetting tax reduction of 20% of her mortgage interest. So at first glance it looks like she is unaffected by the change to interest tax relief.

Where Sinead will feel the sting is on her dividend income. Dividends are always treated as the top slice of income. The first £2,000 of her dividend income will be tax free thanks to the dividend nil rate band but this will take her income up to the £50,270 higher-rate threshold.

All of her remaining dividend income will therefore be taxed at the 32.5% higher rate.

The end result is that, because her taxable rental profits are £12,000 higher than her true rental profit, this will push £12,000 of her dividend income over the higher-rate threshold where it will be taxed at 32.5% instead of 7.5% – an increase of 25%.

Thus her final tax bill will increase by £3,000 (£12,000 x 25%) compared with what it would be if her interest was fully deductible.

Many company owners who are also landlords will find themselves in a similar position and will see their tax bills increase by an amount equivalent to 25% of their mortgage interest (compared with the position if their interest was fully deductible).

For example, a company owner with £20,000 of buy-to-let interest could end up paying £5,000 more tax from 2020/21 onwards.

Tax Planning for Landlords

If you are a company owner and separately own mortgaged rental properties personally you will have to be careful about the amount of dividend income you pay yourself if you want to avoid going over the various tax thresholds.

Example
Jessie owns a small engineering company and some rental property.

Because she earns rental income she decides to pay herself a salary of £8,840 in 2021/22 (Chapter 19 explains why this may be the optimal salary for someone with income from other sources).

Her rental property produces income of £20,000 net of all expenses except mortgage interest. Her mortgage interest is £7,500 so her true rental profit is £12,500.

However, her taxable rental profit is £20,000 and it is this number she must use when deciding how much dividend income to take.

With a salary of £8,840 and taxable rental profit of £20,000 Jessie can pay herself a dividend of up to £21,430 before she becomes a higher-rate taxpayer and has to pay 32.5% tax (£50,270 - £8,840 - £20,000).

Example

Cillian owns a software company and a portfolio of rental properties. Because he earns rental income he decides to pay himself a salary of £8,840 in 2021/22.

His rental property produces income of £50,000 (net of all expenses except interest). His mortgage interest is £15,000 so his true rental profit is £35,000. However, his taxable rental profit is £50,000.

With a salary of £8,840 and taxable rental profit of £50,000 Cillian is a higher-rate taxpayer and will pay 32.5% tax on his dividend income (except the first £2,000 which is always tax free).

Cillian can pay himself a dividend of up to £41,160 before he reaches the £100,000 tax threshold where his personal allowance will be gradually withdrawn. He will then pay tax at an effective rate of 52.5% on the next £25,000 of dividend income he receives (see Chapter 16 for an explanation of how the withdrawal of the personal allowance works).

Interest Income

Most interest income can be sheltered from tax inside an ISA or SIPP. Other tax-free investments include index-linked savings certificates (when they're available) and offset mortgages (instead of earning interest, your savings are used to reduce the interest on your mortgage). Even paying off personal debts is effectively a way to earn tax-free interest.

Wealthier individuals, with large cash balances or holdings of corporate and government bonds may, however, have a significant amount of *taxable* interest income and there may also be times in life when less wealthy taxpayers have significant amounts of taxable interest income:

- You sell your home and have a large cash lump sum
- You lend money to a friend or family member
- You receive a big dividend and put the cash in the bank
- You lend money to your company (see Chapter 25)

This income may need to be factored into the equation when you decide how much income to withdraw from your company.

The £5,000 Starting Rate Band

When it comes to interest income, many company owners are in a fortunate position. They can receive up to £5,000 of interest *tax free* each year thanks to the 0% starting-rate band.

The starting rate is supposed to benefit only those with very low incomes. Hence the £5,000 starting rate band is reduced by any taxable *non-savings* income you have including:

- Employment income
- Self-employment income
- Pension income
- Rental income

If your taxable non-savings income exceeds £5,000, none of your interest income will be covered by the starting rate band.

Of course, most regular salary earners and self-employed business owners will have more than £5,000 of taxable non-savings income. Many *company owners* are in a different position, however. Note that the above list of non-savings income does NOT include dividends. Dividends are the top slice of income and do not use up the starting rate band.

Because company owners often pay themselves small salaries and take the rest of their income as dividends, they will often have little or no taxable non-savings income. As a result, many can earn at least £5,000 of tax-free interest!

Example
Mandy is a company owner with a salary of £12,570, dividend income of £32,700 and interest income of £5,000. Her salary is tax free thanks to her personal allowance and she therefore has no taxable non-savings income that uses up her starting rate band (her dividend income does not count). Her interest income is fully covered by her £5,000 starting rate band and taxed at 0%.

Many company directors will thus pay 0% tax on their interest if:

- They take a small salary from their company,
- Do not have a sole trader or partnership business, and
- Don't earn much, if any, rental income.

It is important to point out that the 0% starting rate band is not given in addition to your basic-rate band (currently £37,700). Instead it is part of your basic-rate band.

If you qualify to use the starting rate band your basic-rate band will be reduced, possibly pushing some of your dividend income into a higher tax bracket.

The Savings Allowance

The savings allowance (also known as the savings nil rate band) exempts the first £1,000 of your interest income from tax if you're a basic-rate taxpayer and the first £500 if you're a higher-rate taxpayer. Additional-rate taxpayers get nothing.

When the allowance was introduced banks were allowed to stop deducting 20% income tax from their customers' interest earnings.

The savings nil rate band operates separately from, and in addition to, the starting rate band. This means some company owners can earn up to £6,000 of tax-free interest every year.

Income that falls within the savings nil rate band uses up some of the band that it falls into. For example, if you have £49,400 of salary and rental income and £1,000 of interest income you will have total income of £50,400.

As a higher-rate taxpayer you will therefore be entitled to a £500 savings nil rate band. Thus £500 of your interest income will be tax free and this will use up £500 of your basic-rate band, leaving £370 taxed at 20%. The final £130 will be taxed at 40%.

The savings nil rate band will be useful to company owners who cannot use the starting rate band because they have too much non-savings income, e.g. rental income. Most can enjoy £1,000 or £500 of tax-free interest. It may also be useful for extracting interest from your own company (see Chapter 25).

Interest Income - Examples

The somewhat complex operation of the starting rate band and savings nil rate band is best explained with some examples:

Example
Samantha is a company owner with a salary of £12,570 and interest income of £5,000. She also has £10,000 of rental income.

Her salary is covered by her personal allowance but thanks to her rental income she has £10,000 of taxable non-savings income. Because her taxable non-savings income exceeds the £5,000 starting rate limit, none of her interest income is covered by the 0% starting rate.

However, because she is a basic-rate taxpayer (her total income is less than £50,270) she is entitled to a £1,000 savings nil rate band. So £1,000 of her interest income will be tax free, the remaining £4,000 will be taxed at 20%.

Example
Elaine is a company owner with a salary of £9,568, rental income of £7,500, interest income of £1,000 and dividends of £20,000 (total income £38,068).

There is no income tax on her salary and the first £3,002 of her rental income is covered by her remaining personal allowance. The final £4,498 of her rental income is taxed at 20% and uses up £4,498 of her £5,000 starting rate band. Thus £502 of her interest income is covered by her remaining starting rate band and is tax free.

As a basic-rate taxpayer she is also entitled to a £1,000 savings nil rate band, so the final £498 of her interest income is also tax free.

The first £2,000 of her dividend income is covered by the dividend nil rate band, the remaining £18,000 is taxed at 7.5%.

Example
Ollie is a company owner with a salary of £12,570 and dividends of £37,700. He also has interest income of £5,500 (total income £55,770).

There is no income tax on his salary and £5,000 of his interest income is tax free thanks to the 0% starting rate band (dividends do not count as non-savings income and do not use up the starting rate band).

Because his total income is £55,770 he is a higher-rate taxpayer and is entitled to a £500 savings nil rate band, so the final £500 of his interest income will also be tax free.

Turning to his dividend income, Ollie has £32,200 of his basic-rate band remaining (£50,270 - £12,570 - £5,500). Of this £2,000 will be tax free thanks to the dividend nil rate band and £30,200 will be taxed at 7.5%. The final £5,500 of his dividend income is taxed at 32.5%.

Although all of Ollie's interest is tax free it uses up some of his basic-rate band, pushing an equivalent amount of his dividend income over the higher-rate threshold where it is taxed at 32.5%.

Example
Mark is a company owner with a salary and rental income totalling £50,000 (his non-savings income) and dividend income of £20,000. He also has interest income of £5,000. His total income is £75,000.

Because his taxable non-savings income exceeds the £5,000 starting rate limit, none of his interest is covered by the 0% starting rate. Furthermore, as a higher-rate taxpayer he is entitled to a £500 savings nil rate band. The final £4,500 of his interest income is taxed at 40%.

Turning to his dividend income, the first £2,000 will be tax free thanks to the dividend nil rate band and the final £18,000 is taxed at 32.5%.

Making the Most of Your Personal Allowance

In Chapter 4 we showed how a small number of company owners may be able to save some tax by allocating some of their personal allowance from their salary to their dividend income.

Those who also have interest income are more likely able to save tax by allocating some of their personal allowance from their interest income to their dividend income. This is because their interest income will still be tax free thanks to the 0% starting rate.

Example
In 2021/22 company owner Jameel has salary income of £9,568, interest income of £4,000 and dividend income of £50,000. If all of his personal allowance is allocated to his salary and interest his tax bill will be calculated as follows:

Salary		**Income Tax**
Personal allowance	£9,568	£0

Interest		
Personal allowance	£3,002	£0
Starting rate	£998	£0

Dividend		
Dividend allowance	£2,000	£0
Taxed at 7.5%	£34,702	£2,603
Taxed at 32.5%	£13,298	£4,322
Total tax		£6,925

This is not the optimal outcome. Jameel can reduce his tax bill by reallocating some of his personal allowance from his interest income to his dividend income. This is because his interest income will still be tax free thanks to the 0% starting rate.

Salary		**Income Tax**
Personal allowance	£9,568	£0

Interest		
Starting rate	£4,000	£0

Dividend		
Personal allowance	£3,002	£0
Dividend allowance	£2,000	£0
Taxed at 7.5%	£31,700	£2,378
Taxed at 32.5%	£13,298	£4,322
Total tax		£6,700

In this case Jameel saves £225 tax. This is because his salary does not use up his personal allowance so £3,002 of his dividend income can be tax free instead of taxed at 7.5%. His interest income remains tax free thanks to the 0% starting rate.

Note, good tax software should perform the optimal tax calculation automatically.

Scottish Company Owners with Interest Income

The Scottish Parliament can tax most types of income but not interest and dividends. So Scottish taxpayers will not pay more tax on their interest income than other taxpayers.

This year it's only when Scottish company owners have salary income and other income subject to Scottish tax of more than £27,393 that they will pay more tax than those living elsewhere in the UK.

Thus in all of the above examples the company owners will pay the same tax on their interest and dividend income if they live in Scotland. Samantha and Elaine will, however, pay less tax on their rental income if they live in Scotland, whereas Mark will pay more tax on his salary and rental income.

Stock Market Dividends

The big difference between dividends from your own company and stock market companies is that stock market dividends can be completely sheltered from income tax in an ISA or SIPP.

In practice, many investors do in fact end up with a mixture of shares held inside and outside the tax protection of ISAs and SIPPs (for example, those who inherit a big share portfolio or want to invest more than the current £20,000 ISA limit but do not want to put money in a pension).

These investors could consider:

- Holding high-income shares inside an ISA (to protect the dividends from income tax), and

- Holding growth shares that produce capital gains outside an ISA (because up to £12,300 of capital gains will be tax free anyway thanks to the annual CGT exemption).

This simplistic strategy will not always produce the biggest tax savings, however. If you bought Apple shares back in 2003 – before their 50,000% rise – you would be kicking yourself if you didn't stick them in an ISA!

Stock Market Dividends – How Big a Problem?

Unlike dividends from your own company, you cannot control the amount of income you receive from stock market companies.

So if you have significant dividends from stock market companies, and the shares are not sheltered inside an ISA or SIPP, you may want to reduce the dividends you extract from your own company to avoid going over one of the key income tax thresholds.

However, my gut feeling is that stock market dividends do not cause a significant tax problem for most small investors.

Even if you own, say, £100,000 worth of shares outside an ISA or SIPP you will probably receive no more than £5,000 per year in dividends, producing an income tax bill of £1,625 for a higher-rate taxpayer.

Short-term (Emergency) Tax Planning

If your total taxable income is higher than expected, there are some steps you can take to reduce it before the end of the tax year:

Pension Contributions

Everyone under age 75 can make a gross pension contribution of £3,600 per year. The taxpayer personally contributes £2,880 and the taxman tops up the pension plan with £720 of basic-rate tax relief. To make bigger pension contributions you require earnings: generally salary income or self-employment profits.

If you have a salary of £9,568 you can make a gross pension contribution of £9,568 (£7,654 from you, £1,914 from the taxman). Your basic-rate band will be increased by £9,568 so £9,568 of your dividends may escape higher-rate tax.

If you have self-employment income you can generally make an additional gross pension contribution equivalent to the taxable profits of the business, thereby eliminating any tax problem caused by this type of income.

See Chapters 27 and 28 for more on pension contributions.

Tax Deductible Expenditure

Self-employed business owners (sole traders and partnerships) can also reduce their taxable income by incurring tax deductible expenditure before the end of the business's tax year.

Possibly the easiest way is to incur expenditure that qualifies for an immediate tax deduction thanks to the annual investment allowance.

The allowance is supposed to be £200,000 per year. However, this has been increased to £1 million until 31st December 2021 to encourage investment and help the economy recover.

Property investors with higher than expected rental profits can spend money on property repairs before the end of the tax year, e.g. replacement kitchens and bathrooms.

Long-term Tax Planning

Company owners with significant amounts of income from other sources may be able to take the following steps to shift income from themselves to another entity or person:

Self-Employment Income

Consider putting the business into a second company (company 2) so that corporation tax is payable rather than income tax.

Dividends can then be extracted from company 2, taking into account dividends withdrawn from company 1. This will allow you to control your income tax bill from year to year.

Of course, it's not always advantageous to incorporate a second business. Sole traders and partnerships enjoy certain tax benefits, including more generous tax treatment of various expenses (including home office, travel and car capital allowances).

Rental Income

- Transferring properties to your spouse if he/she pays income tax at a lower rate.

- Holding commercial properties inside a pension scheme.

- Holding investment properties inside a company, so that corporation tax is payable instead of income tax and the extraction of rental profits (as dividends) can be controlled. See the Taxcafe guide *Using a Property Company to Save Tax* for a full discussion of the benefits and drawbacks of using a company.

- Consider alternative investments (e.g. blue chip shares) that can be sheltered from tax in an ISA or pension scheme.

Interest Income

Some company owners can receive up to £6,000 of tax-free interest and most can receive at least £500 (except additional-rate taxpayers). Where tax is payable on your interest income, or you fear it will push some of your dividend income into the 32.5% tax bracket, the following strategies can be adopted:

- Transfer savings into an ISA or SIPP.

- Use savings to pay off debt or take out an offset mortgage.

- Transfer cash to certain family members who pay tax at a lower rate.

- Invest in assets that produce capital growth rather than interest income.

Stock Market Dividends

- Hold shares in an ISA or SIPP.

- Transfer holdings to a spouse and possibly other family members.

Part 5

Splitting Income with Your Family

Chapter 21

Splitting Income with Your Spouse or Partner

In Chapter 12 we saw that couples can double up the tax-free salary and dividend and the amount of dividend income taxed at just 7.5%.

That's all very well if the couple own and run the company together. But what if your spouse/partner isn't involved in the business, for example if the company was started before you met or if they have a separate career and receive salary income from another employer?

In situations like these it may be possible to save income tax by gifting shares in the company to your spouse. It may even be possible to save tax by paying them a salary as well.

The amount of tax that can be saved depends on individual circumstances, for example how much profit the company makes and how much taxable income each person has already.

Tax savings are typically achieved where one spouse is a higher-rate taxpayer (paying 32.5% tax on their dividend income) and the other spouse has no income at all or is a basic-rate taxpayer.

However, it's not just these couples who can save tax. It's possible to pay income tax at more than 32.5% on dividend income that falls into any of the following tax brackets:

- £50,270-£60,000   Child benefit charge
- £100,000-£125,140   Personal allowance withdrawal
- Over £150,000   Additional-rate tax

If your income falls into one of these tax brackets you may be able to save tax by transferring income to your spouse, even if your spouse is a higher-rate taxpayer.

And because *every* taxpayer is entitled to a dividend allowance, it may be possible to save tax by shifting some dividend income to your spouse/partner, even if they're in the same tax bracket as you or a higher tax bracket. Unfortunately, the potential tax savings are relatively modest because the dividend allowance was cut from £5,000 to £2,000 on 6 April 2018.

Before we look at some sample tax savings it is important to point out that there are also potential dangers when it comes to splitting dividend income with your spouse. We will return to this important issue later in the chapter.

Capital Gains Tax (CGT)

If you wish to split your dividend income with your spouse you generally have to transfer shares in the company to them.

In the case of married couples, a gift of shares would be exempt from capital gains tax. Capital gains tax will, however, be payable if the spouse who receives the gift later disposes of the shares. The original base cost of the spouse who made the transfer will be used to perform the CGT calculation.

Gifts between unmarried couples are normally subject to capital gains tax. However, the couple may be able to jointly elect to claim holdover relief.

Holdover relief allows a chargeable gain to be deferred (held over) when gifts of qualifying business assets are made. The person who receives the shares may eventually have to pay capital gains tax on the original owner's gain, as well as their own, when the shares are sold.

To qualify for holdover relief the company must generally be a regular trading company.

Unmarried couples who want to split their income face a further potential danger (see below).

Giving the Business Away

To successfully split your dividend income with your spouse it is essential that proper ownership of shares in the company is handed over. This means your spouse must be able to do what

156

they like with any dividends paid out and with any capital growth from any sale of the business.

As we shall see shortly, it is also safer to transfer ordinary shares rather than shares that have fewer voting rights or other rights.

It is probably advisable to have any dividends received by your spouse paid into a separate bank account in their name, to illustrate to HMRC that you have not retained control of the money.

Dividends are generally payable in proportion to shareholdings. So if you normally take a dividend of £100,000 and want to transfer £40,000 of this income to your spouse, you will generally have to transfer 40% of the business to them.

Because this sort of tax planning, if done correctly, involves effectively giving away ownership and control of part of your business, it is only suitable where there is a significant amount of trust between the parties involved.

How Much of the Business Should Be Transferred?

For many company owners, a 50:50 ownership split with their spouse or partner will prove optimal, but a smaller stake can be transferred if the founder wants to retain more control over the business.

Example

Steve owns 100% of Steve's Spices, a small trading company. Steve currently pays himself a salary of £15,000 and dividends of £80,000.

His total income is £95,000 which means he is close to the £100,000 threshold. If his income rises above this threshold he will start to lose his income tax personal allowance.

As things stand he will pay income tax of £17,033 on his dividend income in 2021/22 – see Chapter 3 for an explanation of how dividends are taxed.

Steve's wife Lara does not own any shares in the company but she does receive rental income of £13,000 from a buy-to-let property.

This means she can receive dividends of up to £37,270 this year before she becomes a higher-rate taxpayer (£50,270 – £13,000). Of this, £2,000 will be tax-free and the rest will be taxed at just 7.5%.

Steve therefore transfers 45% of the ordinary shares in the business to Lara. The company continues to pay total dividends of £80,000 but now Steve's dividend is £44,000 and Lara's is £36,000.

Lara's total taxable income is now £49,000 and the tax bill on her dividend income is £2,550. Steve's total taxable income is now £59,000 and the tax bill on his dividend income is £5,333.

The tax on the total dividend income has been reduced by £9,150.

Furthermore, Steve's income is now well below the £100,000 threshold which means he doesn't have to worry about losing his income tax personal allowance for now.

Additional tax savings may be achieved if the couple are currently receiving child benefit. As we know from Chapter 15, the child benefit charge is payable if, like Steve, the highest earner in the household has income of more than £50,000.

But if Steve transfers 50% of the business to Lara, instead of 45%, his total taxable income will fall to £55,000. Lara will pay 32.5% tax on most of the additional £4,000 of dividend income she receives. However, because Steve's income is now £55,000 the child benefit charge will be reduced by 40%, saving the couple an additional £731 in 2021/22 if they have two children, with similar savings in future years (see Chapter 15).

Potential Tax Savings

The potential tax savings from transferring dividend income to your spouse will vary from case to case:

Spouse Has No Income

If you are a basic-rate taxpayer (income under £50,270) and your spouse is a 'house-spouse' with no taxable income, they can receive tax-free dividends of up to £14,570 this year (made up of the £12,570 personal allowance and £2,000 dividend allowance). The potential tax saving is £1,093 (£14,570 x 7.5%).

If you are a higher-rate taxpayer and your spouse has no taxable income, they can receive less heavily taxed dividends of up to £50,270 this year. The first £14,570 will be tax free and the remainder will be taxed at 7.5%.

By contrast you as a higher-rate taxpayer could be paying at least 32.5% tax on all of this income.

For example, let's say you gift enough shares in the company so that your spouse receives dividend income of £40,000. Your spouse will pay £1,907 tax (first £14,570 tax free, the remainder taxed at 7.5%). You would have paid £13,000 (at 32.5%), so the total tax saving in this example is £11,093.

The tax saving may be even greater if you have income of more than £100,000 before the transfer. Reducing your income may allow you to claw back some of your personal allowance which will produce an additional tax saving.

Spouse is Basic-Rate Taxpayer

Even if your spouse works and has taxable income, it may be possible to save tax by gifting shares in the business to them. Again, the tax savings will vary from case to case.

Example
Rupert is a company owner who expects to have a taxable income of £70,000 this year, made up of a £60,000 dividend and £10,000 of salary and other income. He will pay 32.5% tax on £19,730 of his dividend income (£70,000 - £50,270 higher-rate threshold).

His wife, Wendy, receives taxable income of £30,000 from another source. Thus she has £20,270 of her basic-rate band left and can receive around £20,270 of dividends that will be less heavily taxed in her hands.

If Rupert gifts one third of the shares to Wendy and the company normally pays dividends of £60,000, she'll receive £20,000. The first £2,000 will be tax free thanks to the dividend allowance and tax of £1,350 will be payable on the remaining £18,000 (at 7.5%). Rupert would've paid £6,433 tax on this income so the tax saving is £5,083.

Spouse is Higher-Rate Taxpayer

If you and your spouse/partner are both higher-rate taxpayers (income over £50,270) it may still be possible to save tax by gifting them shares in the company.

For starters your spouse will have their own dividend allowance which means they can receive up to £2,000 of dividend income tax free, no matter how much other income they have.

If your income exceeds £100,000 some or all of your personal allowance will have been withdrawn and it may be possible to save even more tax by transferring dividend income to your spouse.

Example

Saul is a company owner who expects to have a taxable income of £130,000 this year, made up of £120,000 of dividend income and £10,000 of salary and other income. With this much income all of his personal allowance will be withdrawn.

His wife Kylie has income of £60,000 from another source. If Saul transfers 25% of the company to Kylie she will receive dividend income of £30,000. The first £2,000 will be tax free but she will pay 32.5% tax on the rest (£9,100).

Saul's income will fall from £130,000 to £100,000 which means he will recover all of his personal allowance and his tax bill will fall from £33,925 to £18,840.

All in all the couple will save £5,985 in tax by transferring the dividend income to Kylie, even though she is also a higher-rate taxpayer.

If you have income of more than £150,000 and are an *additional-rate* taxpayer it may be possible to save tax by gifting shares to your spouse who is a higher-rate taxpayer.

The first £2,000 of their dividend income will be tax free and they will pay 32.5% tax on the rest, compared with the 38.1% you would pay as an additional rate taxpayer.

The tax savings are not huge: Your spouse will pay just £56 less tax on every £1,000 of dividend income you transfer to them.

Transferable Tax Allowance for Married Couples

Married couples can transfer 10% of their personal allowances to each other (£1,260 during the current 2021/22 tax year). Only basic-rate taxpayers can benefit, so the potential tax saving is £252 (£1,260 x 20%).

Married couples can generally only benefit if one person earns less than £12,570 (i.e. is wasting some of their personal allowance). However, company owners with small dividends have more scope to benefit from this tax break:

Example
David owns a small company. In 2021/22 he takes a salary of £9,568 and dividend of £25,000, i.e. he's a basic-rate taxpayer. His wife Michelle doesn't own any shares in the company. She's a teacher with a salary of £30,000, i.e. also a basic-rate taxpayer.

If David elects to transfer £1,260 of his personal allowance to Michelle, this will reduce her income tax bill by £252. David will pay 7.5% tax on an additional £1,260 of dividend income: £95. So the overall net saving for the couple is £157.

This strategy won't work if David takes a salary of £12,570 instead. Although Michelle will save tax, David will pay £252 income tax on his own salary.

It also won't work if David takes a salary of £9,568 and dividend of more than £39,442 in 2021/22 – reducing his personal allowance will push some of his dividend income into the higher-rate bracket – higher-rate taxpayers cannot transfer their personal allowances.

Why the Tax Savings May Not Last

There are many reasons why any tax savings that may be achieved in one tax year by splitting income with your spouse may not be achievable in full in future tax years, including:

- Changes to tax rates and thresholds
- Changes to personal circumstances

Changes to Tax Rates & Thresholds

The dividend allowance was cut from £5,000 to £2,000 on 6 April 2018. This has reduced the tax savings that can be achieved by shifting dividend income to a spouse who is in the same tax bracket as you, for example where you are both higher-rate taxpayers.

In the March 2021 Budget the Government announced that the higher-rate threshold will remain fixed at £50,270 until 5th April 2026. As a result more and more basic-rate taxpayers are likely to become higher-rate taxpayers.

This may make it less attractive for some higher-rate taxpayers to shift income to their spouses or partners who are currently basic-rate taxpayers. If their income simply increases with inflation, they will have less of their basic-rate bands left to enjoy dividends taxed at just 7.5%.

Changes to Personal Circumstances

Because every taxpayer can benefit from the £2,000 dividend allowance it is possible to save some tax by shifting income to your spouse, even if your spouse pays tax at a higher rate than you.

Beyond the dividend allowance, income tax savings can generally only be achieved if your spouse has a lower tax rate than you.

It is possible that, over time, your tax rate will fall or your spouse's tax rate will increase. This could eliminate or even reverse any initial income tax saving that is achieved.

Your tax rate could fall if the company's profits fall, resulting in lower dividends. Your spouse's tax rate could rise if their income from other sources increases (for example, if another business they own produces bigger profits).

There are lots of different permutations. The key point is that couples should look further ahead than just one tax year when deciding what proportion of the company each should own.

HMRC's Attacks on Income Shifting

Income splitting arrangements like those described in this chapter have come under attack in the past. In particular, the taxman has tried to prevent dividends being paid to non-working spouses or spouses who do just a small amount of work for the company.

In particular, the taxman's target has been small 'personal service' companies (IT consultants and the like) where most of the work is carried out by one person.

It all came to a head in the notorious 'Arctic Systems' tax case. HMRC tried to use the so-called settlements legislation to prevent Geoff Jones, a computer consultant, from splitting his dividend income with his wife.

The settlements legislation is designed to prevent income being shifted from one individual to another via a 'settlement', for example by transferring an asset or making some other 'arrangement'.

In the Arctic Systems case Mr Jones did most of the work in the company. Mrs Jones did a few hours admin each week. Because Mr Jones only paid himself a small salary despite all the work he did, more money was left to pay out as dividends to Mrs Jones. HMRC therefore decided that a settlement had taken place and tried to have Mrs Jones' dividend income taxed in her husband's hands.

HMRC originally won the case but the decision was overturned by the House of Lords.

The judges agreed with HMRC that a settlement had taken place **but** decided that the settlement provisions could not be applied because in this case the couple were protected by the exemption for gifts between spouses. This exemption applies where:

- There is an outright gift of property to a spouse, and
- The property is not wholly or mainly a right to income

On the first point, the judges ruled that, although Mrs Jones had subscribed for her share when the company was set up (i.e., it was not strictly speaking gifted to her by her husband), her share was essentially a gift because it contained an 'element of bounty': the share provided a benefit that Mr Jones would not have given to a complete stranger.

On the second point, the judges also ruled that a gift of *ordinary* shares is not wholly or mainly a right to income because ordinary shares have other rights: voting rights and the right to capital gains if the company is sold.

Thanks to the courage of Mr and Mrs Jones, who were prepared to fight HMRC all the way to the House of Lords, this exemption should safeguard most types of income splitting arrangements between married couples where ordinary shares are involved.

For this reason many tax advisers are of the opinion that married couples should make hay while the sun shines, i.e. they should split their dividend income with their spouses while they can.

Preference Shares

The outcome of the Arctic Systems case may have been different if another type of share other than ordinary shares had been involved.

In another tax case (*Young v Pearce*), wives were issued with preference shares that paid income but had very few other rights. The shares did not have voting rights and did not entitle the spouses to receive any payout in the event of the company being sold (other than the original £25 payment for the shares).

All that the preference shares provided was a right to receive 30% of the company's profits as a dividend. The court therefore decided that the preference shares provided wholly or mainly a right to income.

Thus the exemption for gifts between spouses was not available and the settlement rules applied. The wives' dividends were therefore taxed in the hands of their husbands.

Unmarried Couples & Other Family Members

Although HMRC was defeated in the Arctic Systems case, the judges did agree that a settlement had taken place. The taxpayers only won the case thanks to the exemption for gifts between *spouses*.

There is still uncertainty as to where this leaves income-splitting arrangements between other groups of individuals, in particular, *unmarried* couples.

HMRC probably does take the view that the settlements legislation applies to unmarried couples and other family members, especially where small personal service companies are involved.

However, to date the taxman has not pursued these individuals aggressively so, again, it may be a case of making hay while the sun shines.

To protect against any potential attack the best defence is probably to have both individuals equally involved in the business (a bit of admin or bookkeeping will not suffice, as Mr and Mrs Jones discovered.)

HMRC's main concern seems to be personal service companies (IT consultants and other businesses where the profits are generated from one person's services). Larger businesses that have other employees, premises, equipment etc may be safer because the profits come from various sources, not just one person's work.

Future Danger?

In 2007 draft income shifting legislation was published but fortunately never made it onto the statute books after being widely condemned for being completely unworkable.

That draft legislation essentially sought to prevent business owners from receiving dividends unless they effectively earned them! This would have undermined the whole basis of shareholder capitalism – dividends are supposed to be a reward for being an entrepreneur and setting up or investing in a business.

Although income shifting legislation is on the back burner for now, it could be introduced in the future and could upset some income splitting arrangements.

Dividend Waivers

Dividend waivers are used by company owners who wish to relinquish their rights to dividends. They can be commercially justifiable, for example if a shareholder waives his dividend to protect the company's cash.

To be effective it is necessary to draw up a formal deed which is executed before the dividend is declared or paid.

Company owners have also tried to use dividend waivers to avoid tax by diverting income to their spouses. For example, a higher-rate taxpayer may try to divert a disproportionate share of the company's profit to his spouse who is a basic-rate taxpayer.

HMRC may use the settlements legislation to attack arrangements where shareholders end up with excessive dividends, i.e. more of the company's distributable profit than their shareholding would normally entitle them to. Because dividend waivers involve simply a transfer of income, not assets, they are not protected by the exemption for outright gifts to spouses (see above).

Example
Mrs M owns 80 ordinary shares in M Limited and also has a significant amount of taxable income from other sources. Mr M owns 20 shares and has no other income. The company has retained profits of £50,000. Mrs M waives her right to a dividend and the company then declares a dividend of £2,000 per share. Mr M thus receives a dividend of £40,000, most of which he hopes will be taxed at no more than 7.5%.

HMRC could apply the settlements legislation in this situation. Clearly a dividend of £2,000 per share could not have been paid on all 100 shares, so the waiver enhanced Mr M's dividend.

This would therefore be seen as a "bounteous arrangement" – it is unlikely Mrs M would have agreed to do the same thing with a third party. £32,000 of the dividend paid to Mr M would therefore be taxed in Mrs M's hands.

Some of the things HMRC will look for when deciding whether to apply the settlements legislation to dividend waivers include:

- Insufficient retained profits to pay the same rate of dividend on all issued share capital.

- Even if there is sufficient profit to pay the same rate of dividend per share for the year in question, there has been a succession of waivers over several years and, in the absence of the waivers, the total dividends payable exceed the company's retained profits.

- Waiving shareholders wish to benefit non-waiving shareholders.

- Non-waiving shareholders pay tax at a lower rate.

In summary, company owners should be careful of entering into arrangements to waive dividends where there is no commercial reason for the waivers and no evidence that the waivers are for non-tax reasons.

Salaries for Spouses

If your spouse/partner also works for your company they can be paid a salary. Please note, you cannot pay them a salary if they do no work for the company. And you cannot pay them more than is justified for the duties they perform. If you do, the company will be denied tax relief for the expense.

If your spouse is a director then the accompanying legal responsibilities will also justify some remuneration being paid.

If your partner has no taxable income from other sources, a small salary will be more tax efficient than simply paying them dividends.

Why? Unlike dividends which are paid out of the company's after-tax profits, salaries are a tax deductible expense for the company. In other words, in addition to any *income tax* savings enjoyed by the couple, a salary will also save the company *corporation tax*.

For example, a small salary of £9,568 will currently save a company £1,737 in tax, taking into account the small amount or national insurance that is usually payable. The tax savings will be even greater after the increase in corporation tax (see Chapter 1).

To avoid national insurance, salary payments should be made monthly instead of as a lump sum. If, however, your spouse is a director the payment can be made as a lump sum because company directors pay national insurance on an annual basis.

Second Jobs

What if your spouse or partner already has income from other sources, e.g. a salary from another job? Is it still tax efficient to get your company to pay them a small salary?

Firstly, it's important to point out that if they work for another employer the employment contract may prevent them working for you as well.

If there is no such restriction, paying your spouse or partner a small salary could lead to an overall saving of several hundred pounds in some cases. Why? Because for basic-rate taxpayers the combined tax rate (corporation tax and income tax) for dividend income is currently roughly 25%, compared with 20% for salaries.

Thus paying your spouse a salary of, say, £8,840 could lead to an overall saving of around £442 (£8,840 x 5%), providing there is no national insurance payable.

The savings may be much smaller or non-existent in other cases, for example for some higher-rate taxpayers, so it may be necessary to do some calculations specific to your circumstances.

When corporation tax increases (see Chapter 1), paying your spouse or partner a salary may become more attractive because that salary may enjoy more corporation tax relief (26.5% or 25% compared with 19% at present).

Chapter 22

Splitting Income with Your Children

Dividends

It is possible to gift shares in your company to your children. Because they will have their own income tax personal allowance and dividend nil-rate band it may be possible for them to receive tax-free dividends of up to £14,570 each in 2021/22, plus an additional £35,700 taxed at just 7.5%.

However, it is important to point out that this type of tax planning generally only works when *adult* children are involved (i.e. children 18 or older).

Transfers of income to minor children are generally ineffective and the income would be taxed in the parent's hands.

This section therefore deals exclusively with adult children.

If you gift shares in the company to your adult children there will potentially be capital gains tax payable, as if you had sold the shares to them for their full market value. However, it may be possible for both the parent and child to jointly elect to hold over the capital gain.

To qualify for holdover relief the company must, generally speaking, be a trading company.

The safest route is probably to use ordinary shares, which means your children will obtain full ownership and voting rights in respect of their share of the business, not just a right to receive dividends.

There is a potential tax trap for family members who are gifted shares and are also employees of the company. In certain cases, where shares are obtained because of an individual's employment, a gift of shares can be subject to employment income tax charges.

However, there is an exemption where shares are given in the 'normal course of domestic, family or personal relationships'. So in most family companies, where shares are transferred to a spouse or adult children, the transfer should not give rise to any employment tax charges.

There is nevertheless a danger that, in certain circumstances, HMRC may argue that the individuals received shares by virtue of their employment, not because they are family members.

For example, if the individual only receives a small salary from the company (i.e. below market rate) HMRC may have more grounds to argue that the gift was made to increase the individual's remuneration from the company.

If shares are transferred to a family member who is an employee and to other employees who are not family members, this could indicate that the gift was made because of the family member's employment.

On the other hand, if shares are gifted to several family members (some of whom are not employees) this may indicate that the gift was made solely because of the family relationship.

It may be wise in such circumstances to document the reasons for the gift and (as always) obtain professional advice.

Salaries for Children

It's often worth getting your company to employ your children (including your minor children) at certain points in time. The salary payments will be a tax deductible expense for the business, providing the payments can be justified by the duties performed. (In one recent tax case a son's wages were disallowed because there were no time records or other evidence to justify the payments.)

The income will generally be tax free in the hands of the children, if they're at school or university and have no other taxable income.

A tax deduction coupled with a tax-free receipt is the best possible outcome when it comes to extracting money from your company!

Those aged under 16 can be paid up to £12,570 in 2021/22 with no income tax or national insurance consequences.

Children who are 16 and over have to pay 12% employee's national insurance on income over £9,568.

Employer's national insurance is payable on salaries over £8,840 (unless the company has spare employment allowance). However, there is no employer's national insurance on salaries paid to under 21s and apprentices under 25 provided they are not higher-rate taxpayers (i.e. they must earn less than £50,270). Note, the exemption is not lost if the employee earns more than £50,270. Employer's national insurance is only payable on the excess salary.

It is important to take note of the restrictions placed on the hours and types of work that children can do because this will affect how much you can pay them.

Restrictions on Work and Hours

Children are of compulsory school age up to the last Friday in June in the academic year of their 16th birthday. After this they are at the 'mandatory school leaving age' and can apply for a national insurance number and work full time.

Until that time there are restrictions on the hours and types of work that can be carried out. For starters, it is generally illegal to employ children under 13 in any capacity (unless they're involved in TV and modelling).

Other children must not work:

- Without an employment permit if local byelaws require it
- In factories or on industrial sites
- During school hours
- Before 7.00 am or after 7.00 pm
- For more than 1 hour before school (local byelaws permitting)
- For more than 4 hours without taking a 1 hour break
- In occupations prohibited by byelaws/legislation (e.g. pubs)
- If the work will harm their health, well-being or education
- Without having a 2 week break during the school holidays in each calendar year

More Restrictions on Hours Worked

During term time children can work for no more than 12 hours per week including a maximum of:

- 2 hours on school days and Sundays
- 5 hours on Saturdays for 13 to 14 year olds; 8 hours for 15 to 16 year olds

During school holidays 13 to 14 year olds may work a maximum of 25 hours per week. This includes a maximum of:

- 5 hours on weekdays and Saturdays
- 2 hours on Sunday

During school holidays 15 to 16 year olds may work a maximum of 35 hours per week. This includes a maximum of:

- 8 hours on weekdays and Saturdays
- 2 hours on Sunday

National Minimum Wage & Living Wage

If your children are below the compulsory school leaving age the national minimum wage does not apply. From 1st April 2021 the hourly rates for older children are as follows:

- £8.91   Living wage, 23 and over
- £8.36   21-22
- £6.56   18-20
- £4.62   16-17 if above school leaving age
- £4.30   apprentice rate

Part 6

Other Profit Extraction Strategies

Chapter 23

Loans to Directors

It used to be illegal for companies to make loans to directors. This is no longer the case. Since October 2007, loans of any size have been permitted.

With the exception of loans for under £10,000 they do generally have to be approved by the company's shareholders.

For most small companies this is obviously not a problem because the shareholders and directors are the same people!

You cannot take a loan from your company for an indefinite period without any tax consequences. If that was possible most company owners would never pay themselves taxable dividends.

The attractiveness of taking a loan from your company is limited by two potential tax charges:

- a 32.5% tax paid by the *company* (the section 455 charge)
- a benefit-in-kind charge paid by the *director*

The section 455 tax charge was increased from 25% to 32.5% for loans made on or after 6 April 2016.

Fortunately, it is possible to avoid or mitigate the damage caused by these taxes, if you understand the rules.

The Section 455 Charge

Most small family companies are "close companies". A close company is one controlled by five or fewer "participators". A close company is also one controlled by any number of participators who are also directors. Broadly, a participator is a shareholder.

If a close company lends money to a participator *the company* will have to pay a 32.5% tax charge on the loan. This is known as the section 455 charge. Failure to pay this charge will result in penalties and interest.

However, there are two reasons why this charge is not as bad as it first appears:

#1 Short-term Loans Escape the Section 455 Charge

The 32.5% tax does not apply if the loan is repaid within nine months of the company's financial year end. This is the normal due date for the company's corporation tax. This means that short-term loans to directors do not attract a company tax charge.

Example
Bill Ltd's financial year ends on 31st December 2021. The company made a £10,000 loan to Bill, the sole shareholder and director, in January 2021.

Bill repays the loan before the end of September 2022. The company will not have to pay the 32.5% tax charge because the loan was repaid within 9 months of the end of the accounting period in which it was made.

Example
The facts are the same as before except only £7,000 is repaid before the end of September 2022. The remaining £3,000 is repaid in October 2023. The company will pay a section 455 tax charge of £975 (£3,000 x 32.5%).

#2 The Section 455 Charge is Refundable

Even if the 32.5% tax does end up being paid because the loan is not repaid early enough, the tax will be refunded when the loan is repaid.

That's the good news. The bad news is the company will only be repaid 9 months after the end of the accounting period in which the loan is repaid.

In Bill Ltd's case this means the £975 tax will be repaid on 1st October 2024.

Exemption for Minority Shareholders

This exemption isn't much use to most small company owners. Nevertheless it is worth mentioning that there is no 32.5% company tax charge if you own 5% or less of the company's ordinary shares.

There are a number of qualifying criteria:

- Total loans to the individual cannot exceed £15,000
- The individual must work full time in the business

When it comes to the 5% limit you must include shares owned by you, your spouse and other 'associates' (e.g. close relatives).

Although there is no company tax charge on small loans to minority shareholders, there will still be a potential benefit-in-kind charge for the individual.

Benefit-in-kind Charge

If no interest is payable on the loan or if the interest paid is less than the 'official rate', the director will have to pay an income tax benefit-in-kind charge.

The official rate of interest is currently 2% (from 6th April 2021), so if the interest charged on the loan is less than 2%, a benefit-in-kind charge is payable.

For example, if the loan is for £20,000 and no interest is charged, the director will face the following benefit-in-kind charge if he is a higher-rate taxpayer:

£20,000 loan x 2% interest x 40% tax = £160

The company will also have to pay class 1A national insurance:

£20,000 loan x 2% interest x 13.8% = £55

The benefit in kind is reduced if interest is paid to the company. For example, if you pay 1.5% interest, the benefit in kind will be calculated using an interest rate of 0.5% (2% less 1.5%).

Note, however, that the benefit in kind is only reduced if there is a formal obligation to pay interest to the company. For this reason it is probably advisable to have a properly drawn up loan agreement.

If you do pay interest on the loan, the good news is that you will be paying the money to your own company rather than a bank. However, the company will pay corporation tax on the interest it receives.

It must also be remembered that money inside a company is generally less valuable than money outside a company. If you wish to withdraw the interest back out as a dividend, there is likely to be an income tax charge.

Should Directors Pay Interest?

Let's compare two scenarios:

- An interest-free loan
- Paying interest at the official rate

We will assume that the loan is for £20,000, the official interest rate is 2% and the director is a 40% taxpayer.

#1 Interest-free loan

The benefit-in-kind charge paid by the director will be:

$$£20,000 \times 2\% \times 40\% = £160$$

The national insurance paid by the company will be:

$$£20,000 \times 2\% \times 13.8\% = £55$$

The employer's national insurance is itself a tax deductible expense, so the net cost would currently be £45 (£55 less 19% corporation tax relief).

$$\text{Total cost of loan: } £160 + £45 = £205$$

#2 Interest at the official rate

On a £20,000 loan the director will pay £400 interest to the company (£20,000 x 2%). The company will then pay corporation tax on this interest, so the cost is £76:

£400 x 19% corporation tax = £76

Even if the after-tax interest is paid out as a dividend, producing an income tax charge of £105 for a higher-rate taxpayer (£324 x 32.5%), the total tax cost will be less than for an interest-free loan.

In summary, it is generally cheaper, at present, to pay interest at the official rate, rather than take an interest-free loan.

Paying interest at the official rate will become less attractive in the future if the company is affected by the corporation tax increase (see Chapter 1). It will be slightly more tax efficient to take an interest-free loan if the company has a marginal tax rate of 26.5%.

The Official Rate of Interest

Back in 2009 the official rate of interest was 6.25%. If interest rates are eventually increased, the official rate of interest will also be increased and this will affect the cost of directors' loans. At present there is no sign of interest rates increasing. In fact, the official rate was reduced from 2.25% to 2% on 6th April 2021.

The current and previous official rates can be found by typing "official rate of interest" into Google.

Exemptions from the Benefit in Kind Charge

There are two important exemptions from benefit in kind charges:

- Loans to invest in another company
- Loans for less than £10,000

Note that neither exemption makes any difference to the requirement to pay the section 455 company tax charge. Remember, however, that the company tax charge does not apply to short-term loans (up to 21 months) and is repayable.

Benefit-in-kind exemption #1
Loans to invest in another company

There is generally no benefit in kind charge on certain *qualifying* loans. A qualifying loan is one where the interest (if interest was charged) would be a tax deductible expense for the director.

An example of a qualifying loan would be one given to an individual so that he can acquire an interest in another close trading company.

The person borrowing the money must generally hold more than 5% of the ordinary shares in the company in which the money is being invested.

Whether this is the most tax-efficient way to finance a new business venture is, of course, another question altogether.

Remember that the section 455 company tax charge still applies, unless the loan is repaid within 9 months of the end of the accounting period in which it is made.

Benefit-in-kind exemption #2
Loans under £10,000

There is no benefit-in-kind charge if all of the loans to the director/shareholder total £10,000 or less throughout the tax year.

It is important to understand that any sum due from the director to the company is counted as a 'loan', including goods or services that have been provided to the director but not paid for.

The section 455 corporation tax charge still applies if the loan is not repaid on time. Nevertheless, this exemption currently allows a director/shareholder to take a loan of up to £10,000 for up to 21 months with no adverse tax consequences.

Larger Short-term Loans

In the above example, by taking a loan for no more than £10,000 and repaying it on time, both the 32.5% section 455 tax charge and the benefit-in-kind charge were avoided.

What if you want to borrow more than the tax-free limit for a short period – how does this compare with paying yourself additional taxable dividends?

Example

Penelope owns Pitstop Hotels Ltd which has a 31st December accounting date. Penelope normally withdraws a small salary and enough dividend income to use up her basic-rate band. It's the beginning of January 2022 and Penelope would like to withdraw some additional money from Pitstop Hotels, over and above her usual salary and dividend income. She needs £13,500 for some home improvements.

If she takes the money as a dividend she will need to withdraw £20,000. There will be an income tax charge of £6,500 payable by 31st January 2023, leaving her with the required £13,500.

Instead she decides to takes a loan of £13,500 from her company on 6th January 2022. Because the loan is for more than £10,000 she will be subject to a benefit-in-kind charge, unless she pays interest to her company at the official rate.

The loan will also be subject to the 32.5% section 455 tax charge unless it is repaid by the end of September 2023 (9 months after the end of the company's accounting period on 31st December 2022).

She decides to pay interest to her company at the official rate and repays the loan on 5th September 2023, after 20 months. Assuming the official rate is 2%, the total interest payable to Pitstop Hotels is £449 and the corporation tax payable on the interest is £96, calculated as follows:

6th January 2022 to 31st December 2022:
£13,500 x 2% x 360/365 = £266 x 19% = £51

1st January 2023 to 5th September 2023:
£13,500 x 2% x 248/365 = £183 x 24.65%* = £45 (*See Appendix A)

To repay the £13,500 loan Penelope withdraws additional dividend income, over and above what she normally takes, of £20,000 on 6th April 2023. The income tax on this additional dividend is £6,500, payable by 31st January 2025.

By taking a loan in 2022 instead of a taxable dividend, Penelope has managed to defer paying income tax of £6,500 for two years. The total cost is just £96.

Additional points to note:

- If Penelope thinks her marginal income tax rate in 2023/24 may be higher than in 2021/22 then she may be better off paying herself a dividend in January 2022 instead of taking a loan. In particular she may have to watch out for the £100,000 and £150,000 thresholds.

- If Penelope can repay the loan out of her regular dividend income taxed at just 7.5% (i.e. without having to withdraw an additional dividend taxed at 32.5%) she may be able to *save* £6,500 in income tax, not just defer paying it.

Loans to Directors – Other Issues

Loans to Family

You cannot necessarily avoid the section 455 tax charge and benefit-in-kind charge by making loans to family members.

For example, both the section 455 charge and the benefit-in-kind charge apply to loans to spouses and children of the director/shareholder and other close relatives. The section 455 charge also applies to loans to business partners.

The charges do not apply to loans to friends and some more distant relatives BUT you will incur the taxman's wrath if the benefit of the loan passes back to you or a close relative.

Loan Written Off

If the loan is formally released or written off by the company, the amount is likely to be treated as a deemed dividend for income tax purposes.

In most instances the amount released will also be subject to national insurance payable by both the employee and employer.

Because of this national insurance cost you may wish to consider declaring a dividend to settle the debt, providing the company has sufficient distributable reserves. One drawback of this is a dividend would have to be paid to all shareholders pro rata.

A loan written off in these circumstances will not be deductible for corporation tax purposes.

Any section 455 tax charge paid is, however, refunded to the company if the loan is released or written off.

The safest course of action may be to ensure that any loan is always repaid, wherever possible, rather than written off.

Paperwork

Although it's simple in small companies to obtain shareholder approval for loans, it's important to get the paperwork right.

There should be a proper loan agreement with written documentation outlining the nature of the loan, the company's liability and the amount and purpose of the loan.

The shareholders should then grant their approval at a meeting or by written resolution, again with all the appropriate documentation.

Shareholder approval is not required for loans of up to £10,000, although it is good practice to continue to produce the same paperwork, where possible, as this may provide more certainty as to the tax treatment of the borrowed money.

Financial Reporting Standard 102 (FRS 102)

A new financial reporting standard (FRS 102) may affect the accounting treatment of directors' loans in certain circumstances.

Where interest is not charged at a market rate the loan may have to be discounted in the company's accounts. For example, if the market interest rate is 5% and an interest-free loan of £100,000 is made to a director and is repayable after three years, the present value of the loan is £86,384:

$$£100,000/(1.05 \times 1.05 \times 1.05) = £86,384$$

The initial shortfall of £13,616 would be treated as a 'distribution'.

The tax treatment does not, however, follow the accounting treatment. The section 455 charge is still based on the total amount of the loan and the director's taxable benefit will be calculated in the way described earlier in this chapter.

To avoid the complexities of FRS 102, tax commentators suggest that it should be specifically recorded that directors' loan accounts are repayable on demand or to make sure that a market rate of interest is charged.

Loan Recycling

HMRC didn't like it when loans to directors were repaid before the section 455 charge was payable, with new loans taken out straight away (known as 'bed and breakfasting'). Thus a number of changes came into operation on 20th March 2013:

The 30 Day Rule

Relief from the section 455 tax is denied if:

- A shareholder makes repayments totalling £5,000 or more to the company and within 30 days...

- new loans totalling £5,000 or more are made to the same person or their associates

For this rule to apply, the original loan and repayment can take place in the same or different accounting periods. The new loan must be in a subsequent accounting period to the original loan.

It's important to point out that the 30-day rule does not apply where the loan is repaid using amounts that give rise to an income tax charge, for example where a taxable dividend is declared and credited to the director's loan account.

Example 1
During accounting period 1 there is a loan outstanding of £6,000. Two days before the end of the accounting period £6,000 is repaid. Three days into accounting period 2 a new £6,000 loan is taken. The repayment will be matched with the new loan, not the old loan. The loan from accounting period 1 is treated as still outstanding and will be subject to the section 455 tax charge if not repaid.

Example 2

C Ltd is a close company in which Jim is a shareholder. C Ltd's accounting period ends on 31st March 2022. On 25th March 2022, Jim borrows £15,000 from C Ltd. If the loan is not repaid within nine months of the end of the accounting period, C Ltd must pay a 32.5% section 455 tax charge (£4,875).

On 1st December 2022, a dividend of £9,000 is declared by C Ltd which is chargeable to income tax. On the same day, Jim repays the remaining £6,000. On 10th December 2022, Jim borrows £3,500 from the company. On 15th December 2022, Jim borrows a further £2,000.

The section 455 tax charge is calculated as follows:

- £9,000 was repaid by applying a chargeable dividend towards the loan. This is ignored when it comes to applying the 30 day rule. The remaining £6,000 that Jim repays exceeds the £5,000 minimum repayment under the 30-day rule.

- Nine days later and 14 days later respectively (i.e. within 30 days) Jim withdraws a further £5,500 (£3,500 + £2,000) which is also in excess of the £5,000 limit for new loans.

- The new loans (£5,500) are less than the repayments (£6,000). Relief from the section 455 tax charge is denied on the lesser amount of £5,500, resulting in a tax charge of £1,788. Only the real repayment of £500 is recognised.

The Arrangements Rule

This rule applies even if the new borrowing takes place after 30 days. Relief from the section 455 tax will be denied if:

- Prior to repaying the loan, the total amount owed by the shareholder to the company is £15,000 or more, and

- At the time of the repayment, arrangements had been made for new loans of £5,000 or more to replace the amounts repaid.

The relief denied is the lower of the amount repaid and the new loan.

'Arrangements' are not defined and HMRC will give the term a wide meaning.

Once again, the arrangements rule does not apply if the loan is repaid with a taxable dividend or bonus. In other words, if a loan account is credited with a taxable dividend this will be treated as a valid loan repayment.

Example
Brigitte owes her company Bard Ltd £25,000 which she borrowed on 1st June 2021 during the accounting period ending 30 June 2021.

After the end of the accounting period, Brigitte takes a 45-day loan from the bank for £25,000 and uses it to repay the loan to her company. 40 days after repaying her company, Brigitte takes a new loan of £30,000 from her company and uses it to repay the bank.

There is a significant risk that HMRC will argue that, at the time she repaid her company, Brigitte had made arrangements to withdraw a new amount from her company (to repay the bank), so the original loan will be treated as not repaid. Thus the section 455 tax will become payable on the initial £25,000 loan, unless a further repayment is made.

What is a Valid Income Tax Charge?

As mentioned above, the anti-avoidance rules do not apply if the amount repaid gives rise to an income tax charge in the hands of the director-shareholder.

This will be the case if a loan is repaid by means of a dividend credited to the director's loan account which is included as income on the director's tax return (or where a bonus is paid subject to PAYE before being credited to the director's loan account).

According to HMRC, if a dividend is first paid out in cash and the money is then paid back into the company and credited to the director's loan account, the exemption does not apply.

HMRC also contends that, if the director owns the business premises and the company pays him rent, the exemption does not apply to rent credited to the director's loan account.

Chapter 24

Rental Income: Better than Dividends

Should you get your company to pay you rent?

Many company owners own their business premises *personally* and the company pays them rent.

Paying yourself rent is often more tax efficient than paying yourself a higher salary. Like salaries, rental payments are a tax deductible expense (providing the rent does not exceed the market rent). But, unlike salaries, there is no national insurance cost.

Following the 2016 increase in dividend tax rates, rental income is also more tax efficient than dividend income and will, in many cases, become even more attractive when corporation tax increases (see Chapter 1).

Of course, there are also non-tax reasons why you may wish to pay yourself rental income instead of withdrawing dividends from your company. For starters, to pay dividends the company must have sufficient distributable profits. There is no such requirement when it comes to paying rent.

Secondly, with rental income it is relatively straightforward to pay yourself a fixed monthly amount throughout the year, for example by setting up a direct debit from your company bank account to your personal bank account. This could be helpful if you have to personally pay various costs associated with the property, especially mortgage interest.

With rental income there is no requirement to continually do all the paperwork that often accompanies dividends, for example holding directors' board meetings and shareholder meetings.

How much better off could you be by paying yourself rental income instead of dividends? It all depends on your personal circumstances, for example how much taxable income you have and the amount of tax deductible mortgage interest you have.

Example – Basic-rate Taxpayer

Warren is a company owner and a basic-rate taxpayer. He personally owns the property out of which the company operates but the company currently doesn't pay him any rent. He does not have any tax deductible mortgage interest to offset.

During the current 2021/22 tax year he decides to pay himself a small salary of £8,840 (see Chapter 19). He also has other taxable income which uses up the balance of his £12,570 income tax personal allowance. He withdraws the rest of the company's profits as dividends.

Let's say he gets the company to pay him rental income of £10,000 per year. After paying income tax at 20% he will be left with £8,000.

If the company had not paid him rent it would have had an extra £8,100 to pay dividends (£10,000 less 19% corporation tax). Warren would have been left with £7,493 after paying 7.5% income tax.

By getting the company to pay him rent Warren is better off by just over £500. This is because, for basic-rate taxpayers, the combined tax rate on dividends is roughly 25% at present, compared with 20% for rental income.

Example 1 – Higher-rate Taxpayer

The facts are exactly the same except the company has bigger profits and so Warren has more dividend income and is a higher-rate taxpayer. If he gets the company to pay him rental income of £10,000, after paying income tax at 20% he will be left with £8,000.

However, his rental income will use up £10,000 of his basic-rate band which means £10,000 of his dividend income will be taxed at 32.5% instead of 7.5%, resulting in additional tax of £2,500. Overall Warren will be left with £5,500 (£8,000 - £2,500).

If the company had not paid him any rental income, it would have been left with an extra £8,100 to pay out as dividends and Warren would have been left with £5,467 after paying income tax at 32.5%.

Rental income is still more tax efficient than dividend income but in this example the saving is very small – just £33 on £10,000 of rental income!

In some other cases higher-rate taxpayers will save more tax by paying themselves rental income:

Example 2 – Higher-rate Taxpayer

This time we'll assume that Warren's premises are more substantial and he gets the company to pay him rental income of £37,700. Along with his salary and other non-dividend income this will take him up to the £50,270 higher-rate threshold. After paying 20% tax on his rental income he will be left with £30,160.

His rental income will use up his entire £37,700 basic-rate band, which means £37,700 of his dividend income will be taxed at 32.5% instead of 7.5%, resulting in additional tax of £9,425. However, because all of his dividend income is now subject to higher-rate tax, this time his £2,000 dividend nil rate band will save him 32.5% tax instead of 7.5% tax, a saving of £500.

Overall Warren will be left with £21,235 (£30,160 - £9,425 + £500).

If the company had not paid him £37,700 rental income, it would have been left with an extra £30,537 to pay out as dividends and Warren would have been left with £20,612 after paying income tax at 32.5%.

Warren is £623 better off by paying himself rental income.

After the Corporation Tax Increase

After the corporation tax increase (see Chapter 1) the tax savings enjoyed from rental income will be even greater in many cases. Whereas rental income will enjoy corporation tax relief, dividends will be paid out of profits that have been taxed at 25% or 26.5%, compared with 19% at present.

If we assume that Warren's company in the above example has a marginal tax rate of 26.5% after the corporation tax increase, he will end up £2,531 better off paying himself rental income. He will also save a little bit more tax by paying himself a salary of £9,568 instead of £8,840.

Mortgage Interest

Many company owners who personally own their business premises will also have a mortgage on which they personally pay the interest. These interest payments can be offset against your rental income, effectively making some or all of it 'tax free'.

Note that, although tax relief on mortgage interest for residential property has been reduced (see Chapter 20), mortgages used to buy commercial properties are unaffected.

Most company owners will instinctively realise that it would be foolish not to receive rental income if they also have mortgage interest to set off (or other tax-deductible property expenses). Tax-free rental income has to be better than a taxable dividend!

Example 3 – Higher-rate Taxpayer

Warren has a salary and other income of £12,570, is a higher-rate taxpayer and has tax deductible mortgage interest of £5,000. If he gets the company to pay him rental income of £10,000, he'll have a taxable rental profit of £5,000. After paying income tax at 20% he will be left with £4,000 (£10,000 - £5,000 interest - £1,000 tax).

His taxable rental income will use up £5,000 of his basic-rate band which means £5,000 of his dividend income will be taxed at 32.5% instead of 7.5%, resulting in additional tax of £1,250. Overall Warren will be left with £2,750 (£4,000 - £1,250).

If the company had not paid him any rental income, it would have been left with an extra £8,100 to pay out as dividends (after paying 19% corporation tax) and Warren would have been left with £5,467, after paying income tax at 32.5%. After paying his interest costs Warren would be left with just £467.

Overall, Warren is £2,283 better off paying himself rental income.

After the Corporation Tax Increase

Once again, after the corporation tax increase Warren will be even better off paying himself rental income. If we assume his company has a marginal tax rate of 26.5%, he will end up £2,789 better off paying himself rental income instead of a dividend which is paid out of profits taxed at 26.5%.

Summary

The above examples illustrate that it is often more tax efficient to get your company to pay you rent instead of dividend income.

Rental income is most tax efficient to the extent that you have tax deductible costs to offset, such as mortgage interest.

The savings vary considerably from case to case so it is essential to do your own number crunching.

The potential tax savings will be even higher after the increase in corporation tax.

Business Asset Disposal Relief (BADR)

Although you may be able to save income tax by paying yourself as much rental income as possible, there is one reason why you may prefer to get your company to pay you a below-market rent.

If you sell your business, you may be able to claim Business Asset Disposal Relief (previously called Entrepreneurs Relief), which means you may be able to pay capital gains tax at just 10%.

Trading premises can also qualify for Business Asset Disposal Relief, even if you own them personally. But you cannot claim the relief if your company has paid you a full market rent (although rent paid for periods before 6th April 2008 is ignored). If your company pays you a rent that is lower than the market rent, or if you owned the property before 6th April 2008, then a partial claim for Business Asset Disposal Relief can usually be made.

If Business Asset Disposal Relief is not available when you dispose of your premises you will be subject to capital gains tax at the normal rates for commercial property. Higher-rate taxpayers pay 20% capital gains tax and 10% tax is payable to the extent that your basic-rate band is not used up by your income.

So it's possible that, even without Business Asset Disposal Relief, company owners will be able to benefit from a 10% tax rate on at least some of their capital gains by making sure they don't have much taxable income in the year they sell their trading premises.

Chapter 25

Pay Yourself Tax-free Interest Income

If your company owes you money you can make it pay you interest. In some cases the interest will be both a tax deductible expense for the company and tax free in your hands – the best case scenario when it comes to extracting money from your company.

In this situation extracting interest income may be more tax efficient than other types of income, including dividends.

How can interest income be tax free? For starters, interest is not subject to national insurance. As for income tax, there is a 0% "starting rate band" for up to £5,000 of savings income.

There's also a savings allowance which shelters up to £1,000 of interest income from tax if you're a basic-rate taxpayer and £500 if you're a higher-rate taxpayer (additional-rate taxpayers do not benefit from the savings allowance).

In Chapter 20 we were looking at company owners with income from *other sources*, including interest from investments. In this chapter we're looking at a different type of interest income: interest that comes out of your own company.

The £5,000 Starting Rate Band

Not everyone can benefit from the 0% starting rate. It's designed to benefit those with very low income. Hence the £5,000 starting rate band is reduced if you have any *taxable non-savings income*.

Non-savings income includes income from employment, self-employment, pensions and rental properties. Crucially, it does not include dividend income.

For example, if you have a salary of £12,570 this year and no other income apart from dividends, you won't have any taxable non-savings income and can receive £5,000 of tax-free interest.

You may also be able to receive up to £1,000 of additional tax-free interest thanks to the savings allowance.

But if you have a salary of £12,570 and rental income of more than £5,000, your rental income will eat up all of your starting rate band, so none of your interest income will be tax-free under the 0% starting rate.

You may, however, be able to receive up to £1,000 of tax-free interest thanks to the savings allowance.

The £5,000 starting rate band is not given in addition to the basic-rate band – it is part of the basic-rate band. In other words, if you have £5,000 of interest income your basic-rate band will be reduced by £5,000.

This means some of your dividend income may be pushed into the higher-rate tax bracket.

This may reduce the attractiveness of extracting interest income from your company but may not eliminate the benefit altogether.

The Savings Allowance

The savings allowance (also known as the savings nil rate band) operates separately from, and in addition to, the starting rate band. This means some company owners will be able to pay themselves up to £6,000 of tax-free interest every year.

The savings allowance is especially useful to company owners who cannot use the starting rate band because they have too much non-savings income, e.g. rental income.

They can typically extract £1,000 (basic-rate taxpayers) or £500 (higher-rate taxpayers) of tax-free interest from their companies.

Lending to Your Company

There are lots of circumstances in which company owners may lend money to their companies. For example, it may be a new company that needs some cash to get started or a well-established company that needs money to buy a major asset.

In some cases company owners lend money to their companies indirectly, for example when a dividend is declared but the cash is not withdrawn immediately, perhaps because the company owner wants to reinvest it to help the business grow.

The Mechanics of Extracting Interest Income

There is no requirement for a director to charge interest on a loan account with their own company but if they do it must not exceed a reasonable commercial rate.

If the company pays more than a commercial rate the excess payment could be treated as salary income and subject to income tax and national insurance.

Interest paid to a director on their loan account will usually be an allowable expense for the company, providing the money is used for business purposes. The interest will therefore provide corporation tax relief.

Although your interest income may ultimately be tax free, the company will have to deduct 20% income tax and pay this to HMRC quarterly, using form CT61 which can be requested online.

If this results in a tax overpayment, the director can reclaim the excess through his self-assessment tax return.

Nevertheless, the additional reporting duties and payments may put some company owners off paying themselves any interest.

The company should also issue you an annual interest certificate.

How Much Tax Can You Save?

This will depend on *how much* and what *type* of income you earn.

Example 1
Basic-Rate Taxpayer, No Taxable Non-Savings Income

Gillian is a company director with salary and other non-savings income (e.g. rental income) of £12,570. She has £15,000 of dividend income. She charges her company £5,000 interest for a substantial loan she made to help it buy new equipment. Interest is charged at a commercial rate.

The interest will be a tax deductible business expense, saving the company £950 in corporation tax (£5,000 x 19%). Gillian has no taxable non-savings income so all of her interest income will be tax free, being covered by the £5,000 starting rate band (although the company will initially have to withhold 20% tax and pay this to HMRC).

If instead Gillian decided to NOT pay herself interest, the company would have an extra £5,000 of taxable profit. After paying £950 corporation tax there would be an extra £4,050 that could be paid out as dividends taxed at 7.5%, leaving Gillian with £3,746.

The potential tax saving is £1,254.

Example 2
Higher-Rate Taxpayer, No Taxable Non-Savings Income

As before Gillian has £12,570 of salary and other non-savings income and £5,000 of interest from her company. However, this time she has dividend income of £50,000 which means she pays 32.5% tax.

Gillian can enjoy £5,000 of tax-free interest income but because the starting rate band is part of the basic-rate band an additional £5,000 of her dividends will be taxed at 32.5% instead of 7.5%, resulting in additional tax of £1,250. So effectively Gillian receives £3,750 after tax.

If she did not pay herself interest, the company would have an extra £5,000 profit. After paying £950 corporation tax there would be an extra £4,050 to pay out as dividends, leaving her with £2,734 after tax.

For a higher-rate taxpayer with no taxable non-savings income the potential saving is £1,016 (£3,750 - £2,734).

Example 3
Basic-Rate Taxpayer, No Starting Rate Band Available

This time Gillian has £17,570 of salary and rental income, £5,000 of interest income and £15,000 of dividend income.

Because she has £5,000 of taxable non-savings income (£17,570 - £12,570 personal allowance) she will have no starting rate band available. However, thanks to the new savings allowance, £1,000 of her interest income will be tax free and the rest will be taxed at 20%, leaving her with £4,200.

If Gillian did not pay herself interest, the company would have an extra £5,000 of taxable profit. After paying £950 corporation tax there would be an extra £4,050 that could be paid out as dividends taxed at 7.5%, leaving her with £3,746.

So in this case Gillian is £454 better off paying herself interest. Not only is £1,000 of her interest income tax free, the remaining £4,000 is taxed at just 20% (remember the total combined tax rate on dividend income is currently 25% if you are a basic-rate taxpayer).

Example 4
Higher-Rate Taxpayer, No Starting Rate Band Available

This time Gillian has £17,570 of salary and rental income, £5,000 of interest income and £50,000 of dividend income.

Once again she will have no starting rate band available. However, thanks to the new savings allowance, £500 of her interest income will be tax free and the rest will be taxed at 20%, leaving her with £4,100.

An additional £5,000 of her dividend income will be taxed at 32.5% instead of 7.5%, resulting in an additional income tax charge of £1,250. So effectively Gillian ends up with £2,850 after tax.

If instead she had decided to not pay herself interest, the company would have an extra £5,000 of taxable profit. After paying £950 corporation tax there would be an extra £4,050 that could be paid out as dividends, leaving her with £2,734 after tax.

So in this case Gillian is just £116 better off paying herself interest.

Making the Most of Your Personal Allowance

If you pay yourself a salary of £9,568 and do not have any rental income or other non-savings income, you will have spare personal allowance of £3,002 (£12,570 - £9,568) to set off against your interest or dividends.

In Chapter 20 we saw how you can save tax by allocating your spare personal allowance to your dividend income rather than your interest income (if your interest is tax free anyway).

In that chapter we were focusing on interest income from investments but the same principle applies when you extract interest income from your own company.

Example 5
Higher-Rate Taxpayer, Spare Personal Allowance

Roisin's company pays her a salary of £9,568 and she extracts the remaining profits as dividends totalling £50,000. She has no other income and therefore has spare personal allowance of £3,002 to use against her dividends. She ends up with after-tax income of £53,869.

Let's now assume Roisin receives £5,000 of interest from her company (which also reduces the amount of profit that can be distributed as dividends).

*If her spare personal allowance of £3,002 is set against her **interest income** she will end up with after-tax income of £54,660 – £791 more than before.*

*But if her spare personal allowance is set against her **dividend income** she will end up with £54,885 – an additional £225.*

Overall Roisin ends up £1,016 better off by extracting £5,000 of interest from her company but the maximum saving is only achieved if she allocates her personal allowance correctly.

After the Corporation Tax Increase

Getting your company to pay you interest income instead of dividend income will become even more attractive after the increase in corporation tax.

Whereas an interest payment will enjoy full corporation tax relief, dividends will be paid out of profits that may have already suffered corporation tax of 25% or 26.5%, compared with 19% at present.

For example, for Gillian in Example 2 the potential saving will rise from £1,016 to £1,269.

Tax-free Loan Repayments

Apart from the beneficial tax treatment of interest income, it's worth pointing out that some or all of the outstanding balance on a director's loan account can be paid out tax free at any time.

Having such an amount 'banked' inside your company that can be withdrawn tax free at any time could prove useful, for example if the director unexpectedly requires additional money that would be taxed heavily as a salary or dividend.

Summary

Some company owners may be able to save over £1,000 by getting their companies to pay them interest.

The potential tax saving is a lot smaller if there is no starting rate band available, for example if the taxpayer has a significant amount of salary income or rental income.

For many taxpayers the additional tax paperwork will nullify the tax savings.

Finally, it's important to point out that relatively few small company owners will be able to pay themselves as much as £5,000 of interest income because the interest you charge your company must be at a commercial rate.

Chapter 26

Charitable Donations: You or the Company?

Who should donate to charity: you or your company?

In this chapter we'll focus on the tax benefits and drawbacks of both types of donation, although *non-tax* factors may be more important.

For example, charitable donations by your company could enhance its reputation and good standing in the community which in turn could help its business.

Donations by Your Company

Charitable donations are a tax deductible expense for corporation tax purposes. So if your company donates £100 its taxable profits will be reduced by £100, currently saving it £19 corporation tax.

The company can also enjoy tax relief when it gives money to community amateur sports clubs, a list of which can be obtained by entering "community amateur sports clubs registered with HMRC" into a search engine like Google.

No gift aid declaration is necessary for company donations (see below for more on gift aid declarations).

Nevertheless you should still obtain documentation from the charity to support the donation, just as you would for any other business expense.

Charitable donations cannot create or increase a trading loss. If the donation exceeds the company's taxable profit, the excess will not enjoy any corporation tax relief and cannot be carried forward to the next year.

Donations do not enjoy corporation tax relief if there are strings attached, for example a condition that the charity will buy goods from the company (or anyone connected with the company).

Companies don't have to donate money, they can also donate:

- Equipment
- Stock (the goods they sell)
- Employees' time

If a company donates equipment (e.g. furniture and computers) on which capital allowances have been claimed the disposal value used in the capital allowances calculation is zero. Normally when a business gives away an asset on which capital allowances have been claimed the disposal value is the market value of the asset.

If a company donates its trading stock it can claim the cost of the goods as an expense for corporation tax purposes.

If the company is VAT registered it will need to account for VAT on the items given to charity. However, you can apply VAT at the zero rate if the charity will sell, hire out or export the item donated. This means you can still reclaim the VAT on the cost of the stock donated.

If a company lends an employee to a charity the employee's salary can still be claimed as a business cost for corporation tax purposes.

Grassroots Sports

A new corporation tax deduction was introduced from April 2017 for contributions to grassroots sports, even where the beneficiary is not a registered charity.

The rules allow companies to deduct all contributions to grassroots sports through recognised sport governing bodies, and deductions of up to £2,500 annually for contributions made directly to grassroots sports, without the involvement of a qualifying sports body.

Donations by You Personally

If you make a charitable donation of, say, £80 the charity can claim £20 gift aid.

Essentially what the charity is doing is reclaiming from HMRC the 20% basic-rate tax you will typically have paid on £80 of after-tax income.

The charity will require you to make a gift aid declaration. This entails stating that you have paid sufficient tax to cover the basic-rate tax the charity reclaims.

It is important that you are actually liable for the tax the charity reclaims. The tax can be either income tax or capital gains tax.

For example, a company owner with a salary of £9,568 and dividend of £30,000 will face an income tax bill of £1,875 in 2021/22.

If that company owner makes an £8,000 charitable donation, the gift aid rules require that the donor has paid tax of £2,000. The company owner will therefore have to make up the shortfall of £125.

Higher-rate Taxpayers

Higher-rate taxpayers who make charitable donations can claim higher-rate tax relief when they submit their tax returns.

Example
Melinda, a company owner who takes most of her income as dividends, donates £80 to a charity. The gift aid on the donation is £20, resulting in a gross donation of £100.

Melinda's basic-rate band is extended by £100 which means she will pay 7.5% tax instead of 32.5% tax on £100 of her dividend income. This will save her £25 income tax.

In summary, Melinda has effectively made a £100 donation with a net cost to her of £55. The basic-rate tax relief goes to the charity, the higher-rate tax relief goes to the person making the donation.

Protecting Child Benefit & Personal Allowance

Your family's child benefit is gradually taken away when the highest earner in the household has adjusted net income of more than £50,000. All the child benefit will be withdrawn when that person's income exceeds £60,000.

Your personal allowance is also gradually taken away when your adjusted net income exceeds £100,000. All of your personal allowance is withdrawn when your income exceeds £125,140 in 2021/22.

Like pension contributions, gift aid donations reduce your adjusted net income and can therefore be used to increase your personal allowance or protect your family's child benefit payments, in addition to enjoying higher-rate tax relief.

Example
Hassan is a company owner with salary and dividend income of £110,000. He donates £4,000 to his favourite charity and the gift aid on the donation is £1,000, resulting in a gross donation of £5,000. As a result his adjusted net income is reduced by £5,000 from £110,000 to £105,000. This in turn increases his personal allowance by £2,500.

Carrying Back Donations to the Previous Tax Year

You can claim tax relief on donations a year early if you like. For example, you can claim tax relief for donations you have made during the current 2021/22 tax year when you submit your tax return for 2020/21.

Understandably, you can only claim tax relief for donations made between 6th April 2021 and the date you file your 2020/21 tax return.

This option to carry back donations is attractive if you want the tax relief sooner or if you were a higher-rate taxpayer during the previous tax year but you are not certain whether you will be a higher-rate taxpayer this year.

When you come to submit your 2020/21 tax return you will know for certain your taxable income for that year and thus how much tax relief you will obtain.

Similarly, carrying back donations may be attractive if your income in the previous 2020/21 tax year was in the £50,000-£60,000 bracket (child benefit withdrawal) or the £100,000-£125,000 bracket (personal allowance withdrawal).

In these cases you may enjoy extra tax relief on your charitable donations if you do not expect your income to fall into those tax brackets this year.

Company versus Personal Donations

In this section we will compare the tax relief enjoyed by companies on their charitable donations with the tax relief enjoyed by individuals.

Example – Basic-rate taxpayer

Beric's company has £1,000 in its bank account which he would like to give to charity. If the company makes the donation it will enjoy corporation tax relief so the whole £1,000 can be paid directly to the charity with no further tax consequences.

If instead Beric decides to make the donation personally, the company will currently pay 19% corporation tax, leaving £810 to pay out as additional dividend income.

Let's say Beric holds onto £10 and gives £800 to the charity. The taxman will add £200 of gift aid, leaving the charity with the same amount – £1,000.

But that's not the end of the matter: Beric will still have to pay 7.5% tax on his £810 dividend – roughly £60. Beric is worse of by about £50 (£60 less the £10 of dividend income he held onto).

Thus, if you're a basic-rate taxpayer, for every £1,000 that ends up with the charity you will have to pay an additional 5% in tax.

In this case a company donation is clearly more tax efficient than a donation made personally by the company owner.

Example – Higher-rate taxpayer

This time we'll assume Beric is a higher-rate taxpayer. If the company makes the donation it can pay £1,000 directly to the charity. Alternatively Beric can pay himself additional dividend income of £810, hold onto £10 and give £800 to the charity. The taxman will add £200 of gift aid, resulting in the same donation of £1,000.

Again, that's not the end of the matter. Beric still has to pay income tax on the additional dividend.

With a gross donation of £1,000, Beric's basic-rate band will be increased by £1,000. This means the £810 dividend will be taxed at just 7.5%, not 32.5%, so the tax will be roughly £61.

Furthermore, an additional £190 of his other dividend income will also be taxed at 7.5% instead of 32.5%, saving him an extra £48.

All in all a £1,000 donation made by the company owner is only £3 more expensive than a donation made by the company:

£61 income tax - £48 higher-rate relief - £10 saved dividend = £3

In this case a company donation is again more tax efficient than a contribution made personally by the director but the difference is tiny.

Because the saving is so small it will probably be other factors that determine whether the company or the individual makes the donation.

After the Corporation Tax Increase

Company donations will enjoy tax relief at up to 26.5% (compared with 19% at present) and will therefore, in many cases, become significantly more attractive than donations made personally out of dividend income.

Example – Higher-rate taxpayer

Beric's company has a marginal tax rate of 26.5% and has £1,000 in its bank account which he would like to give to charity. If the company makes the donation it will enjoy corporation tax relief so the whole

£1,000 can be paid directly to the charity with no further tax consequences.

Alternatively Beric can pay himself a £735 dividend (£1,000 profit less £265 corporation tax). Let's say he holds onto £15 and makes a donation of £720. The taxman will add £180 of gift aid, leaving the charity with £900.

With a gross donation of £900, Beric's basic-rate band will be increased by £900. This means the £735 dividend will be taxed at just 7.5%, not 32.5%, so the tax will be £55.

Furthermore, an additional £165 of his other dividend income will also be taxed at 7.5% instead of 32.5%, saving him an additional £41.

His additional tax relief plus the £15 of dividend income he held onto are almost exactly equal to the tax he has to pay on the dividend:

£41 tax relief + £15 saved dividend - £55 income tax = £1

All in all, the charity will receive 10% less money if Beric makes the donation personally.

Should the Company Postpone Making Donations?

Some company owners may be wondering whether it's worth postponing or reducing charitable donations until corporation tax increases, so that more tax relief can be enjoyed.

A company which will have a marginal tax rate of 26.5% will be able to enjoy up to £75 of additional tax relief for every £1,000 of charitable donations it postpones. A company which will have a marginal tax rate of 25% will enjoy £60 of additional tax relief.

The company may have to wait quite some time to enjoy the maximum tax relief. For a company with a January to December tax year, only donations made from January 2024 onwards will enjoy up to 26.5% tax relief, although donations made between January and December 2023 will enjoy up to 24.65% tax relief (see Appendix A). Some company owners may be willing to postpone making donations for this amount of time; others may feel that their favoured charities require help sooner.

Chapter 27

Pension Contributions: Better than Dividends

Following the increase in dividend tax rates in 2016, some company owners have probably been paying themselves smaller dividends and getting their companies to make pension contributions instead.

When corporation tax increases many companies will enjoy more tax relief on any pension contributions they make for their directors and employees. Thus some company owners may find it even more appealing to make pension contributions instead of paying themselves additional dividend income (because dividends will be paid out of profits that have been taxed more heavily).

At present companies enjoy 19% tax relief on their pension contributions but this will rise to 26.5% for companies with profits between £50,000 and £250,000 and 25% for companies with profits in excess of £250,000.

Thus a company with profits of £100,000 will currently save £1,900 corporation tax by making a pension contribution of £10,000. When the company's marginal tax rate increases to 26.5% it will save £2,650 tax.

There are several reasons why pension contributions are currently an attractive alternative to dividends and may become even more attractive when corporation tax increases:

- Like salaries, company pension contributions enjoy corporation tax relief. In other words, they're a tax deductible business expense.

- Unlike salaries, there is no national insurance on the income you eventually withdraw from your pension.

- When you eventually withdraw money from your pension, 25% can be taken tax free.

- Pension income is taxed at the "regular" income tax rates, typically 20% or 40%. By contrast, the combined tax rate (corporation tax and income tax) on dividend income is currently around 25% for basic-rate taxpayers and 45% for higher-rate taxpayers. When corporation tax increases these combined tax rates will rise to approximately 31% and 49% respectively for owners of companies with profits in excess of £250,000. Similar rates will be payable by many owners of smaller companies.

- When you start withdrawing money from your pension, you could find yourself in a lower tax bracket than you are now (many retirees are basic-rate taxpayers).

Putting all this together, it's possible that you will ultimately pay income tax on your pension withdrawals at an effective rate no higher than 15%. By contrast, you may face a combined tax rate that is possibly two to three times higher if the same money is paid out as dividend income.

There is, of course, a major drawback with pensions: your money is locked away until you are 55 (rising to 57 in 2028). Nevertheless, when you do reach the minimum retirement age you can make unlimited withdrawals.

Another drawback with pensions is you are potentially exposed to any future increase in income tax rates. Essentially your savings are at the mercy of future governments. Having said this, we do believe pension contributions are still worth making in most cases.

Example – Higher-rate Taxpayer
Before Corporation Tax Increase

Lesleyanne is a company owner and a higher-rate taxpayer (i.e. her taxable income is more than £50,270).

Let's say she is trying to choose between taking an additional £1,000 of the company's profit as a dividend and getting the company to invest £1,000 in her self-invested personal pension (SIPP).

With a dividend the company will first pay corporation tax at 19% (£190), leaving £810 to distribute. Lesleyanne will then pay income tax at 32.5%: £263. The total combined tax rate on the dividend is roughly 45%.

A company pension contribution will enjoy corporation tax relief so the whole £1,000 will go straight into Lesleyanne's SIPP. Ignoring investment growth, when she eventually withdraws the money from her pension the first £250 will be tax free and the remaining £750 will be subject to income tax.

If Lesleyanne is a basic-rate taxpayer when she retires she will pay 20% tax (£150), leaving her with £850 overall. Thus her effective overall tax rate will be 15%. If Lesleyanne is a higher-rate taxpayer when she retires (for example, if she ends up with a significant amount of rental income from buy-to-let properties) she will effectively pay 40% tax on her taxable pension income (£300), leaving her with £700 overall. Thus the effective tax rate on her pension withdrawals will be 30%.

If Lesleyanne does not have much income from other sources when she retires (except perhaps her state pension), it's also possible that some of her pension withdrawals will be covered by her income tax personal allowance and therefore tax free. Although this is a distinct possibility for many retirees, we will ignore it for the remainder of this chapter so as not to overstate the potential benefits of pensions.

In summary, Lesleyanne's choice is between paying tax at roughly 45% now on her additional dividend income and paying tax at 15% and possibly 30% on her pension withdrawals in the future.

Example – Higher-rate Taxpayer
After Corporation Tax Increase

Let's say after the increase in corporation tax Lesleyanne's company makes profits of approximately £100,000 and she is once again trying to choose between the same additional dividend and pension contribution.

With a dividend the company will face a marginal corporation tax rate of 26.5% which means it will pay £265 tax, leaving £735 to distribute. Lesleyanne will then pay income tax at 32.5%: £239. The total combined tax rate on the dividend will be roughly 50%.

With a company pension contribution the whole £1,000 will go straight into Lesleyanne's SIPP. The effective tax rate on her pension

*withdrawals will be either 15% if she is a basic-rate taxpayer when she
retires or 30% as a higher-rate taxpayer.*

*In summary, Lesleyanne's choice will be between paying tax at roughly
50% on her additional dividend income and paying tax at 15% and
possibly 30% on her pension withdrawals.*

What these examples show is that, for company owners who have
not already built up significant pension savings, a company
pension contribution is currently an extremely attractive
alternative to additional dividend income and will become even
more attractive when corporation tax increases.

Of course, one must never lose sight of the fact that your pension
savings are placed in a locked box until you are at least 55. So a
company pension contribution is only an attractive alternative to
a dividend if you have already withdrawn enough money from
your company to cover your living costs.

In the above example we have assumed that the company will
have a marginal tax rate of 26.5% after the increase in corporation
tax. If its profits are greater than £250,000 it will face a marginal
tax rate of 25%. In this case Lesleyanne's choice will be between
paying tax at roughly 49% on her additional dividend income and
paying tax at 15% and possibly 30% on her pension withdrawals.

Are company pension contributions attractive if you're a basic-rate
taxpayer with taxable income of less than £50,270? Let's find out:

Example – Basic-rate Taxpayer
Before Corporation Tax Increase

Poppy is a company owner and a basic-rate taxpayer.

*She too is trying to choose between taking £1,000 of the company's
profit as a dividend and a £1,000 company pension contribution.*

*With a dividend the company will first pay corporation tax rate at 19%
(£190), leaving £810 to distribute. Poppy will then pay income tax at
7.5%: £61. The total combined tax rate on the dividend is roughly 25%.*

*With a company pension contribution the whole £1,000 will go straight
into Poppy's SIPP. As with Lesleyanne, the effective tax rate on her*

pension withdrawals will be either 15% if she is a basic-rate taxpayer when she retires or 30% if she is a higher-rate taxpayer.

In summary, Poppy's choice is between paying tax at roughly 25% on her additional dividend income now and paying tax at 15% and possibly 30% on her future pension withdrawals.

Example – Basic-rate Taxpayer
After Corporation Tax Increase

If the company's profits do not exceed £50,000 in the future it will continue to pay corporation tax at 19% and the outcome will be the same as the above example.

With a dividend, if the company has profits in the £50,000-£250,000 bracket it will face a marginal corporation tax rate of 26.5% which means it will pay £265 tax on the £1,000 of profit, leaving £735 to distribute. Poppy will then pay income tax at 7.5%: £55. The total combined tax rate on the dividend will be 32%.

In summary, Poppy's choice will be between paying tax at 32% on her additional dividend income and paying tax at 15% and possibly 30% on her future pension withdrawals.

What this example shows is that, if you are a basic-rate taxpayer, a company pension contribution is currently a reasonably attractive alternative to additional dividend income and will become even more attractive when corporation tax increases.

However, pension contributions will not be very attractive if Poppy ends up wealthier in retirement and becomes a higher-rate taxpayer. This could happen if, for example, she inherits or accumulates a significant amount of assets and the income takes her over the higher-rate threshold before she starts withdrawing money from her pension.

Periods Straddling the Date of Change

The above examples all use the corporation tax rate that currently applies or the rates that will apply when the increase is in full force. However, we also have to consider the rates that will apply to accounting periods that straddle 1st April 2023, the date corporation tax changes. Pension contributions in those years will be more attractive than at present but not quite as attractive as when the corporation tax increase is in full force.

Example

Three Trees Ltd has accounting periods that run from 1st January to 31st December and has taxable profits of more than £50,000 but less than £250,000 per year. The company faces the following marginal rates of corporation tax:

- *Year ended 31st December 2021   19%*
- *Year ended 31st December 2022   19%*
- *Year ended 31st December 2023   24.65%*
- *Year ended 31st December 2024   26.5%*

The company's marginal tax rate for 2023 is 24.65% because 90 days' worth of profit will be subject to the existing 19% rate and 275 days' worth of profit will be subject to the new rates.

If the company makes any pension contributions between 1st January 2021 and 31st December 2022 it will enjoy 19% tax relief. Any contributions between 1st January 2023 and 31st December 2023 will enjoy up to 24.65% tax relief. Any contributions made from 1st January 2024 onwards will enjoy up to 26.5% tax relief.

Postponing Pension Contributions

Some company owners may be wondering whether it is worth postponing or reducing pension contributions until corporation tax increases, so that more tax relief can be enjoyed. (Note, here we are talking about voluntary pension contributions, typically for the directors, rather than the compulsory ones that are due under auto-enrolment.)

A company with profits of £50,000-£250,000 will eventually face a marginal tax rate of 26.5% and will be able to enjoy up to £75 of additional tax relief for every £1,000 of pension contributions it postpones. A company with profits of more than £250,000 will enjoy up to £60 of additional tax relief.

It's certainly worth considering postponing contributions but this strategy is not without its risks and practical problems.

For starters, the company may have to wait quite some time to enjoy the maximum tax relief. From the previous example we can see that, for Three Trees Ltd, only pension contributions made from January 2024 onwards will enjoy up to 26.5% tax relief, although contributions made between January and December 2023 will enjoy up to 24.65% tax relief.

Some company owners may be willing to postpone making contributions for this amount of time; others may prefer to make more steady contributions.

One reason why it may be worth making pension contributions sooner rather than later is because cash kept inside a company is arguably more vulnerable to commercial risk than cash stored away in a pension.

Another reason is that it is possible changes could be made to the pension contribution rules that make it harder to make bigger catch-up contributions. For example, at present the annual allowance is £40,000 which means your company can make contributions of up to £40,000 per year on your behalf. It's also possible to make use of any unused annual allowance from the three previous tax years.

But what if the annual allowance is reduced to, say, £20,000 or less? That could make it more difficult for some company owners to receive catch-up contributions.

Furthermore, rumours have been circulating that tax relief on pension contributions will be reduced at some point in the future. We don't know if these rumours have any substance and how any changes would affect company pension contributions.

In summary, postponing or perhaps partly reducing pension contributions, where possible, may produce greater tax savings but you will have to keep your eyes open for changes to pension tax relief that may scupper your plans.

Auto-Enrolment

In recent years the Government has rolled out a system of compulsory pensions called auto-enrolment. Essentially it's an extra tax on employers.

Only employees earning more than £10,000 and aged from 22 to state pension age need to be *automatically* enrolled into a pension. Some older and younger employees and those who earn less than £10,000 also have certain workplace pension rights.

According to the Pension Regulator a company does not have any automatic-enrolment duties when:

- It has just one director, with no other staff

- It has a number of directors, none of whom has an employment contract, with no other staff

- It has a number of directors, only one of whom has an employment contract, with no other staff

A contract of employment does not have to be in writing. However, according to the Pension Regulator, if there is no written contract of employment, or other evidence of an intention to create an employer/worker relationship between the company and the director, it will not argue that an employment contract exists.

If a director does not have an employment contract they are always exempt from automatic enrolment. If a director has a contract of employment and there are other people working for the company with an employment contract, they are not exempt.

Depending on their age and earnings, they may qualify for automatic enrolment but the company can decide whether to automatically enrol them into a pension. However, the director has the right to join a pension scheme at any time and the company cannot refuse to enrol them (although in practice this problem will not arise in most owner-managed companies).

If the company decides not to enrol any employed director who is eligible for automatic enrolment, and it has no other eligible staff, it does not need to set up a pension scheme. However, it will need to make a 'declaration of compliance'.

Chapter 28

Pension Contributions: You or the Company?

In the previous chapter we showed that company pension contributions can be an attractive alternative to dividends.

However, company directors can also make pension contributions *personally*, so a key question is:

"Who should make the contributions: the director or the company?"

Before the increase in dividend tax rates it was often more tax efficient for a small pension contribution to be made by the company director personally.

At present it is often tax efficient to get your company to make the pension contributions.

Company Owner Pension Contributions

When you make pension contributions *personally* (as opposed to getting your company to make them) the taxman will top up your savings by paying cash directly into your pension.

Effectively for every £80 you invest, the taxman will put in an extra £20.

Why £20? Your contributions are treated as having been paid out of income that has already been taxed at the 20% basic rate of income tax.

The company that manages your pension plan – usually an insurance company or SIPP provider – will claim this money for you from the taxman and credit it to your account.

So whatever contribution you make personally, divide it by 0.80 and you'll get the total amount that is invested in your pension pot. This is known as your *gross pension contribution*.

Example

Peter is a company owner who takes most of his income as dividends. He invests £800 in a self-invested personal pension (SIPP). The taxman will top up his pension with £200 of basic-rate tax relief which means he'll have £1,000 in his pension pot:

$$£800/0.80 = £1,000$$

If Peter is a higher-rate taxpayer he can also claim higher-rate tax relief when he completes his tax return. This is given by increasing his basic-rate band by the amount of his gross pension contribution.

Example continued

Peter's gross pension contribution is £1,000 so his basic-rate band will be increased by £1,000. This means £1,000 of his dividend income will be taxed at 7.5% instead of 32.5%, i.e. a 25% saving. Thus, Peter's higher-rate tax relief is:

$$£1,000 \times 25\% = £250$$

In total Peter will enjoy £450 of tax relief (£200 basic-rate relief plus £250 higher-rate tax relief). Peter's total tax relief is 45% of his £1,000 gross pension contribution.

Company Directors with Small Salaries

To obtain tax relief on your pension contributions they have to stay within certain limits:

- **Earnings.** Contributions made by you *personally* must not exceed your 'relevant UK earnings'. Earnings include your salary, bonus and taxable benefits in kind but do NOT include your dividends.

- **The £40,000 Annual Allowance.** Total pension contributions by you and your company must not exceed £40,000 per year, although it is possible to carry forward any unused annual allowance from the three previous tax years. The annual allowance is reduced if your "adjusted income" exceeds £240,000 (see Chapter 17).

For a company director taking a salary of £9,568 (see Chapter 8) the maximum pension contribution that can be made in 2021/22 is therefore £9,568.

This is the maximum *gross* contribution. The director would personally invest £7,654 (£9,568 x 80%) and the taxman will top this up with £1,914 of basic-rate tax relief for a total gross contribution of £9,568.

For a company director taking a salary of £12,570, the maximum gross pension contribution is £12,570. The director would personally invest £10,056 (£12,570 x 80%) and the taxman will top this up with £2,514 of basic-rate tax relief for a total gross contribution of £12,570.

Directors who want to make bigger pension contributions personally have to pay themselves bigger salaries. However, this is usually not an attractive option because a bigger salary may be subject to both employee's and employer's national insurance (at 12% and 13.8% respectively).

Company Pension Contributions

As a company owner you can also get your company (your employer) to make pension contributions on your behalf. Company pension contributions are always paid *gross* (there is no top up from the taxman) but the company will normally enjoy corporation tax relief on the payment. For example, a company currently paying 19% corporation tax can make a pension contribution of £10,000 and enjoy £1,900 tax relief.

Note you do not need a dedicated company pension scheme to make company pension contributions. Most firms that offer SIPPs have special forms that allow your company to pay directly into your pension.

How much can your company contribute? Unlike the contributions that you make personally, the company's contributions are NOT restricted by the size of your salary.

In other words, the company can make a pension contribution that is bigger than your salary.

However, there are other restrictions on company contributions:

- Total pension contributions by you and your company must not exceed the annual allowance (typically £40,000), although you can carry forward any unused allowance from the previous three tax years.

- The company may be denied corporation tax relief on any pension contributions made on behalf of directors, if the taxman views them as 'excessive'.

Corporation Tax Relief on Pension Contributions

Unlike the pension contributions that you make personally, tax relief for company pension contributions is not automatic.

Company contributions will only be a tax deductible expense for corporation tax purposes if they are incurred wholly and exclusively for the purposes of the trade.

There is a danger that HMRC will deny corporation tax relief for 'excessive' pension contributions. In practice this is relatively rare.

When determining whether company pension contributions qualify for corporation tax relief, HMRC will look at the total remuneration package of the director. The total package (including salary, pension contributions and other benefits in kind) must not be excessive relative to the work the individual carries out and his or her responsibilities.

Relevant factors may include:

- The number of hours you work, your experience and your level of responsibility in the company.

- The pay of unconnected employees in your company and other companies who perform duties of similar value.

- The pay required to recruit someone to take over your duties.

- The company's financial performance.

Extra care may be necessary in the event of a large one-off company pension contribution.

It may be sensible to document the commercial justification (e.g. strong recent financial performance of the company) in the minutes of a directors' board meeting and hold a shareholders' meeting to approve the contribution.

In some cases, when a much larger than normal contribution is made, it may be necessary to spread tax relief over a number of years. These spreading rules will not affect most small companies and only kick in when the excess contributions amount to £500,000 or more.

In conclusion, although the risk that your company will be denied corporation tax relief may be small, it is important to stress that, when it comes to company pension contributions, unlike contributions made by individuals, there is no cast-iron guarantee that the company will enjoy tax relief.

That's why I would recommend speaking to a tax advisor before your company starts making significant contributions.

Pension Contributions – You or the Company?

Using a couple of case studies we will now compare company pension contributions with pension contributions made personally by company owners to see which is most tax efficient.

Case Study 1 – Basic-rate Taxpayer

Eva owns Cassidy Ltd. She is a basic-rate taxpayer and pays herself a small tax-free salary of £9,568 this year (2021/22) and takes the rest of her income as dividends.

She also decides to make a £1,000 pension contribution. If Cassidy Ltd makes the contribution it can pay £1,000 directly into Eva's SIPP.

If instead Eva pays herself a dividend to fund a pension contribution that she makes personally, the company will pay 19% corporation tax leaving Eva with £810.

Eva holds onto £10 and invests £800 in her SIPP. The taxman will add £200 of basic-rate tax relief, leaving her with the same amount in her pension – £1,000.

But that's not the end of the matter: Eva will still have to pay 7.5% tax on her £810 dividend – £61.

Eva is worse off by about £50 (£61 - £10 saved dividend income).

Thus, if you're a basic-rate taxpayer, for every £1,000 that ends up in your pension you will have to pay an additional 5% in tax.

In this case a company pension contribution is clearly more tax efficient than a contribution made personally by the director.

Other Important Points

If Eva wants more than £9,568 invested in her pension, making the contribution personally will be even more expensive.

She would have to pay herself a bigger salary and this could result in a significant amount of national insurance becoming payable. This is because any pension contribution you make personally cannot exceed your earnings (i.e. salary).

The additional salary would attract 12% employee's national insurance and 13.8% employer's national insurance (unless there is spare employment allowance).

Case Study 2 – Higher-rate Taxpayer

This time we'll assume Eva is a *higher-rate taxpayer* and again wants to make a £1,000 pension contribution.

If Cassidy Ltd makes the contribution it can pay £1,000 directly into Eva's SIPP. Alternatively Eva can pay herself an £810 dividend, hold onto £10 and invest £800 in her SIPP. The taxman will add £200 of basic-rate tax relief, resulting in the same gross pension contribution of £1,000.

Again, that's not the end of the matter. Eva still has to pay income tax on the additional dividend.

With a gross pension contribution of £1,000, Eva's basic-rate band will be increased by £1,000. This means the £810 dividend will be taxed at just 7.5%, not 32.5%, so the tax is £61.

Furthermore, an additional £190 of her other dividend income will also be taxed at 7.5% instead of 32.5%, saving her an extra £48.

All in all a £1,000 pension contribution made by the director is only £3 more expensive than a company contribution:

£61 income tax - £48 higher-rate relief - £10 saved dividend = £3

In this case a company pension contribution is again more tax efficient than a contribution made personally by the director but the difference is tiny.

Because the saving is so small it will probably be other factors that determine whether the company or the individual makes the pension contributions.

Other Important Points

Note that if Eva wants to enjoy full higher-rate tax relief on a gross pension contribution of £9,568 (i.e. equal to her salary), she must have at least £9,568 of dividend income above the higher-rate threshold (income of at least £59,838 in 2021/22). If Eva wants to make a pension contribution bigger than £9,568 personally she will have to pay herself a bigger salary. This may result in significant national insurance becoming payable.

When Personal Contributions Are Attractive

Making pension contributions personally is still worth considering in some situations. Take the example of a director who unexpectedly finds himself with income of £120,000, which means most of his personal allowance will be withdrawn.

Let's also say he has received a salary of £8,840 this year. If he makes a gross pension contribution of £8,840 he will enjoy full income tax relief on the contribution. Furthermore, his adjusted net income will fall by £8,840 which means £4,420 of his personal allowance will be clawed back, saving him even more tax.

Lifetime ISAs

Those aged 18 to 39 can open a Lifetime ISA which can be used to save for a first home or for retirement.

Up to £4,000 per year can be invested and receives a 25% Government bonus. So if you put in £4,000, the Government will add £1,000. This is the same as the basic-rate tax relief enjoyed on pension contributions.

It is possible to continue making contributions up to age 50.

This means you can invest up to £128,000 between age 18 and 50 with a Government bonus of up to £32,000.

Unlike a pension, your savings are not locked up inside a Lifetime ISA. However, if you withdraw money before reaching age 60, for any reason other than to buy your first home, there will be a 25% early withdrawal charge. This will claw back all of the Government bonus, plus an additional 6.25% of the amount you invested.

Lifetime ISA versus Company Pension Contribution

The Lifetime ISA is an attractive alternative to saving in a pension if you are a basic-rate taxpayer. Like pensions they attract a top up from the Government but, unlike pensions, ALL the money you take out will be tax free.

For example, let's say a company owner who is a basic-rate taxpayer is trying to decide between a £1,000 company pension contribution and using a dividend to fund a Lifetime ISA contribution.

A £1,000 pension contribution will attract corporation tax relief so the whole £1,000 will go directly into the company owner's pension.

If the same money is used to fund a dividend, the company will currently pay 19% corporation tax leaving £810 to pay out. After paying 7.5% income tax the company owner will be left with around £750 to invest in a Lifetime ISA. Adding the Government bonus the company owner will end up with £938 in his Lifetime ISA.

However, when the company owner retires all withdrawals from the Lifetime ISA will be tax free, whereas only 25% of the money withdrawn from the pension will be tax free. The rest will be taxed at 20% if he is a basic-rate taxpayer.

If we ignore investment growth to keep the example simple (it doesn't affect the outcome), with a Lifetime ISA the company owner will end up with £938, with a pension he will end up with just £850 after tax.

Thus, if you're a basic-rate taxpayer, your retirement income could be 10.3% higher with a <u>Lifetime ISA</u>!

What about higher-rate taxpayers?

Once again a £1,000 pension contribution will attract corporation tax relief so the whole £1,000 will go directly into the company owner's pension.

If the same money is used to fund a dividend, the company will currently pay 19% corporation tax leaving £810 to pay out. After paying 32.5% income tax the company owner will be left with £547 to invest in his Lifetime ISA. Adding the Government bonus the company owner will end up with £684 in his Lifetime ISA.

When the company owner retires all withdrawals from the Lifetime ISA will be tax free, whereas only 25% of the money withdrawn from the pension will be tax free. The rest will be taxed at 20% if he is now a basic-rate taxpayer (most retirees end up as basic-rate taxpayers).

Ignoring investment growth again, with a Lifetime ISA the company owner will end up with £684, with a pension he will end up with £850 after tax.

Thus, your retirement income could be 24% higher with a <u>pension</u>.

However, if the company owner is a higher-rate taxpayer when he retires (for example if he has a lot of income from other sources, e.g. rental property) he will end up with £700 from a pension, compared with £684 from a Lifetime ISA. The difference is small and the investment decision will probably be based on other factors.

Finally, it's also important to remember that you can only invest £4,000 per year in a Lifetime ISA (with an additional £1,000 bonus from the Government), compared with the maximum gross pension contribution of £40,000 per year. Furthermore, you can only open a Lifetime ISA if you're under 40 years of age and it's only possible to continue making contributions up to age 50.

After the Rise in Corporation Tax

Company pension contributions will become even more attractive once the corporation tax rate increases (assuming, of course, that your company has profits of more than £50,000 and therefore pays higher tax). Let's look at another couple of case studies to see why.

Case Study 3 – Basic-rate Taxpayer

Eva has £1,000 of pre-tax profit in Cassidy Ltd that she would like to use to fund a pension contribution. We will assume that her company has a marginal tax rate of 26.5%. If Cassidy Ltd makes the contribution it can pay £1,000 directly into Eva's SIPP.

Alternatively, Eva can use that same £1,000 to pays herself a dividend to fund a pension contribution that she makes personally. The company will pay 26.5% corporation tax leaving Eva with a £735 dividend.

Eva will also have to pay income tax of £55 on the dividend (7.5%), leaving her with £680 to invest in her pension. The taxman will add £170 of basic-rate tax relief, resulting in a total gross pension contribution of £850.

In summary, Eva's pension contribution will be 15% smaller if she decides to make it personally.

Case Study 4 – Higher-rate Taxpayer

This time we'll assume Eva is a *higher-rate taxpayer* and again has £1,000 of pre-tax profit in Cassidy Ltd that she would like to use to fund a pension contribution.

If Cassidy Ltd makes the contribution it can pay £1,000 directly into Eva's SIPP. Alternatively Eva can pay herself a £735 dividend.

Let's say she holds onto £15 and invests £720 in her SIPP. The taxman will add £180 of basic-rate tax relief, resulting in a gross pension contribution of £900.

With a gross pension contribution of £900, Eva's basic-rate band will be increased by £900. This means the £735 dividend will be taxed at just 7.5%, not 32.5%, so the tax is roughly £55.

Furthermore, an additional £165 of her other dividend income will also be taxed at 7.5% instead of 32.5%, providing additional tax relief of £41.

Her additional tax relief plus the £15 of dividend income she held onto are almost exactly equal to the tax she has to pay on the dividend:

£41 tax relief + £15 saved dividend - £55 income tax = £1

All in all, Eva's pension contribution will be 10% smaller if she decides to make it personally.

Lifetime ISA versus Company Pension Contribution After the Rise in Corporation Tax

Let's say a company owner who is a basic-rate taxpayer and whose company has a marginal tax rate of 26.5% is trying to decide between a £1,000 company pension contribution and using a dividend to fund a Lifetime ISA contribution.

A £1,000 pension contribution will attract corporation tax relief so the whole £1,000 will go directly into the company owner's pension. When the company owner retires he or she could end up with £850 after tax (first 25% tax free, remainder taxed at 20%).

If the same money is used to pay a dividend to fund a Lifetime ISA contribution, the company will pay 26.5% corporation tax leaving £735 to pay out.

After paying 7.5% income tax the company owner will be left with £680 to invest in a Lifetime ISA. Adding the Government bonus the company owner will end up with £850 in the Lifetime ISA.

Thus, if you're a basic-rate taxpayer, a company pension contribution and Lifetime ISA will produce exactly the same outcome.

What about higher-rate taxpayers? Once again a £1,000 pension contribution will attract corporation tax relief so the whole £1,000 will go directly into the company owner's pension.

When the company owner retires he will end up with £850 after tax if he is a basic-rate taxpayer when he retires (first 25% tax free, remainder taxed at 20%). If he is a higher-rate taxpayer he will end up with £700 (first 25% tax free, remainder taxed at 40%).

If the same money is used to pay a dividend to fund a Lifetime ISA contribution, the company will pay 26.5% corporation tax leaving £735 to pay out.

After paying 32.5% income tax the company owner will be left with £496 to invest in his Lifetime ISA. Adding the Government bonus the company owner will end up with £620 in his Lifetime ISA.

Thus, if you're a basic-rate taxpayer when you retire your retirement income could be 37% higher with a pension.

If you're a higher-rate taxpayer, your retirement income could be 13% higher.

Summary

- Company pension contributions are currently more tax efficient than contributions made personally by directors.

- The additional saving is very small if the director is a higher-rate taxpayer.

- If you want to make a pension contribution bigger than your existing company salary it is usually more tax efficient to get the company to make the contribution rather than pay yourself a bigger salary which may have a significant national insurance cost.

- Tax relief for company pension contributions is not automatic – tax relief could be denied if the contributions are viewed as excessive, although this is rare in practice.

- A Lifetime ISA is currently an attractive alternative to a company pension contribution if you are a basic-rate taxpayer, although you can only invest £4,000 per year and must be under 40 to open one. Pension contributions remain a more attractive alternative if you are a higher-rate taxpayer.

- When corporation tax increases, Lifetime ISAs and company pension contributions may produce the same outcome if you are a basic-rate taxpayer. Company pension contributions may become even more attractive for many higher-rate taxpayers.

Chapter 29

Putting Property into a Pension

In Chapter 24 we explained that company owners who own their business premises personally can get the company to pay them rent and this may be an attractive alternative to dividends.

Some company owners also use a SIPP or other pension plan to hold their business premises and in this chapter we'll take a look at the benefits and drawbacks of this alternative.

Note that you can put commercial property into a pension but not residential property, so this option is not available to buy-to-let landlords.

Holding business property in a pension has a number of benefits:

- **Tax-free rent**. The rent your company pays into your pension plan is tax free, i.e. there is no income tax payable by you.

- **Corporation tax relief**. The company can still claim the rent as a business expense, saving it corporation tax.

- **No capital gains tax**. When a property held inside a pension is sold there is no capital gains tax payable.

- **Inheritance tax exemption**. Assets held in a pension fall outside your estate for inheritance tax purposes.

Although the ability to roll up rental income tax free inside a pension is enticing, you must never lose sight of the fact that all the money you eventually withdraw from your pension, over and above your 25% tax-free lump sum, will be subject to income tax.

If you are a higher-rate taxpayer at present but expect to be a basic-rate taxpayer when you retire (most retirees end up as basic-rate taxpayers), it's possible the rental income will ultimately be much less heavily taxed by going the pension route.

Similarly, although property held inside a pension can be sold without incurring capital gains tax, when you eventually withdraw the capital gain most of it (75%) will be subject to income tax. If you are a basic-rate taxpayer when you retire you will pay 20% tax and if you are a higher-rate taxpayer you will pay 40% tax.

By contrast, when you sell business premises that you own personally you will be subject to capital gains tax. Commercial property benefits from the lower 20% CGT rate and it's possible some of the gain will be taxed at just 10% if your basic-rate band isn't used up by your other income. Some of the gain may also be covered by your annual exemption, currently £12,300.

In some cases, as we shall see in Chapter 32, a sale of business premises that you own personally will qualify for Business Asset Disposal Relief. If so, a tax rate of 10% may apply to the whole gain, although this relief is generally not available if your company has paid you rent at a full commercial rate.

A property held inside a pension doesn't have to be sold when you retire. If your own business ceases to occupy the property it can be rented out to someone else who will pay rent to your pension which will roll up tax free.

Although property held inside your pension may fall outside your estate for inheritance tax purposes, in most cases the family members that inherit your pension pot will have to pay income tax on any money they subsequently withdraw, typically at 20% or 40%.

By contrast, if you own a business property personally it may qualify for 50% business property relief, i.e. inheritance tax will only be payable on half its value.

Finally, when it comes to tucking away money inside a pension we must never lose sight of the fact that you will not be able to get your hands on any of the money until you are at least 55 (rising to 57 in 2028).

Clearly there are benefits to holding business property inside a pension but it is by no means a 'no brainer'. There are benefits but also drawbacks and each case would have to be decided on its merits with help from a professional.

Funding the Property Purchase

The purchase of a business property by a pension can be funded in several ways.

Typically the company owner will use his or her existing pension savings, topped up with fresh contributions made by the company and/or the company owner personally.

It is also possible for your pension fund to borrow money but only up to 50% of its net assets. For example, if you have pension savings of £100,000 an additional £50,000 can be borrowed.

Some pension providers allow a part share in a property to be acquired by the pension plan, with the balance owned outside the pension.

Several individuals can also pool their pension savings to collectively buy a property.

Transferring Existing Property

If you already own the property you can sell it to your SIPP and this may allow you to release a sizeable amount of cash from your pension savings.

Transferring an existing property into a pension is likely to result in capital gains tax becoming payable if the property has risen in value since you bought it.

As stated earlier, commercial property benefits from the lower 20% CGT rate and some of the gain may be taxed at just 10% and some may be tax-free thanks to the annual exemption. It is unlikely Business Asset Disposal Relief would be available in such cases.

A sizeable capital gains tax bill may put off many existing property owners going down the pension route but others may still be tempted by the prospect of receiving a large cash payment out of their pension savings.

The transfer may also result in a stamp duty land tax bill and VAT may also be payable in certain circumstances, although a refund can usually be claimed.

In Specie Contributions

Properties have also been transferred into pensions as *in specie* pension contributions, with the member claiming income tax relief. Under this method a property worth, say, £100,000 would be transferred into the pension scheme with the pension scheme administrator claiming £25,000 of basic-rate tax relief to add to the member's pension pot and the member himself claiming up to £25,000 of higher-rate tax relief when he submitted his tax return.

In specie contributions are not permitted by most pension firms following a clamp down by HMRC because of perceived abuse. In a recent First-tier Tribunal decision it was decided that tax relief should be allowed on an in specie contribution of shares. However, HMRC appealed the decision and the Upper Tribunal ruled that tax relief was not available. Some in the pensions industry fear that HMRC may now attempt to reclaim millions of pounds of tax relief on past in-specie contributions.

Costs and other Formalities

Not all pension providers deal with property purchases so you may need to transfer your existing pension savings to a specialist provider.

When your property is held inside a pension your company will have to be treated just like any other tenant, with no special favours, which means rent will have to be paid at a full market rate come hell or high water.

If rent is not paid this will be treated as an unauthorised payment by your SIPP and HMRC may levy a charge of 40% on you personally and a charge of up to 40% on the SIPP itself.

Property SIPPs are also much more expensive to run than those that only allow you to invest in traditional 'stocks and shares'.

Initial set up costs include legal fees, surveyor fees, lenders fees and fees to the pension company managing your SIPP.

Fees will have to be paid for regular rent revaluations and a third party property manager may have to be appointed to collect the rent from you.

Chapter 30

Company Cars, Vans and Motoring Costs

Use of Own Car

When you use *your own car* for business journeys, your company can pay you back using the following mileage rates:

	First 10,000 miles	**Above 10,000**
Cars and vans	45p	25p
Motorbikes	24p	24p
Bicycle	20p	20p

If you take one of your employees in your car on a business journey you can claim an extra 5p per mile.

These are known as the approved mileage allowance payment (AMAP) rates. They are supposed to cover not just your fuel costs but also wear and tear on the vehicle.

The amount will be tax free in your hands and a tax deductible expense for the company.

For example, if during the current tax year you rack up 5,000 business miles in your own car your company can pay you £2,250 tax free (5,000 x 0.45). The company can also claim the expense, saving it corporation tax.

If your business mileage comes to 12,000 your company can pay you £5,000 tax free (10,000 x 45p + 2,000 x 25p).

Business mileage does not include travel from your home to your permanent place of work.

Using the above mileage rates is a simple way to obtain tax relief for your business travel, although it is necessary to keep a record of your business journeys (using a log book, for example).

If your company is VAT registered it is also possible to recover the VAT element of your business fuel costs.

The portion of the 45p/25p mileage rate that is for fuel is generally calculated using HMRC's advisory fuel rates:

www.gov.uk/guidance/advisory-fuel-rates

For example, if your car has a 1600cc petrol engine the rate at the time of writing is 13p per mile and the VAT element would be 2.17p (13p/6). So for each business mile you can recover 2.17p in VAT.

For example, if you drive 1,000 miles on business during the period you can recover £22 of VAT (1,000 x 2.17p).

You will have to keep VAT fuel receipts that contain enough VAT to cover the claim you are making. Possibly more trouble than it's worth, unless there is a lot of business mileage.

Exemption for Workplace Charging

If a company provides electricity to charge electric or hybrid cars owned by employees there will not be any taxable benefit in kind.

The charging facilities must, however, be provided at or near the company's workplace. There will be a benefit in kind charge if the company pays for an employee to charge their car away from the workplace, for example at home or at a motorway service station.

Charging must be available to all employees or all employees at a particular location. If the company has multiple workplaces, charging facilities do not have to be available at all of them.

Where an employee incurs electricity costs charging their vehicle away from their employer's premises, *business* mileage can be reimbursed using the approved mileage rates (i.e. 45p per mile for the first 10,000 miles and 25p thereafter).

Company Cars

You can also get your company to buy a car for your business and private use. The company will be able to claim tax relief on the running costs and capital allowances on the cost of the car.

That's the good news. The bad news is that you will have to pay income tax each year on the benefit in kind and your company will have to pay employer's national insurance. In many cases these charges are high enough to put off most small company owners going down the company car route.

The taxable benefit (the amount added to your income) is found by multiplying the manufacturer's list price by a percentage that depends on the car's CO_2 emissions and the type of fuel it uses. The list price is not the same as the price you pay for the car (the list price is probably higher).

For zero emission cars the benefit-in-kind percentage is 1% this year, for the highest emission cars it is 37%. The various taxable percentages can be found here:

https://tinyurl.com/companycartax2021

There are two tables: one for cars registered on or after 6th April 2020 and one for cars registered before this date.

For a petrol car registered before 6th April 2020 with CO_2 emissions of 119g/km and a list price of £25,000 the taxable percentage is 28%, which means £7,000 will be added to your taxable income:

£25,000 x 28% = £7,000

If you are a basic-rate taxpayer you will pay 20% tax (£1,400) and if you are a higher-rate taxpayer you will pay 40% tax (£2,800).

There is no *employee's* national insurance payable.

The taxable percentages generally increase each year. However, for cars registered before 6th April 2020 the taxable percentages are the same for the current 2021/22 tax year right through to the end of 2024/25. One exception is cars with zero emissions – their taxable percentage is 1% this year and 2% for the next three years.

Employer's National Insurance

As a company owner you also have to take account of the costs your company will pay. The employer's national insurance cost on the above car benefit will be as follows:

$$£25,000 \times 28\% \times 13.8\% = £966$$

However employer's national insurance is a tax deductible expense for the business so the net cost is lower.

Private Fuel Costs

If the company pays your private fuel costs there is an additional fuel benefit charge which is £24,600 in 2021/22. The taxable amount is found by multiplying the above fuel benefit charge by the benefit-in-kind percentage.

For example, if the benefit-in-kind percentage is 28%, the taxable amount is £6,888 (£24,600 x 28%). This amount is added to your income and taxed. Thus a basic-rate taxpayer will pay £1,378 and a higher-rate taxpayer will pay £2,755.

The company will pay £951 national insurance (£6,888 x 13.8%).

Company car users can pay for their own fuel and recover the cost of *business travel* using the advisory fuel rates (see above). No income tax or employer's national insurance will be payable.

Cars with Zero or Low Emissions

The taxable percentage for zero-emission cars (electric cars) is 1% this year and will rise to 2% in 2022/23 and remain at 2% for 2023/24 and 2024/25.

For cars with emissions of 1-50g/km the taxable percentage varies from 1% to 14% depending on the electric range in miles of the vehicle and the date the car is registered. Again, the taxable percentages for 2022/23 will also apply in 2023/24 and 2024/25.

If your company provides electricity to charge a fully electric company car there is no benefit in kind charge, regardless of the level of private mileage you do or where the car is charged.

The company can also pay for a charging point at your home for a fully electric car without a taxable benefit arising.

If you pay for electricity personally but use a fully electric company car for business travel, an advisory fuel rate of 4p per mile can be used to reimburse you tax free for business mileage.

Capital Allowances

The company can claim tax relief on the car's cost in the form of capital allowances. From 1st April 2021 the emission thresholds for capital allowances are as follows:

- Over 50g/km   6% per year
- 1 to 50g/km   18% per year
- Zero   100%

The 100% first-year allowance for zero emission cars (electric cars) is available until 31st March 2025. This relief allows your company to claim the whole cost of the car as a tax deductible expense in the year of purchase.

Electric cars have to be new to qualify for the 100% first-year allowance. The car doesn't have to be new to qualify for the 6% or 18% writing down allowances. In other words, you can claim these smaller capital allowances on second-hand cars.

If a loan is taken out to buy the vehicle the interest costs are also an allowable expense, as are running costs such as repairs, insurance and road tax.

VAT cannot be recovered on the purchase price of company cars in the vast majority of cases, although VAT can be recovered on repair costs if the car is used for business purposes.

The 18% and 6% writing down allowances are rather stingy because they're calculated using the 'reducing balance' basis, instead of the more generous 'straight line method'.

For example, if your company buys a car for £10,000 that qualifies for a 6% writing down allowance, it can claim £600 in year 1 but only £564 in year 2:

$$(£10,000 - £600) \times 18\% = £564$$

Each year the amount that can be claimed gets smaller, so it takes many years to recover all the tax relief.

Unlike sole traders and partnerships, companies cannot claim a balancing allowance when they sell a car for less than its written down value. If a car with a written down value of £5,000 is sold for £2,000 a sole trader can claim a balancing allowance of £3,000.

Companies cannot do this. A company will have to claim writing down allowances at 6% or 18% on the £3,000 balance, meaning it could take many years to claim all the tax relief.

Leased Cars

If the vehicle is leased the monthly payments are generally a tax deductible expense for the company, although 15% of the payments are disallowed if the car has emissions above 50g/km (from April 2021).

Capital allowances cannot be claimed as well.

For cars that have some private use 50% of the VAT on the lease payments can be recovered. All of the VAT for repair and maintenance costs can be recovered.

Company Vans

The cost of vans is usually allowable in full thanks to the annual investment allowance.

Some of the VAT can also be reclaimed to the extent the van is used for business purposes.

Vans don't just include Ford Transits and the like. Many double cab pickups are more like 4x4s but qualify as vans for tax purposes.

If the van is used regularly for private purposes the annual benefit-in-kind charge in 2021/22 is £3,500, resulting in income tax of £700 for basic-rate taxpayers and £1,400 for higher-rate taxpayers. There will also be employer's national insurance of £483.

The fuel benefit charge for vans is just £669.

The benefit-in-kind charge for zero emission (electric) vans is 80% of the normal benefit-in-kind for company vans for 2020/21.

There is no van benefit charge for zero-emission vans (from 6th April 2021).

Chapter 31

Mobile Phones

"I turn now to what I regard as one of the greatest scourges of modern life. I refer to the mobile telephone."

With these words former Chancellor of the Exchequer Norman Lamont announced a new tax on mobile phones in his 1991 Budget.

"I hope that, as a result of this measure, restaurants will be quieter and the roads will be safer," he concluded.

His words look rather quaint now, although I'm sure many readers would echo his sentiments!

Fortunately the tax treatment has changed and mobile phones are now a tax-free benefit.

The benefit is limited to one mobile phone per employee, although a second phone may be exempt if private use is insignificant. Phones supplied to family members do not qualify, unless they too are employees.

Also, the contract must be in the name of the *company*.

These days HMRC accepts that smart phones are mobile phones and not computers. Tablets and laptops are excluded. Thus you can get your company to provide you with an iPhone and this will not give rise to a taxable benefit. The company must retain ownership, however.

Chapter 32

Sell Your Business and Pay 10% Tax!

One of the most tax-efficient ways to grow your wealth is to build up a successful company and then sell it. This allows you to convert heavily taxed income into a less heavily taxed capital gain.

Many company owners who receive dividends now have a marginal income tax rate of 32.5%. Those with income over £150,000 have a marginal tax rate of 38.1%.

But when you sell a company and receive a cash lump sum, which replaces all of this heavily taxed income, you could end up paying just 10% tax thanks to Business Asset Disposal Relief (previously known as Entrepreneurs Relief, which was a much better name).

The lifetime limit used to be £10 million of capital gains per person. But in the March 2020 Budget the Government slashed this to £1 million with immediate effect (from 11 March 2020).

The announcement could have been a lot worse. There were fears in some quarters that the relief would be abolished altogether. And because it applies on a per person basis, couples can still enjoy £2 million of capital gains taxed at 10%.

Business Asset Disposal Relief is, however, no longer very attractive to serial entrepreneurs, who build up and sell many businesses during their careers. Many will have already exhausted their new £1 million allowance.

Even if you have no immediate plan to sell your company or wind it up, it's still a good idea to have a basic understanding of the Business Asset Disposal Relief rules. There are certain things you need to check and do *before* you take any action.

However, if you are denied the relief all is not lost. You could end up paying capital gains tax at 20% instead of 10% which is a lot more attractive than the top tax rates for dividends.

Qualifying for Business Asset Disposal Relief

Company owners are entitled to Business Asset Disposal Relief when they sell their shares or wind up the company. The main qualifying criteria are the following:

- The company must be your "personal company" which, generally speaking, means you must own at least 5% of it (but matters can get more complicated – see below)

- You must be an officer or employee of the company

- The company must be a 'trading' company

Each of these rules must be satisfied for at least **two years** before the company is sold or wound up.

Where the company has ceased trading each of the rules must be satisfied for at least two years before it ceases trading. The disposal of the company must then take place within three years after trading has stopped.

It used to be one year instead of two years. The new two year rule applies for disposals taking place on or after 6 April 2019.

Selling a Recently Incorporated Business

Under the previous one-year rule business owners had to be wary of incorporating any business within one year of selling it. To qualify for Business Asset Disposal Relief you had to own the shares of the newly formed company for at least a year.

Under the new two-year rule you don't have to own the shares of the newly formed company for at least two years. The period you own the unincorporated business is added to the period you own the company shares.

Transferring Shares to Your Spouse

You do, however, have to be wary of transferring shares to your spouse within two years of selling the company. Transfers to spouses are exempt from capital gains tax and your spouse can then claim Business Asset Disposal Relief when the business is sold, providing they satisfy the necessary conditions outlined above.

Spouse transfers weren't always necessary when the lifetime limit for the relief was £10 million but are probably more important now that it is just £1 million. Many company owners also transfer shares to their spouse to reduce the income tax payable on dividends.

For disposals taking place after 5 April 2019, the transfer must have taken place at least two years before selling the company.

What is a Personal Company?

As stated above, to qualify for Business Asset Disposal Relief the company must be your personal company. This means you must:

- Own at least 5% of the ordinary share capital

- Have at least 5% of the voting rights

HMRC was concerned that ordinary shares encompass a very broad range of share arrangements, including those where the shareholders have restricted rights to dividends and the company's assets.

As a result, you must now also meet at least one of the following two new conditions to qualify for Business Asset Disposal Relief:

- You must be entitled to at least 5% of the profits available for distribution and at least 5% of the assets available for distribution if the company is wound up, or

- In the event of a disposal of all of the ordinary share capital of the company, you would be entitled to at least 5% of the disposal proceeds

According to the Government: *"These changes improve the effectiveness of ER by ensuring that claimants disposing of shares have a minimum economic stake in the company. The government considers this to be more characteristic of entrepreneurial activity."*

Initially the Government introduced just one additional condition (the first bullet point above). However, several expert tax commentators pointed out that this would have prevented owners of alphabet shares (common in many small family companies) from claiming Business Asset Disposal Relief.

For example, where a company has A and B shares and a different rate of dividend can be declared on each type, it could be argued that neither type of shareholder is entitled to "at least 5% of the profits available for distribution" because there is no dividend entitlement until the dividends are declared.

As a result the second new condition was tagged on. This allows the company owner to instead enjoy Business Asset Disposal Relief if they are entitled to at least 5% of the proceeds when the company is sold.

What is an Officer?

Company officers include non-executive directors and company secretaries, so you don't even have to work full-time at the company to qualify for Business Asset Disposal Relief.

What is a Trading Company?

To qualify for Entrepreneurs Relief the company must be a trading company. HMRC regards the following as non-trading activities:

- Holding investment property
- Holding shares or securities
- Holding surplus cash

If there is substantial non-trading activity you could be denied Business Asset Disposal Relief. Unfortunately to the taxman 'substantial' means as little as 20% of the company's:

- Assets
- Turnover
- Expenses
- Profits
- Directors' and employees' time

So, for example, if just 20% of the assets or income of the business are not trading assets or income, you may be denied Business Asset Disposal Relief when you sell your business. As a result you may end up paying capital gains tax at 20% instead of 10%. (Note, 20% is simply a rule of thumb and has no statutory basis.)

If your company doesn't own investment property or invest in other companies, the most serious danger is holding too much cash. If the taxman believes the cash is held for non-trading reasons (e.g. to avoid declaring taxable dividends), trading status could be revoked and Business Asset Disposal Relief taken away.

However, this should not be a problem if you can prove that the cash was required for business purposes, for example as part of a well-documented expansion plan.

Some tax advisors argue that having a large cash balance may not pose a threat if the cash was generated from trading activities and is not 'actively managed' like an investment (i.e. if the cash is left to earn deposit interest only).

It's all a bit of a grey area and professional advice is recommended.

If the company has surplus cash it may be necessary to extract it at least two years in advance to prevent the company's trading status being challenged.

You then have to weigh up the potential costs and benefits: the benefit being a CGT rate of 10% instead of 20% and the cost being the income tax on any additional dividends.

Business Premises – 'Associated Disposals'

Many business owners purchase business premises *personally* and rent them back to their company. The good news is Business Asset Disposal Relief is available when "associated" assets like these are sold. The bad news is many company owners will not qualify!

The asset will only qualify for Business Asset Disposal Relief if you also make a "material disposal" of shares in your company. The stake being disposed of must generally be at least 5%.

It is possible to claim Business Asset Disposal Relief on an associated disposal even if the stake in the business is sold or gifted to a family member, for example an adult child.

However, there must also be no "share purchase arrangements" in place at the time of disposal. This rule is designed to prevent you from taking back your stake in the business after the property has been sold and Business Asset Disposal Relief has been claimed.

For disposals taking place on or after 6 April 2019, to qualify for Business Asset Disposal Relief the 'associated' asset must have been in use in the business for at least two years (previously one year).

For assets acquired since 13 June 2016, the asset must have been held for at least three years to qualify for the relief.

The relief is also restricted if you've received any payment for the use of the property since 5th April 2008 (for example, if your company has paid you rent to use the property).

Where the property was acquired after 5 April 2008 and a full market rent was received throughout the period of its use in the company's trade, no Business Asset Disposal Relief is available.

Where the property was acquired at an earlier date or rent was charged at a lower rate there will be a partial restriction in Business Asset Disposal Relief.

As we saw in Chapter 24, getting your company to pay you rent is an attractive alternative to dividends, especially when the company owner (who owns the property) has expenses that can be deducted from the rent for tax purposes, such as mortgage interest.

Another advantage of charging your company rent is so that capital allowances can be claimed on the qualifying fixtures in the property. If a market rent is not charged the property owner will not be treated as having a proper 'property business', which is necessary for them to make a full capital allowances claim.

In summary, company owners who own their business premises personally have to weigh the benefits of Business Asset Disposal Relief against the benefits of paying themselves rental income. The reduction in the relief's lifetime limit from £10 million to £1 million has made paying rent more attractive than previously.

Winding Up Your Company

It is not always possible to sell your company shares to a third party. Buyers are often fearful of acquiring companies outright for fear of taking on any unknown liabilities. Instead they often prefer to buy the assets (e.g. premises, goodwill, stock and customers).

The disadvantage of an asset sale such as this is the double tax charge: The company will pay corporation tax on the proceeds and you will pay tax (income tax or capital gains tax) when you extract the after-tax proceeds.

Providing you meet the qualifying criteria, Business Asset Disposal Relief is still available if you wind up your company following an asset sale and extract the cash as a capital distribution.

There are generally two ways to wind up a company:

- Dissolution under the Companies Act
- Voluntary liquidation under the Insolvency Act

With a *dissolution* capital gains tax treatment is only possible if the total distributions are less than £25,000. Where the total distributions exceed £25,000 they are taxed as dividends, possibly at 32.5% or 38.1%.

A *voluntary liquidation* ensures that payments to shareholders are treated as capital distributions for capital gains tax purposes. However, voluntary liquidation requires the appointment of a licensed insolvency practitioner with fees running to many thousands of pounds in some cases (the fees may be less if the company's affairs are simple and its main asset is cash).

To qualify for Business Asset Disposal Relief the capital distribution must be made within three years of the cessation of trading.

For disposals taking place on or after 6 April 2019, in the two years before the cessation of trading the following criteria must be met:

- The company must be your 'personal company' (see earlier explanation)
- You must be an officer or employee of the company
- The company must be a 'trading' company

In some cases a large cash balance (a non-trading asset) may throw in doubt the ability to claim Business Asset Disposal Relief.

It goes without saying that in all cases where a winding up of the company is to be carried out, professional advice should be obtained to ensure the desired tax treatment of the distributions.

Anti-Avoidance Rule

An anti-avoidance rule has applied since 6th April 2016 and means that a distribution made when winding up a company will sometimes be taxed as a dividend. This is to prevent company owners continually winding up companies and starting new ones to enjoy the much lower capital gains tax rates.

The new rule applies where all of the following conditions are met:

- **Condition A & B**. The individual holds at least 5% of the ordinary share capital and voting rights immediately before the winding up and the company is a close company at some point in the two years before the winding up

- **Condition C**. Within two years of the distribution the company owner carries on the same or a similar trade or activity to the company being wound up

- **Condition D**. It is reasonable to assume that the main purpose or one of the main purposes of the winding up is to avoid income tax

With regards to Condition C, it makes no difference whether you operate as a sole trader or through a partnership or new company in which you have at least a 5% interest or through a person with whom you are connected (e.g. your spouse or other close relative).

The test is clearly very subjective and it is feared that it could catch many innocent situations, for example where a company owner retires, winds up his company and a year later decides to take on a few clients or do some work for a family member involved in the same trade.

It is also feared that the third test could be applied broadly. For example, HMRC could argue that if a company owner decides not to pay surplus funds out as dividends prior to the winding up, there is as an 'arrangement' to reduce income tax.

HMRC has provided the following examples which are intended to allay these fears and explain when the new rules will apply:

Example 1
Mr A has been the sole shareholder of a company which carries on the trade of landscape gardening for 10 years. Mr A decides to wind up the business and retire. Because he no longer needs a company he liquidates the company and receives a distribution in a winding up. To subsidise his pension, Mr A continues to do a small amount of gardening in his local village.

Conditions A to C are met, because gardening is a similar trade or activity to landscape gardening. However, when viewed as a whole, these arrangements do not appear to have tax as a main purpose. It is natural for Mr A to have wound up his company because it is no longer needed once the trade has ceased.

Although Mr A continues to do some gardening, there is no reason why he would need a company for this, and it does not seem that he set the company up, wound it up and then continued a trade all with a view to receive the profits as capital rather than income.

In these circumstances, Mr A's distribution in the winding up will continue to be treated as capital.

Example 2
Mrs B is an IT contractor. Whenever she receives a new contract, she sets up a limited company to carry out that contract. When the work is completed and the client has paid, Mrs B winds up the company and receives the profits as capital.

Again, conditions A to C are met because Mrs B has a new company which carries on the same or a similar trade to the previously wound up company. Here, though, it looks like there is a main purpose of obtaining a tax advantage. All of the contracts could have been operated through the same company, and apart from the tax savings it would seem that would have been the most sensible option for Mrs B.

Where the distribution from the winding up is made on or after 6th April 2016, in these circumstances the distribution will be treated as a dividend and subject to income tax.

Example 3

Mrs C is an accountant who has operated through a limited company for three years. She decides that the risk involved with running her own business is not worth her effort, and so decides to accept a job at her brother's accountancy firm as an employee. Her brother's firm has been operating for eight years. Mrs C winds up her company and begins life as an employee.

Conditions A to C are met because Mrs C is continuing a similar activity to the trade that was carried on by the company. She is continuing it as an employee of a connected party, triggering Condition C.

But looking at the arrangements as a whole it is not reasonable to assume that they have tax advantage as a main purpose, so Condition D will not be met. Mrs C's company was incorporated and wound up for commercial, not tax, reasons; although she works for a connected party it is clear that the other business was not set up to facilitate a tax advantage because it has been operating for some time.

In these circumstances, the distribution from the winding up will continue to be treated as capital, absent any other considerations.

Transaction in Securities

HMRC can also use the so-called "transaction in securities" rules to attack distributions when a company is wound up if it thinks the main reason for the liquidation is to save income tax.

The transaction in securities rules are contained in vague legislation that can be used to convert capital gains into income subject to the dividend tax rates if HMRC takes the view that income has been incorrectly extracted as capital gain.

This introduces a second obstacle for business owners who wish to liquidate their companies.

Many tax advisors therefore recommend obtaining pre-transaction clearance from HMRC.

The transaction in securities rules cannot apply if there is a genuine third-party sale of the company, even if one of the main reasons for the sale is to save tax.

Overdrawn Directors Loan Accounts

When a director owes his company money, the overdrawn loan account is an *asset* of the company. When there is a members' voluntary liquidation, it is common practice to distribute this asset to the shareholders *in specie* (i.e. not as a cash payment).

In other words, instead of the director repaying the company and receiving the cash back as a liquidation distribution in his capacity as a shareholder, the distribution is handled as a paper transaction.

In the past the distribution of the director's loan account during a liquidation was treated as a capital distribution and taxed at just 10% if the company owner was entitled to Business Asset Disposal Relief.

Apparently HMRC is now taking the approach that such distributions are subject to income tax at the dividend tax rates (i.e. at up to 38.1%).

For this reason several expert tax commentators recommend that directors with overdrawn loan accounts should pay back their loans to the company before the company enters liquidation.

Conclusion

There is uncertainty amongst tax professionals as to how the various anti-avoidance measures will be applied in practice when a company is liquidated.

Where capital gains treatment is in doubt it may make sense to pay actual dividends over several tax years, rather than making a single large distribution when you wind up the company.

Adopting a phased approach to the withdrawal of profits from your company may allow you to enjoy the 7.5% tax rate that applies to basic-rate taxpayers, rather than the 32.5% or 38.1% tax rates that apply to higher and additional-rate taxpayers.

Adopting this strategy over several tax years could allow a significant amount of cash to be extracted from the company, especially when the amounts taxed at 7.5% can be doubled up in the case of a company owned by a couple.

A Final Note on Business Asset Disposal Relief

Business Asset Disposal Relief is complicated and constantly changing. This chapter is by no means a definitive guide.

There are various quirks in the legislation that I have deliberately ignored for simplicity's sake but could see the relief denied in certain circumstances. For this reason anyone who wants to benefit from Business Asset Disposal Relief should seek advice from a tax professional with experience in this area.

Chapter 33

Employee Ownership Trusts

In the previous chapter we saw how, thanks to Business Asset Disposal Relief (previously Entrepreneurs Relief), company owners can pay just 10% capital gains tax when they sell their businesses.

Many company owners have heard about Business Asset Disposal Relief but did you know that you can also sell your company TAX FREE to something called an employee ownership trust?

With an employee ownership trust the company ends up being owned by a trust for the benefit of employees generally (shares are not earmarked for individual employees).

Note, employee ownership trusts are not to be confused with the much discredited use of employee benefit trusts to give employees interest-free loans that were supposedly tax free.

The capital gains tax relief for the sale of company shares to employee ownership trusts was introduced in the 2014 Finance Act and therefore has the Government's blessing.

A typical business sale would take place as follows:

- An employee ownership trust is established.

- Shares in the company are sold to the trustees of the employee ownership trust. An independent valuation will be required so that the correct market value is used.

- The trust does not need to have any money to buy the company. The purchase consideration will typically take the form of a debt owed to the original shareholders.

- The company will then gift its earnings to the employee ownership trust to pay off the original owners over a number of years. These gifts of earnings are not an allowable expense for corporation tax purposes, so money will need to be retained by the company to settle its corporation tax bills.

- Payments from the employee ownership trust to the original owners will be exempt from capital gains tax, providing various conditions are met (see below).

The employees will only be indirect owners of the company and will therefore not receive dividends. Instead the trustees of the employee ownership trust can arrange for bonuses to be paid by the company. Annual cash bonuses of up to £3,600 per employee are allowed free from income tax (but not national insurance).

Qualifying Requirements

There are, of course, a number of conditions that have to be satisfied to qualify for the tax benefits:

- The company must be a trading company or the holding company of a trading group

- The trustees of the employee ownership trust must provide benefits to all eligible employees on the same terms. It is, however, possible to distinguish between employees based on their levels of pay, length of service and hours worked.

- The trustees of the employee ownership trust must acquire at least 51% of the company and thus have a controlling interest. Up to 49% of the shares can, however, remain in direct ownership.

- The directors can remain at the company following the sale. However, the number of continuing shareholders (and any other 5% participators) who are directors or employees (or persons connected to them, such as close relatives) must not exceed 40% of the total number of employees. So if a company has five employees only two of them can be the original shareholders. This is to show that there has been a genuine change of ownership in the business. This condition must also be met for one year before the sale of the business.

It is possible for the capital gains tax relief to be clawed back if a disqualifying event occurs in the same tax year that the employee ownership trust acquires shares in the company or in the following tax year.

The original owners will then be subject to capital gains tax under the normal rules, as laid out in the previous chapter.

If any of the conditions for CGT relief are breached in a later tax year it is the trustees who will be liable for capital gains tax. The capital gains tax bill will be calculated using the original owners' base cost in the shares.

Employee ownership trusts are supposed to be long-term ownership vehicles but it is possible that the 51% controlling interest requirement could be breached if, for example, the trustees decide to sell shares in the business to a third party on the basis that the offer is in the interest of the beneficiaries of the employee ownership trust.

The sale of the business to the employee ownership trust must not be for tax avoidance purposes and could fall foul of the so-called "transactions in securities" rules if one of the main purposes is to obtain a tax benefit.

For this reason several tax commentators recommend obtaining advance clearance from HMRC to ensure that the payments from the trustees to the original owners will not be treated as disguised dividends.

Of course, selling to an employee ownership trust will not appeal to all business owners. In particular, many will be put off by the potentially long delay receiving payment for their sale of the business. If the company starts making losses the employee ownership trust may be unable to pay the original owners.

Apart from the tax benefits, selling to an employee ownership trust is also seen as a useful way to solve succession issues, where there are no family members willing to carry on with the business and the owners are unwilling to sell to a competitor or third party with all the hassle this may involve.

Part 7

Salary & Dividends: Practical Issues & Dangers

Chapter 34

How to Avoid the Minimum Wage Rules

If you take a small salary from your company (for example, £8,840, £9,568 or £12,570) there is a danger of falling foul of the national living wage (NLW).

Where wages are too low, HMRC will force the company to make up the shortfall. Bigger wage payments may result in bigger national insurance bills for both the company and the director.

There is also a penalty equivalent to 200% of the unpaid wages with a maximum penalty of £20,000 per worker. Those found guilty will also be considered for disqualification from being a company director for up to 15 years.

However, the key point to note about the NLW is that it only applies to directors who have a contract of employment.

Due to the informal set up in many small companies, there may be some uncertainty as to whether an employment contract exists between the director and the company (employment contracts do not need to be in writing).

However, it is generally accepted amongst the tax profession that if you do not issue yourself with an explicit contract of employment the minimum wage regulations will not apply.

This means you should be able to continue paying yourself a small salary, even if it is less than the national living wage.

However, risk averse company owners (those worried about potential penalties) should consider paying themselves enough salary to satisfy the minimum wage regulations.

National Living Wage Rates

The national living wage applies to those aged 23 and over. From April 2021 the rate is £8.91 per hour.

If you spend, say, 35 hours per week actively managing your business, the total salary due for 2021/22 will be:

$$35 \times 52 \text{ weeks} \times £8.91 = £16,216$$

Fortunately this is not hugely higher than the optimal salary amounts but will still result in unwelcome national insurance charges.

The national insurance payable on this salary by the director would be £798 and £1,018 would be payable by the company (£0 if the company has spare employment allowance).

Of course, every case is different and some directors will be able to argue that they spend fewer hours actively managing the business.

Although it may seem that the best strategy is to simply not have a contract of employment, there may be other reasons why having such a contract is important.

Family Members Who Aren't Directors

It is possible that some family members will be employees of the company but not directors. These individuals are subject to the national minimum wage or living wage for all hours spent working in the business (although directors are exempt with respect to hours spent performing their duties as directors).

However, it is possible that if they only work part time, the salary that must be paid to them will still be within the optimal amounts of £8,840, £9,568 or £12,570.

Chapter 35

Is My Salary Tax Deductible?

One of the benefits of getting your company to pay you a salary is that the amount will normally be a tax deductible expense and reduce the company's corporation tax bill.

However, it is important to point out that there is no automatic right to corporation tax relief. The amount paid has to be justified by the work carried out for the business and the individual's level of responsibility.

While this may not be an important issue for company owners who work full time in the business and pay themselves a small salary, it may be important if you start paying salaries to other family members, in particular those who only work on a part time basis.

The question of whether your employment income will attract corporation tax relief may also become an issue if you decide to pay yourself a large one-off bonus.

Some of the factors that may determine whether a salary or bonus payment is tax deductible include:

- The number of hours worked in the business

- The individual's legal obligations and responsibilities (e.g. directors' duties)

- The amount of pay received by the company's other employees

- The pay received by employees at other companies performing similar roles

- The company's performance and ability to pay salaries/bonuses.

In the case of large one-off bonus payments made only to the company's directors/shareholders it may be necessary to document the commercial rationale for the payment to show that the payment is justifiable. This can be done in the minutes of a directors' board meeting.

It may also be advisable to record the approval of any bonus in the minutes of a shareholders' meeting.

Chapter 36

Salary vs Dividends: Non-Tax Factors

Most of this guide focuses on choosing the most tax efficient *level* of income and the most tax efficient *mix* of income (i.e. salary versus dividends).

However, when it comes to withdrawing money from your company there are lots of other non-tax factors that may need to be considered.

This chapter provides a short overview of some of the issues but is not definitive.

Cashflow and Working Capital Needs

When deciding how much income you withdraw from your company you must consider the cashflow and working capital requirements of the business.

It would naturally be irresponsible to pay yourself a large bonus or dividend if this affects the company's ability to carry on its business.

If you prefer to retain the cash in your company, it may be possible for a dividend to be declared but not paid out. The dividend can simply be credited to the director's loan account and withdrawn at a later date when it is more convenient.

Income tax will still be payable on any dividends declared but not paid.

Dividends & Company Insolvency

Dividends should not be declared when the company is insolvent or if the payment of those dividends will render the company insolvent.

Dividends that are deemed illegal may have to be repaid, even if this results in the director being made bankrupt or being forced into an individual voluntary arrangement (IVA).

Company's Profitability

The payment of a large salary or bonus will depress the company's profits. This may affect the company's ability to borrow.

Directors Ability to Borrow

If you take a small salary and the rest of your income as dividends there is a possibility that this will affect your ability to borrow money personally.

Some lenders may only be interested in the level of your salary and ignore your dividends, being unfamiliar with this sort of pay structuring.

Other lenders, on the other hand, will look at the complete picture and will look at your recent tax returns and the company's most recent accounts when assessing your ability to repay a loan.

Affect on Share Value

The value of a company is usually based on a multiple of its after-tax profits. A small minority shareholder's stake, however, is often valued according to the dividend history of the company. A consistent or steadily increasing annual dividend may enhance the value of the shares.

Chapter 37

Paying Salaries & Dividends: Profits & Paperwork

Salaries – Real Time Information

Since April 2013 employers have had to report salary payments to HMRC under the Real Time Information (RTI) regime. Under real time information, employers are required to submit a Full Payment Submission (FPS) to HMRC at the same time or before each payment is made to a director or employee.

The idea is to make sure the right amount of tax is paid at the right time. Under the previous system, employers generally only had to report payroll information to HMRC at the end of the year.

Under RTI the directors own salaries could result in additional payroll costs (for example, in small husband and wife companies or 'one man band' companies, where the only salaries paid are those of the directors themselves).

Where the directors receive small salaries, it may be cheaper and easier to register with HMRC as an annual scheme and pay salaries as a single annual lump sum (e.g. in March just before the end of the tax year).

With annual schemes an FPS is only expected in the month of payment and HMRC only has to be paid once a year. However, it is only possible to register as an annual scheme if all employees are paid annually at the same time.

Once a business is registered as an annual scheme, an Employer Payment Summary (EPS) is not required for the 11 months of the tax year where no payments are made to the directors. Schemes not registered as annual schemes have to make monthly submissions, even if no salaries are paid.

An additional problem may arise where directors withdraw cash from their companies and only later decide how these payments are to be treated (for example, as salaries or dividends).

Where the director's loan account is overdrawn, an amount withdrawn and subsequently designated as salary could result in a late filing penalty under RTI.

When directors withdraw money from their companies it is essential to decide up front the nature of the payment (e.g. salary, loan, dividend, reimbursement of expenses) and to have evidence supporting that decision.

For example, where a director borrows money from the company, the terms of the loan should be set out in writing. Withdrawals by directors that cannot be categorised might be treated as earnings by HMRC unless the company can prove otherwise.

Dividends

Distributable Profits

Under the Companies Act a company cannot legally pay a dividend unless it has sufficient distributable profits to cover it. This is an important point to remember, with many companies expecting smaller profits because of the pandemic.

A company's distributable profits are its accumulated realised profits, less accumulated realised losses. This information can generally be found in the company's most recent annual accounts.

It is not necessary for the company to actually make a profit in the year the dividend is paid, as long as there are sufficient accumulated profits (after tax) from previous years.

So all is not necessarily lost if your company has been experiencing difficult trading conditions in recent times. As long as there are sufficient distributable profits from previous years, it may be possible to continue paying dividends.

Where the most recent annual accounts do not show sufficient profits, interim or management accounts can be prepared with more up to date information. This may be useful if business conditions have improved since the last accounts were prepared.

It's also important to remember that directors have a duty to promote the company's success, protect its assets and take reasonable action to ensure that the company can pay its debts.

If future trading losses are expected, this is a factor that should be taken into account when considering the cash flow implications of any proposed dividend.

Thus, even if the most recent set of accounts show that there are sufficient distributable profits, the directors must take account of any change in the company's financial position since the accounts date and consider whether the company will remain solvent after any proposed dividend is paid. The key point is that directors must act honestly and reasonably at all times.

Before paying any dividends it is probably wise to speak to your accountant to check whether the company does indeed have sufficient distributable profits.

If the company does not have sufficient distributable profits to cover its dividend payments, the dividends will be illegal and the shareholder will be liable to repay the company.

Dividend Formalities & Paperwork

It is possible that HMRC will try to tax dividends as employment income. To help avoid any such challenge it is essential to ensure that dividends are properly declared and you have the supporting paperwork to prove it.

This includes:

- Holding a directors' board meeting to recommend the dividend payment (with printed minutes to prove the meeting took place)

- Holding a general meeting of the company's members (i.e. shareholders) to approve the dividend payment (with printed minutes to prove the meeting took place).

- Issuing a dividend confirmation to each shareholder.

See Appendix B for sample documentation.

Some commentators also argue that it is not advisable to declare dividends monthly because this will look more like salary income, especially if the above formalities are neglected.

A better alternative would be an infrequent dividend credited to the director's loan account which can then be drawn down throughout the year.

Paying a dividend towards the end of the tax year, when it may be easier to work out how much income tax will be payable, is possibly best in timing terms. If a dividend is paid at the beginning of the year and income from other sources (e.g. rental income) turns out to be higher than expected, the company owner could end up paying tax at a higher rate on his dividend income.

Interim versus Final Dividends

A final dividend must be recommended by the directors and endorsed by a shareholders meeting. For tax purposes the dividend is treated as paid on that date (unless a later date is specified).

Interim dividends can be authorised at the discretion of directors and are recognised for tax purposes only when they are paid, for example by crediting the director's loan account.

Chapter 38

Dividends Taxed as Earnings

Tax cases in recent years demonstrate the potential danger that dividends paid to a director/shareholder may in some circumstances be vulnerable to a national insurance liability and possibly a full PAYE charge.

It remains to be seen how HMRC will choose to use these decisions in the context of family companies:

P A Holdings

PA Holdings switched from a conventional bonus arrangement to a more intricate structure whereby an employee benefit trust was funded by the company, which in turn awarded preference shares to employees. These preference shares duly paid a dividend after which they were redeemed.

The company and its employees argued that the dividends should be taxed as dividends using dividend tax rates and without any PAYE or national insurance implications.

By contrast, HMRC took the view that the dividends simply amounted to earnings and that the normal PAYE and national insurance payments should have been deducted from them and accounted for to HMRC.

The Court of Appeal overturned the decisions of the First Tier Tribunal and the Upper Tribunal and decided that the dividends were indeed earnings for employment and should therefore suffer deductions of income tax at source through PAYE. Both employers and employees national insurance deductions should also have been made.

PA Holdings initially decided to appeal to the Supreme Court but later threw in the towel. This led to fears that HMRC could attack director/shareholders who take most of their income as dividends.

Many tax advisers argue that the aggressive tax planning undertaken by PA Holdings (trying to change bonuses into dividends for a large chunk of employees) is entirely different to the profit extraction model of most small companies.

In other words, most director/shareholders should be able to continue paying themselves small salaries and taking the rest of their income as dividends with limited risk of challenge from HMRC.

Uniplex (UK) Ltd

Uniplex was sold a scheme aimed at giving employees dividend income instead of remuneration, issuing different classes of share to each employee. This type of arrangement is generally known as alphabet shares.

The scheme failed as it was not implemented as planned. However, the First Tier Tribunal judge added that the scheme, even if implemented correctly, might still have failed.

Stewart Fraser Ltd

This case involved a write off of loans by a close company to an employee shareholder. The loan write offs were treated as distributions taxable on the employee. HMRC successfully argued that national insurance liabilities were payable by the company on the loan write offs.

Practical Implications

The practical implications relate to the boundary between normal dividend payments and those which under the PA Holdings/Uniplex/Stewart Fraser case principles would be treated as employment earnings and hence attract income tax and national insurance deductions through PAYE. For instance in PA Holdings the First Tier Tribunal said:

"if something is paid out as a distribution by a company to an investing shareholder then the issue of derivation may arise if the shareholder is also an employee. The facts may show that the derivation of a dividend

from a share may not be related to earnings because the acquisition and ownership of the share was not related to earnings or more generally to the status of the individual as an employee of the company".

In Uniplex, the First Tier Tribunal said:

"The PA Holdings case is authority for the proposition that payments from a party other than the employer can be from an employee's employment" and *"It may well have still been the case that the full amount would have been taxable because employees had given no consideration for the payment other than their services".*

Summary

Dividends paid to an employee-shareholder may in some circumstances be vulnerable to a national insurance liability, and possibly to a full PAYE charge. It remains to be seen how HMRC will choose to use these decisions in the context of family companies and remuneration planning generally.

Dividends from certain alphabet share arrangements, that allow profits to be shared in a way that relates to the amount of work carried out in the business, are at risk of being taxed as employment income.

Most at risk are shares that have no capital or voting rights other than a right to dividend income.

Alphabet share arrangements could also fall foul of the settlements legislation if they are used to divert dividend income to another person.

Chapter 39

Small Salary, Big Dividends: Potential Dangers

It is quite common practice for company owners to pay themselves a small salary and take the rest of their income as dividends. Many accountants have been recommending this strategy for years.

However, it is important to point out that some tax advisors are cautious about certain aspects of this tax planning technique, especially in light of court decisions like *PA Holdings*, where the Court of Appeal decided that certain dividends should be subject to PAYE and national insurance (see Chapter 38).

There is a fear that cases like this will create a wide precedent for any employer that pays dividends to its staff. It is difficult to quantify the potential danger, however, because a lot depends on HMRC's willingness to act. The most vulnerable, arguably, are those that use tax planning techniques that HMRC may view as aggressive, including possibly:

- Large scale contrived arrangements where dividends are created for tax avoidance purposes (as in *PA Holdings*).

- Directors' loans that are written off and taxed as dividends.

- Dividend waivers that are used to divert income to other shareholders, for example where a director waives his own dividends so that his wife can receive more income. HMRC succeeded in challenging dividend waivers in the case of *Donovan & McLaren v HMRC*.

- Certain 'Alphabet' share arrangements, where different classes of shares (A, B, C etc) have no substantive rights other than to dividends. These arrangements are often used to substitute dividends for bonuses.

- Situations where previous salaries have been reduced in favour of dividends.

The sixty-four thousand dollar question is: where does this leave the average small company owner taking a small salary and the rest of his income as dividends?

At the time of writing it would appear that most small companies are not under attack but this state of affairs could change at any time. The small salary/big dividend tax planning technique does not produce *guaranteed* tax savings. There is a danger, no matter how small, that HMRC may try to tax your dividends as earnings, if not now then at some point in the future.

Also, with regards to the last point in the above list, please note that some (more conservative) tax advisors argue that if you are currently taking a salary that is larger than the 'optimal' amounts listed in Chapter 8 you should not reduce it.

Other tax advisors recommend taking a salary slightly larger than the 'optimal' amounts, so that at least some income tax and national insurance is paid by the director.

Chapter 40

Personal Service Companies

If your company is classed as a personal service company, many of the tax planning opportunities available to other company owners may not be available, for example, the ability to take dividends that are free from national insurance.

Personal service companies often have to operate the infamous 'IR35' regime which means the company may be forced to calculate a notional salary for the director/shareholder.

This deemed income will be subject to PAYE and national insurance.

Essentially, HMRC may ignore the company set up and treat most of the company's income as employment income.

Which Companies Are Affected by IR35?

This is where it all becomes a bit of a grey area (which is why professional advice is essential!)

A personal service company is, generally speaking, a firm that receives all or most of its income from services provided by the director/shareholder.

Often the work will be carried out for just one client, often for a long period of time, and the client will probably only want the personal services of the company owner (hence IR35 often applies to 'one man band' companies).

Essentially HMRC is looking for cases of 'disguised employment'. In other words, ignoring the fact that there is an intermediary company, the relationship is more like that between an employer and employee rather than the kind of relationship that exists between independent self-employed business owners and their clients.

Where such 'disguised employment' exists, the company must apply the IR35 regime to the payments received from that client – effectively treating most of those payments as if they were salary paid to the director/shareholder.

A typical situation which might be caught under the IR35 rules is where the individual resigns as an employee and then goes back to the same job but working through a company.

However, it's all very subjective with a long line of legal cases adding to the confusion.

Personal service companies can be found in many different business sectors: the most cited example is IT consultants.

They also came under the media spotlight in recent times when it was disclosed that some BBC presenters had been operating as 'freelancers' via personal service companies, when many would argue that they are in fact nothing but employees of the BBC.

Recent Changes

Since 6th April 2017 the onus has been on the 'employer' in the public sector to put payments to contractors' personal service companies on the payroll where there appears to be an employment relationship falling under the provisions of IR35.

In the October 2018 Budget the Government announced that, from 6th April 2020, *private sector* employers would become responsible for deciding whether the IR35 rules apply. However, shortly after the March 2020 Budget, the Government announced that the reforms will only come in on 6th April 2021 as part of the response to the coronavirus pandemic.

In the March 2021 Budget it was confirmed that there will be no further delay.

Small organizations are exempt from the new rules. Where small businesses are engaging workers through an intermediary, the responsibility for applying the IR35 rules remains with the intermediary.

As a result it may become more attractive for owners of personal service companies to work for small businesses.

A business will generally be treated as small if it satisfies two or more of the following requirements:

- Annual turnover does not exceed £10.2 million
- Assets not more than £5.1 million
- No more than 50 employees

Where an individual works for a medium or large organization in the private sector through their own personal service company and falls under the IR35 rules, the organization paying them is treated as their employer and must deduct income tax and national insurance from the payments made to the personal service company.

A 5% allowance has been available to personal service companies to reflect the costs of administering the off-payroll working rules. Because responsibility has shifted from personal service companies to the organisations hiring them, this allowance has been removed from 6th April 2021 for those engagements with medium and large-sized organisations in the private and voluntary sectors.

The allowance will continue to be available to personal service companies for engagements with small organisations outside the public sector.

Personal service companies and IR35 are beyond the scope of this guide.

Part 8

More Tax Planning Ideas

Chapter 41

How to Pay Less CGT by Postponing Dividends

The main capital gains tax rates were reduced in April 2016:

- From 18% to 10% Basic rate taxpayers
- From 28% to 20% Higher rate taxpayers

Sadly, the 18% and 28% rates still apply to gains arising on disposals of *residential* property.

Where the individual is entitled to Business Asset Disposal Relief (previously called Entrepreneurs Relief), the gain is taxed at 10%. This relief is generally only available when you sell or wind up a trading business. In other cases the capital gains tax rate depends on how much income you've earned during the tax year.

In the absence of Business Asset Disposal Relief, the maximum amount of capital gains that you can have taxed at 10% or 18% during the current tax year is £37,700. This is the current level of the basic-rate tax band.

Basic-rate taxpayers pay 10% less capital gains tax than higher-rate taxpayers. This means the basic-rate tax band can save each person £3,770 in capital gains tax this year: £37,700 x 10% = £3,770.

Postponing Dividends

If you expect to realise a large capital gain, for example by disposing of a buy-to-let property, you may be able to save quite a lot of tax by making sure the disposal takes place during a tax year in which your taxable income is quite low.

In this respect, company owners can manipulate their incomes more easily than regular employees, sole traders or business partners. The company itself can keep trading and generating profits but the company owner can make sure very little of these profits are extracted and taxed in his or her hands.

Example

Richard, a company owner, sells his second home, realising a gain of £50,000 after deducting all buying and selling costs. Deducting his annual CGT exemption of £12,300 leaves a taxable gain of £37,700.

Richard hasn't paid himself any dividends during the current tax year and decides to postpone paying any so that his £37,700 capital gain is taxed at 18% instead of 28%. This simple piece of tax planning saves Richard £3,770 in capital gains tax.

Note that Richard can still pay himself a tax-free salary of up to £12,570 to utilise his income tax personal allowance. The income tax personal allowance does not interfere with the capital gains tax calculation. (In practice he may be better off paying himself a slightly smaller salary of £9,568 and a tax-free dividend of £3,002 if his company doesn't have any spare employment allowance.)

Limitations

Although postponing dividends could help you pay less capital gains tax, it's probably not worth doing this unless you can withdraw the postponed dividends in a future tax year and pay no more than 7.5% tax. If you take a bigger dividend in a later tax year, and end up paying 32.5% income tax, you may end up worse off overall.

Example continued

In the above example Richard postponed taking a dividend of £37,700 to free up his basic-rate band and pay 18% capital gains tax.

If during 2022/23 he takes an additional dividend of £37,700, on top off his usual salary and maximum dividend taxed at 7.5%, he will pay additional income tax of £12,253 (£37,700 x 32.5%). However, if he had taken that income in 2021/22 he would have paid income tax of £2,678 – so he ends up paying £9,575 more income tax.

He saved £3,770 in capital gains tax in 2021/22 but pays an additional £9,575 in income tax in 2022/23. Overall Richard is £5,805 worse off.

Chapter 42

Emigrating to Save Tax

Possibly the most drastic step you can take to save tax is leave the country!

By becoming non-resident you may be able to avoid both capital gains tax (when you sell your company) and income tax (if you want to withdraw big dividends).

Capital Gains Tax

In the past it was possible to go and live in certain countries for just one year and completely avoid paying capital gains tax.

This was a fantastic loophole, especially when capital gains tax was levied at rates of up to 40%.

Unfortunately that loophole was closed and most UK taxpayers who move abroad temporarily to avoid capital gains tax will be taxed when they return, if the period of non residence lasts for five years or less.

With a capital gains tax rate of just 10% applying to many company sales (where Business Asset Disposal Relief applies), many company owners would be unwilling to exile themselves from the UK for five years just to increase their bank accounts by 10%.

Moving abroad is an expensive and time-consuming business and these costs would eat into your tax savings.

Having said this, the reduction in the lifetime allowance for Business Asset Disposal Relief from £10 million of gains to just £1 million of gains means that many business owners will now pay the higher 20% capital gains tax rate when they sell their companies.

If you plan to emigrate one day anyway, this is all academic. You may be able to live in the country of your dreams **and** reduce your tax bill at the same time.

Income Tax

Where a company has built up significant distributable profits it was possible in the past to withdraw these profits as tax-free dividends during a short period of non-residence.

This tax planning opportunity is no longer available following the introduction of some anti-avoidance rules.

Income from "closely controlled companies" (most small companies) will be taxed if the recipient becomes UK resident again after a temporary period of non residence of five years or less.

This anti-avoidance rule does not apply to dividends paid out of "post-departure" profits, ie profits built up while you are non-resident.

It is not meant to apply to employment and self-employment earnings or regular investment income, eg dividends from stock market companies and bank interest.

Furthermore, the anti-avoidance rule will only apply where an individual has been resident in four or more of the seven tax years prior to the tax year in which they become non-resident.

While it may no longer be possible to avoid income tax by becoming non-resident for a short period, this tax planning strategy may still work for genuine emigrants who decide to leave the UK permanently.

Professional advice should be obtained before attempting to become non-resident to reduce UK taxes.

Statutory Residence Test

So how do you become non-resident?

A statutory residence test has been in operation since 6th April 2013. This test is supposed to make it a lot easier to determine your residence status and hence where you stand when it comes to paying UK tax.

Automatic Overseas Tests

You start with the automatic overseas tests. You will be automatically *non-resident* for the tax year if you meet *any* of the following tests:

- You spend fewer than 16 days in the UK during the tax year. This test is used if you were UK resident in *any* of the previous 3 tax years.

- You spend fewer than 46 days in the UK during the tax year. This test is used if you were UK resident in *none* of the previous three tax years.

- If you work sufficient hours overseas (generally 35 hours or more per week on average) without a significant break, and during the tax year:

  - You spend fewer than 91 days in the UK, and
  - You spend fewer than 31 days working in the UK (a work day means more than three hours work).

If you do not meet any of these automatic overseas tests, you should move onto the 'automatic UK tests'.

Automatic UK Tests

You will be automatically *UK resident* for the tax year if you meet *any* of the following tests:

- You spend 183 days or more in the UK during the tax year.

- You have a home in the UK and are present in that home on 30 or more days during the tax year. This test only applies if you do not have an overseas home or, if you do have an overseas home, you are present in that home on fewer than 30 days during the tax year.

- You work full time in the UK for any period of 365 days (all or part of which falls into the tax year) with no significant break.

If any of the automatic UK tests apply to you for a particular tax year and none of the automatic overseas tests apply, you are UK resident for tax purposes for that tax year.

If you do not meet any of the automatic overseas tests and do not meet any of the automatic UK tests you have to use the sufficient ties test to determine your residence status for the tax year.

Sufficient Ties Test

This test takes into account your UK ties and the number of days you spend in the UK. The more ties you have, the more likely it is that you will be UK resident for tax purposes:

- **Family tie** – your spouse or common-law partner (unless separated) or children under 18 (with some exceptions) are UK resident.

- **Accommodation tie** – you have a place to live in the UK that is available for a continuous period of 91 days or more during the tax year. You don't have to own the property but must spend at least one night there during the tax year or, if it is the home of a close relative, you must spend at least 16 nights in it to have an accommodation tie.

- **Work tie** – you do more than three hours work a day in the UK for a total of at least 40 days. Includes employment and self-employment.

- **90-day tie** – you have spent more than 90 days in the UK in either or both of the previous two tax years.

- **Country tie** – the UK is the country in which you were present for the greatest number of days during the tax year. This tie only applies if you were UK resident in any of the previous three tax years.

These ties are then combined with days spent in the UK to determine your residence status.

The scoring is different for people who have recently left the UK (i.e. were UK resident in any of the previous three tax years) and those who have recently arrived (i.e. were not resident in any of the previous three tax years).

UK Resident in Any of Previous 3 Tax Years – Leavers

UK ties are combined with days spent in the UK as follows:

Days in UK	Residence status
Fewer than 16 days	Always non-resident
16 – 45 days	UK Resident if 4 or more ties
46 – 90 days	UK Resident if 3 or more ties
91 – 120 days	UK Resident if 2 or more ties
121-182 days	UK Resident if 1 or more ties
183 days or more	Always UK resident

Not Resident in All 3 Previous Tax Years – Arrivers

UK ties are combined with days spent in the UK as follows:

Days in UK	Resident Status
Fewer than 16 days	Always non-resident
16 – 45 days	Always non-resident
46 – 90 days	UK resident if all 4 ties
91 – 120 days	UK resident if 3 or more ties
121-182 days	UK resident if 2 or more ties
183 days or more	Always UK resident

Further Information

Finally, please note that many of the terms used in this chapter have complex definitions and there is more to the statutory residence test than can be covered in just a few pages.

For more information see the Taxcafe guide *Tax Planning for Non-Residents & Non Doms*.

Chapter 43

Venture Capital Trusts (VCTs)

One of the easiest ways to cut your income tax bill is by investing in a venture capital trust (VCT). Venture capital trusts are funds that invest in small unquoted companies, including companies quoted on the Alternative Investment Market (AIM).

VCT investments provide 30% income tax relief, so if you invest £10,000 your income tax bill will be cut by £3,000.

An investment of roughly £8,927 is sufficient to wipe out the entire income tax bill of a company owner who pays himself income of £50,270 in 2021/22.

Example
Leanne, a company owner, pays herself a salary of £9,568 and dividend of £40,702 in 2021/22 – a total of £50,270. Her salary is tax free in her hands, as is £5,002 of her dividend income (being covered by the remainder of her personal allowance and the dividend allowance). She stands to pay 7.5% income tax on the remaining £35,700 dividend: £2,678.

Leanne has a significant amount of money tucked away in a bank savings account. So before the end of the tax year she withdraws £8,927 and invests it in a venture capital trust. This reduces her income tax for the year by £2,678 (£8,927 x 30%). When she submits her tax return for 2021/22 she will not have any income tax to pay and will not have to make any payments on account (see Chapter 5).

A VCT can also be used to head off an unexpectedly high tax bill:

Example
Tony owns a catering company and a few rental properties. Just before the end of the tax year he works out that his taxable rental profit will be higher than expected. He took a dividend from his company early in the tax year but only now realises that an additional £12,000 of this income will be taxed at 32.5% instead of 7.5%, producing an unexpected tax bill of £3,000. Tony decides to invest £10,000 in a VCT. This will provide income tax relief of £3,000, wiping out the additional income tax he otherwise would have had to pay.

There are some other points to note about VCT income tax relief:

- The maximum investment is £200,000 per tax year, so the maximum initial tax saving is £60,000.

- The 30% up-front tax relief is available only if your income tax bill for the year is high enough. So if you invest £10,000, your maximum tax relief is £3,000. But if your tax bill is only £2,000, your tax relief will be limited to £2,000.

- VCTs provide income tax relief only. They do not reduce your capital gains tax or national insurance.

- You can no longer defer capital gains tax from the sale of property or other assets by investing in a VCT.

VCTs also offer two further tax benefits:

- Tax-free dividends
- Tax-free capital gains

ISAs also offer tax-free dividends and capital gains so tax-free VCT dividends, in particular, will be most appealing to company owners who are higher-rate taxpayers or additional-rate taxpayers and max out their ISA allowance each year.

These taxpayers would normally pay 32.5% tax or 38.1% tax on any additional dividend income they receive outside a VCT or ISA.

A lot of the return from a VCT investment will often come in the form of dividends.

VCTs vs ISAs & Pensions

What makes VCTs more attractive on paper than other tax shelters like ISAs and pensions is the double tax relief: when you put your money in AND when you take it out.

Pensions provide tax relief when you put your money in but your withdrawals are taxed. You can withdraw 25% of your fund as a tax-free lump sum when you retire but you have to pay income tax on everything else.

ISAs, by contrast, allow you to make tax-free withdrawals of income and capital gains but do not provide any up-front tax relief for your initial contributions.

An exception is the Lifetime ISA which provides a 25% Government bonus and allows tax-free withdrawals. However, you cannot open one if you're 40 or older and the maximum investment is £4,000 per year.

So venture capital trusts offer the best of both worlds and are arguably one of the most generous tax shelters available. Even if you only receive back your original money after five years, with no capital gains or dividends, you will still have enjoyed a return of around 7.5% per year, thanks to the initial tax relief.

VCTs may also appeal to those who have already made the maximum investment allowed in ISAs and pensions.

VCTS Drawbacks

Five Year Minimum

The first catch with VCTs is you have to invest for a minimum period of five years, otherwise you will lose the income tax relief.

Pensions can be even more restrictive depending on your age: you cannot touch your money at all until you reach age 55 at least. With ISAs you can withdraw your money tax free at any time.

With the new and more generous Lifetime ISA withdrawals before age 60 attract a penalty (unless you use the money to buy your first home).

A traditional ISA is therefore the only tax shelter that comes with no strings attached and is arguably the best investment for those who want easy access to their money.

Small, Risky Companies

The second and most important catch with VCTs is they have to invest most of your money in the smallest and arguably most risky companies. This, after all, is why the Government created such a generous tax shelter in the first place: it wants to encourage investment in small, expanding companies.

With pensions and ISAs, on the other hand, you can invest in the biggest blue chip companies, as well as small companies, corporate bonds and cash.

VCTs have to put at least 80% of the money they raise in 'qualifying' companies. The remaining money can be invested in pretty much anything, including bigger companies and other less risky investments.

For companies to qualify for VCT funding they must:

- Have gross assets of £15 million or less.

- Have fewer than 250 employees (500 for "knowledge-intensive" companies).

- Be unquoted companies, i.e. not stock exchange companies (AIM companies are treated as unquoted and there are several well-established AIM VCTs).

- Raise their first VCT or other risk finance investment within 7 years of making their first commercial sale. For "knowledge-intensive" companies the time limit is 10 years from either the date of their first commercial sale or their turnover reaching £200,000.

- Not be involved to a substantial extent in certain activities, including energy generation, dealing in land or financial assets, providing finance or insurance, legal and accountancy services, leasing or receiving royalties, and certain property-based trades (e.g. property development, farming, hotels and nursing homes).

- Be seeking genuine long-term growth with a significant risk that there will be a loss of capital. Tax-motivated investments, where the tax relief provides most of the return for an investor with limited risk, will no longer be eligible.

Companies are no longer allowed to use the money they raise from VCTs to acquire other existing businesses (they're supposed to use it to grow organically). VCTs are also prohibited from investing in management buy-outs (MBOs). These were a particularly lucrative source of returns in the past.

There are other investment rules and if a VCT doesn't comply it could lose its special tax status which means that investors may have to pay back the income tax relief they received. This almost happened to one well-known fund in recent times.

The £15 million ceiling on assets means that VCTs have to invest most of the money they raise in very small (usually privately-owned) firms. VCTs generally also have to invest in relatively young companies that have not been selling for more than 7 years (10 years if knowledge intensive). Very small and very young businesses are arguably the riskiest.

Having said this, if you take part in a fund raising by a large established VCT you will end up owning shares in a fund that also has an established portfolio of companies, some of which may be quite large and profitable businesses.

For example, looking at the 10 biggest holdings in a sample fund, the Hargreave Hale AIM VCT, many have a market capitalisation of over £100 million.

If a VCT with a portfolio worth £80 million raises a further £20 million from investors (including you), 80% of your shareholding will be in the existing holdings, some of which may be more established companies, and only 20% in new investments.

Illiquid Investments

A major drawback of VCTs is their lack of liquidity. The trusts themselves are quoted on the London Stock Exchange but you may struggle to sell your shares at a decent price when the five-year period is up.

Why? Because the 30% income tax relief – the only reason most people invest in venture capital trusts – is only available on *new* VCT shares.

Investors who buy 'second-hand' VCT shares are entitled to tax-free dividends but the all-important 30% tax refund is denied. For this reason, there are very few people willing to buy VCT shares from exiting investors.

Some VCTs do, however, offer to buy back shares from investors who wish to exit. This will typically be at a discount to net asset value of, for example, 5% to 10%.

Previously, some VCTs offered a buy-back facility that allowed investors to sell back their shares and buy new ones in the same VCT with another round of income tax relief. VCTs are no longer able to carry out these enhanced share buybacks that offer a fresh round of income tax relief.

Investors are also not able to obtain a second round of income tax relief if they sell their VCT shares and invest in a new issue of shares in the same fund within six months.

Higher Charges

VCTS have higher charges than more mainstream investment funds such as unit trusts and OEICs.

Initial charges can be as much as 5%, whereas most traditional investment funds have no initial charges these days when you invest through one of the big investment platforms such as Hargreaves Lansdown. However, discounts on VCT investments are generally available when you invest through a platform.

Annual management fees are in the region of 2% per year or more, also higher than the charges levied by mainstream funds. There may also be a performance fee.

These initial and ongoing charges, coupled with the fact that you may have to eventually sell your investment at a discount, mean that a significant portion of your initial income tax relief (possibly over half your income tax relief) could be swallowed up by additional charges.

Our View of VCTs

It's important not to invest in VCTs solely for the tax savings. You must want to invest in small companies (for example to diversify your investment portfolio).

Some readers may feel that they already have ample exposure to small companies... namely their own companies! The share prices of many VCTs fell dramatically at the onset of the coronavirus crisis but recovered strongly thereafter.

For those who do want to invest in small companies, investing in a VCT with 30% income tax relief may be more attractive than investing in a regular small company fund, especially for those who have already made the maximum permitted investment in ISAs and pensions.

VCTs are typically associated with "year-end tax planning" – steps you take just before the end of the tax year to head off an unwelcome tax bill. However, in recent times demand for some of the best VCT offers has outstripped supply and it has been essential to invest well before the end of the tax year on 5th April.

The minimum investment period is five years but a longer time horizon is arguably necessary because of the inherent riskiness of this type of investment. Company owners who have volatile income and are not comfortable with having their savings locked up for at least five years should arguably steer clear of VCTs.

Although a VCT investment could be a useful way to cut your income tax bill it should also be remembered that the easiest way for company owners to avoid unwanted income tax bills is by paying themselves smaller dividends!

Financial advice may be necessary to help you decide whether to invest and what type of VCT to buy.

Marginal Corporation Tax Rates

Year Ending:	Small Profits Rate	Marginal Rate	Main Rate
31-Mar-2018 to 31-Mar-2023	n/a	n/a	19.000%
30-Apr-2023	19.000%	19.616%	19.493%
31-May-2023	19.000%	20.253%	20.003%
30-Jun-2023	19.000%	20.870%	20.496%
31-Jul-2023	19.000%	21.507%	21.005%
31-Aug-2023	19.000%	22.144%	21.515%
30-Sep-2023	19.000%	22.760%	22.008%
31-Oct-2023	19.000%	23.397%	22.518%
30-Nov-2023	19.000%	24.014%	23.011%
31-Dec-2023	19.000%	24.651%	23.521%
31-Jan-2024	19.000%	25.288%	24.030%
29-Feb-2024	19.000%	25.865%	24.492%
31-Mar-2024	19.000%	26.500%	25.000%

Sample Dividend Documentation

1. Director's Board Meeting Minute

BOARD MINUTE

Minutes of a Meeting of Directors of Standard Ltd held at 100 London Road, Newtown, ZZ10 1AA on 31st March 2022.

Present: Mr A B Crown – Director
                 Mrs D E Crown – Director
                 Mr E F Bloodaxe – Director

In attendance: Mr H Godwinson – Company Secretary

Motions:
1) It was recommended that the company pay a dividend of £2.50 per ordinary share out of the profits for the year ended 31st December 2021, to be paid on 1st April 2022.
2) The directors noted the company's excellent trading results for the year ended 31st December 2021 with satisfaction.
3) No other motions.

Signed _____   Date _____
           (Mr A B Crown)

Notes (Not Part of the Minute)
The minutes of a directors' board meeting should:
   a) *Indicate the persons present.*
   b) *Include sufficient information to describe how directors reasonably came to reasonable decisions.*
   c) *Include details of any conflicts of interest or abstainment from voting.*
   d) *Be signed by a director present at the meeting.*
   e) *Be retained with the company's statutory records.*

Regarding point (a) above, a quorum may need to be present for the meeting to be valid. This depends on the company's own constitution as set out in its Articles of Association.

2. Member's General Meeting Minute

GENERAL MEETING OF MEMBERS

Minutes of an Extraordinary General Meeting of the Ordinary Shareholders of Standard Ltd held at 100 London Road, Newtown, ZZ10 1AA on 31st March 2022.

Present: Mr A B Crown – Ordinary shareholder
               Mrs D E Crown – Ordinary Shareholder
               Mr E F Bloodaxe – Ordinary Shareholder

In attendance: Mr H Godwinson – Company Secretary

Motions:
1) The members, all being present, agreed to accept the short notice period for the meeting.
2) The members approved the recommendation of the directors that the company pay a dividend of £2.50 per ordinary share for the year ended 31st December 2021. Payment to be made on 1st April 2022.
3) No other motions.

Signed _____   Date _____
        (Mr A B Crown)

3. Dividend Confirmation

Dividend Confirmation

Standard Limited

100 London Road, Newtown, ZZ10 1AA

Ordinary shares of £1 each

Mr A B Crown   1st April 2022
1 Viking Crescent
York
Y1 1AA

Payment of the final dividend in respect of the year ended 31st December 2021, at the rate of £2.50 per share on the ordinary shares registered in your name on 31st March 2022 is enclosed herewith.

H. Godwinson, Company Secretary

Shareholding	Dividend Payable	Payment Number
10,000	£25,000.00	11

This dividend confirmation should be kept with your tax records.

Lightning Source UK Ltd.
Milton Keynes UK
UKHW021415280621
386289UK00002B/25